PRAISE FOR

SUPERFORECASTING

"*Superforecasting* is a rare book that will make you smarter and wiser. One of the giants of behavioral science reveals how to improve at predicting the future."

—ADAM GRANT,
New York Times bestselling author of *Give and Take*

"Good judgment and good forecasting are rare, but they turn out to be made of teachable skills. By forcing forecasters to compete, Tetlock discovered what the skills are and how they work, and this book teaches the ability to any interested reader."

—STEWART BRAND,
president, The Long Now Foundation

"Philip Tetlock is renowned for demonstrating that most experts are no better than 'dart-throwing monkeys' at predicting elections, wars, economic collapses, and other events. In his brilliant new book, Tetlock offers a much more hopeful message, based once again on his own groundbreaking research. He shows that certain people can forecast events with accuracy much better than chance—and so, perhaps, can the rest of us, if we emulate the critical thinking of these 'superforecasters.' The self-empowerment genre doesn't get any smarter and more sophisticated than this."

—JOHN HORGAN,
director, Center for Science Writings, Stevens Institute of Technology

"*Superforecasting* is the rare book that is both scholarly and engaging. The lessons are scientific, compelling, and enormously practical. Anyone who is in the forecasting business—and that's all of us—should drop what they are doing and read it."

—MICHAEL J. MAUBOUSSIN,
head, Global Financial Strategies, Credit Suisse

"There isn't a social scientist in the world I admire more than Phil Tetlock."

—TIM HARFORD,
author of *The Undercover Economist*

"From the Oracle of Delphi to medieval astrologers to modern overconfident experts, forecasters have been either deluded or fraudulent. For the first time, *Superforecasting* reveals the secret of making honest, reliable, effective, useful judgments about the future."

—AARON BROWN,
chief risk officer, AQR Capital Management, and
author of *The Poker Face of Wall Street*

"Socrates had the insight in 'know thyself,' Kahneman delivered the science in *Thinking, Fast and Slow,* and now Tetlock has something we can all apply in *Superforecasting.*"

—JUAN LUIS PEREZ,
global head, UBS Group Research

SUPERFORECASTING

The Art and Science of Prediction

PHILIP E. TETLOCK
DAN GARDNER

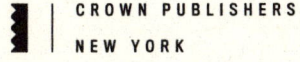

CROWN PUBLISHERS
NEW YORK

2015 Crown Publishers International Edition

Copyright © 2015 by Philip Tetlock Consulting, Inc. and Connaught Street, Inc.

Published in the United States by Crown Publishers,
an imprint of the Crown Publishing Group,
a division of Penguin Random House LLC, New York.
www.crownpublishing.com

CROWN is a registered trademark and the Crown colophon
is a trademark of Penguin Random House LLC.

Simultaneously published in hardcover in the
United States by Crown Publishers, an imprint of the Crown Publishing
Group, a division of Penguin Random House LLC, New York.

Library of Congress Cataloging-in-Publication Data

Tetlock, Philip E. (Philip Eyrikson), 1954–
Superforecasting : the art and science of prediction / Philip E. Tetlock, Dan Gardner.
pages cm
1. Economic forecasting. 2. Forecasting. I. Gardner, Dan, 1968– II. Title.

HB3730.T47 2015
303.49—dc23

2015007310

ISBN 978-1-101-90556-2
eBook ISBN 978-0-8041-3670-9

Printed in the United States of America

Illustrations by Joe LeMonnier
Cover design by Christopher Brand

10 9 8 7 6 5 4 3 2 1

Jenny, alive forever in the hearts of your mother and father, as if that day were yesterday

CONTENTS

SUPERFORECASTING

1

An Optimistic Skeptic

We are all forecasters. When we think about changing jobs, getting married, buying a home, making an investment, launching a product, or retiring, we decide based on how we expect the future will unfold. These expectations are forecasts. Often we do our own forecasting. But when big events happen—markets crash, wars loom, leaders tremble—we turn to the experts, those in the know. We look to people like Tom Friedman.

If you are a White House staffer, you might find him in the Oval Office with the president of the United States, talking about the Middle East. If you are a Fortune 500 CEO, you might spot him in Davos, chatting in the lounge with hedge fund billionaires and Saudi princes. And if you don't frequent the White House or swanky Swiss hotels, you can read his *New York Times* columns and bestselling books that tell you what's happening now, why, and what will come next.[1] Millions do.

Like Tom Friedman, Bill Flack forecasts global events. But there is a lot less demand for his insights.

For years, Bill worked for the US Department of Agriculture in Arizona—"part pick-and-shovel work, part spreadsheet"—but now he lives in Kearney, Nebraska. Bill is a native Cornhusker. He grew up in Madison, Nebraska, a farm town where his parents owned and published the *Madison Star-Mail*, a newspaper with lots of stories about local sports and county fairs. He was a good student in high school and he went on to get a bachelor of science degree from the University of Nebraska. From there, he went to the University of

Arizona. He was aiming for a PhD in math, but he realized it was beyond his abilities—"I had my nose rubbed in my limitations" is how he puts it—and he dropped out. It wasn't wasted time, however. Classes in ornithology made Bill an avid bird-watcher, and because Arizona is a great place to see birds, he did fieldwork part-time for scientists, then got a job with the Department of Agriculture and stayed for a while.

Bill is fifty-five and retired, although he says if someone offered him a job he would consider it. So he has free time. And he spends some of it forecasting.

Bill has answered roughly three hundred questions like "Will Russia officially annex additional Ukrainian territory in the next three months?" and "In the next year, will any country withdraw from the eurozone?" They are questions that matter. And they're difficult. Corporations, banks, embassies, and intelligence agencies struggle to answer such questions all the time. "Will North Korea detonate a nuclear device before the end of this year?" "How many additional countries will report cases of the Ebola virus in the next eight months?" "Will India or Brazil become a permanent member of the UN Security Council in the next two years?" Some of the questions are downright obscure, at least for most of us. "Will NATO invite new countries to join the Membership Action Plan (MAP) in the next nine months?" "Will the Kurdistan Regional Government hold a referendum on national independence this year?" "If a non-Chinese telecommunications firm wins a contract to provide Internet services in the Shanghai Free Trade Zone in the next two years, will Chinese citizens have access to Facebook and/or Twitter?" When Bill first sees one of these questions, he may have no clue how to answer it. "What on earth is the Shanghai Free Trade Zone?" he may think. But he does his homework. He gathers facts, balances clashing arguments, and settles on an answer.

No one bases decisions on Bill Flack's forecasts, or asks Bill to share his thoughts on CNN. He has never been invited to Davos to sit on a panel with Tom Friedman. And that's unfortunate. Because Bill Flack is a remarkable forecaster. We know that because each one of Bill's predictions has been dated, recorded, and assessed for accuracy by independent scientific observers. His track record is excellent.

Bill is not alone. There are thousands of others answering the same questions. All are volunteers. Most aren't as good as Bill, but about 2% are. They include engineers and lawyers, artists and scientists, Wall Streeters and Main Streeters, professors and students. We will meet many of them, including a mathematician, a filmmaker, and some retirees eager to share their underused talents. I call them *superforecasters* because that is what they are. Reliable evidence proves it. Explaining why they're so good, and how others can learn to do what they do, is my goal in this book.

How our low-profile superforecasters compare with cerebral celebrities like Tom Friedman is an intriguing question, but it can't be answered because the accuracy of Friedman's forecasting has never been rigorously tested. Of course Friedman's fans and critics have opinions one way or the other—"he nailed the Arab Spring" or "he screwed up on the 2003 invasion of Iraq" or "he was prescient on NATO expansion." But there are no hard facts about Tom Friedman's track record, just endless opinions—and opinions on opinions.[2] And that is business as usual. Every day, the news media deliver forecasts without reporting, or even asking, how good the forecasters who made the forecasts really are. Every day, corporations and governments pay for forecasts that may be prescient or worthless or something in between. And every day, all of us—leaders of nations, corporate executives, investors, and voters—make critical decisions on the basis of forecasts whose quality is unknown. Baseball managers wouldn't dream of getting out the checkbook to hire a player without consulting performance statistics. Even fans expect to see player stats on scoreboards and TV screens. And yet when it comes to the forecasters who help us make decisions that matter far more than any baseball game, we're content to be ignorant.[3]

In that light, relying on Bill Flack's forecasts looks quite reasonable. Indeed, relying on the forecasts of many readers of this book may prove quite reasonable, for it turns out that forecasting is not a "you have it or you don't" talent. It is a skill that can be cultivated. This book will show you how.

THE ONE ABOUT THE CHIMP

I want to spoil the joke, so I'll give away the punch line: the average expert was roughly as accurate as a dart-throwing chimpanzee.

You've probably heard that one before. It's famous—in some circles, infamous. It has popped up in the *New York Times*, the *Wall Street Journal*, the *Financial Times*, the *Economist*, and other outlets around the world. It goes like this: A researcher gathered a big group of experts—academics, pundits, and the like—to make thousands of predictions about the economy, stocks, elections, wars, and other issues of the day. Time passed, and when the researcher checked the accuracy of the predictions, he found that the average expert did about as well as random guessing. Except that's not the punch line because "random guessing" isn't funny. The punch line is about a dart-throwing chimpanzee. Because chimpanzees are funny.

I am that researcher and for a while I didn't mind the joke. My study was the most comprehensive assessment of expert judgment in the scientific literature. It was a long slog that took about twenty years, from 1984 to 2004, and the results were far richer and more constructive than the punch line suggested. But I didn't mind the joke because it raised awareness of my research (and, yes, scientists savor their fifteen minutes of fame too). And I myself had used the old "dart-throwing chimp" metaphor, so I couldn't complain too loudly.

I also didn't mind because the joke makes a valid point. Open any newspaper, watch any TV news show, and you find experts who forecast what's coming. Some are cautious. More are bold and confident. A handful claim to be Olympian visionaries able to see decades into the future. With few exceptions, they are not in front of the cameras because they possess any proven skill at forecasting. Accuracy is seldom even mentioned. Old forecasts are like old news—soon forgotten—and pundits are almost never asked to reconcile what they said with what actually happened. The one undeniable talent that talking heads have is their skill at telling a compelling story with conviction, and that is enough. Many have become wealthy peddling forecasting of untested value to corporate executives, government officials, and ordinary people who would never think of swallowing medicine of unknown efficacy and safety but who routinely pay for forecasts that are as dubious as elixirs sold from the back of a wagon. These people—and their customers—deserve a nudge in the ribs. I was happy to see my research used to give it to them.

But I realized that as word of my work spread, its apparent meaning was mutating. What my research had shown was that the average expert had done little better than guessing on many of the political and economic questions I had posed. "Many" does not equal all. It was easiest to beat chance on the shortest-range questions that only required looking one year out, and accuracy fell off the further out experts tried to forecast—approaching the dart-throwing-chimpanzee level three to five years out. That was an important finding. It tells us something about the limits of expertise in a complex world—and the limits on what it might be possible for even superforecasters to achieve. But as in the children's game of "telephone," in which a phrase is whispered to one child who passes it on to another, and so on, and everyone is shocked at the end to discover how much it has changed, the actual message was garbled in the constant retelling and the subtleties were lost entirely. The message became "all expert forecasts are useless," which is nonsense. Some variations were even cruder—like "experts know no more than chimpanzees." My research had become a backstop reference for nihilists who see the future as inherently unpredictable and know-nothing populists who insist on preceding "expert" with "so-called."

So I tired of the joke. My research did not support these more extreme conclusions, nor did I feel any affinity for them. Today, that is all the more true.

There is plenty of room to stake out reasonable positions between the debunkers and the defenders of experts and their forecasts. On the one hand, the debunkers have a point. There are shady peddlers of questionable insights in the forecasting marketplace. There are also limits to foresight that may just not be surmountable. Our desire to reach into the future will always exceed our grasp. But debunkers go too far when they dismiss all forecasting as a fool's errand. I believe it is possible to see into the future, at least in some situations and to some extent, and that any intelligent, open-minded, and hardworking person can cultivate the requisite skills.

Call me an "optimistic skeptic."

THE SKEPTIC

To understand the "skeptic" half of that label, consider a young Tunisian man pushing a wooden handcart loaded with fruits and vegetables down a dusty road to a market in the Tunisian town of Sidi Bouzid. When the man was three, his father died. He supports his family by borrowing money to fill his cart, hoping to earn enough selling the produce to pay off the debt and have a little left over. It's the same grind every day. But this morning, the police approach the man and say they're going to take his scales because he has violated some regulation. He knows it's a lie. They're shaking him down. But he has no money. A policewoman slaps him and insults his dead father. They take his scales and his cart. The man goes to a town office to complain. He is told the official is busy in a meeting. Humiliated, furious, powerless, the man leaves.

He returns with fuel. Outside the town office he douses himself, lights a match, and burns.

Only the conclusion of this story is unusual. There are countless poor street vendors in Tunisia and across the Arab world. Police corruption is rife, and humiliations like those inflicted on this man are a daily occurrence. They matter to no one aside from the police and their victims.

But this particular humiliation, on December 17, 2010, caused Mohamed Bouazizi, aged twenty-six, to set himself on fire, and Bouazizi's self-immolation sparked protests. The police responded with typical brutality. The protests spread. Hoping to assuage the public, the dictator of Tunisia, President Zine el-Abidine Ben Ali, visited Bouazizi in the hospital.

Bouazizi died on January 4, 2011. The unrest grew. On January 14, Ben Ali fled to a cushy exile in Saudi Arabia, ending his twenty-three-year kleptocracy.

The Arab world watched, stunned. Then protests erupted in Egypt, Libya, Syria, Jordan, Kuwait, and Bahrain. After three decades in power, the Egyptian dictator Hosni Mubarak was driven from office. Elsewhere, protests swelled into rebellions, rebellions into civil wars. This was the Arab Spring—and it started with one poor man, no different from countless others, being harassed by police, as so many have been, before and since, with no apparent ripple effects.

It is one thing to look backward and sketch a narrative arc, as I did here, connecting Mohamed Bouazizi to all the events that flowed out of his lonely protest. Tom Friedman, like many elite pundits, is skilled at that sort of reconstruction, particularly in the Middle East, which he knows so well, having made his name in journalism as a

New York Times correspondent in Lebanon. But could even Tom Friedman, if he had been present that fatal morning, have peered into the future and foreseen the self-immolation, the unrest, the toppling of the Tunisian dictator, and all that followed? Of course not. No one could. Maybe, given how much Friedman knew about the region, he would have mused that poverty and unemployment were high, the number of desperate young people was growing, corruption was rampant, repression was relentless, and therefore Tunisia and other Arab countries were powder kegs waiting to blow. But an observer could have drawn exactly the same conclusion the year before. And the year before that. Indeed, you could have said that about Tunisia, Egypt, and several other countries for decades. They may have been powder kegs but they never blew—until December 17, 2010, when the police pushed that one poor man too far.

In 1972 the American meteorologist Edward Lorenz wrote a paper with an arresting title: "Predictability: Does the Flap of a Butterfly's Wings in Brazil Set Off a Tornado in Texas?" A decade earlier, Lorenz had discovered by accident that tiny data entry variations in computer simulations of weather patterns—like replacing 0.506127 with 0.506—could produce dramatically different long-term forecasts. It was an insight that would inspire "chaos theory": in nonlinear systems like the atmosphere, even small changes in initial conditions can mushroom to enormous proportions. So, in principle, a lone butterfly in Brazil could flap its wings and set off a tornado in Texas—even though swarms of other Brazilian butterflies could flap frantically their whole lives and never cause a noticeable gust a few miles away. Of course Lorenz didn't mean that the butterfly "causes" the tornado in the same sense that I cause a wineglass to break when I hit it with a hammer. He meant that if that particular butterfly hadn't flapped its wings at that moment, the unfathomably complex network of atmospheric actions and reactions would have behaved differently, and the tornado might never have formed—just as the

Arab Spring might never have happened, at least not when and as it did, if the police had just let Mohamed Bouazizi sell his fruits and vegetables that morning in 2010.

Edward Lorenz shifted scientific opinion toward the view that there are hard limits on predictability, a deeply philosophical question.[4] For centuries, scientists had supposed that growing knowledge must lead to greater predictability because reality was like a clock—an awesomely big and complicated clock but still a clock—and the more scientists learned about its innards, how the gears grind together, how the weights and springs function, the better they could capture its operations with deterministic equations and predict what it would do. In 1814 the French mathematician and astronomer Pierre-Simon Laplace took this dream to its logical extreme:

> *We may regard the present state of the universe as the effect of its past and the cause of its future. An intellect which at a certain moment would know all forces that set nature in motion, and all positions of all items of which nature is composed, if this intellect were also vast enough to submit these data to analysis, it would embrace in a single formula the movements of the greatest bodies of the universe and those of the tiniest atom; for such an intellect nothing would be uncertain and the future just like the past would be present before its eyes.*

Laplace called his imaginary entity a "demon." If it knew everything about the present, Laplace thought, it could predict everything about the future. It would be omniscient.[5]

Lorenz poured cold rainwater on that dream. If the clock symbolizes perfect Laplacean predictability, its opposite is the Lorenzian cloud. High school science tells us that clouds form when water vapor coalesces around dust particles. This sounds simple but exactly how a particular cloud develops—the shape it takes—depends on complex feedback interactions among droplets. To capture these interactions, computer modelers need equations that are highly sensitive to tiny butterfly-effect errors in data collection. So even if we learn all that is knowable about how clouds form, we will not be able to predict the shape a particular cloud will take. We can only wait and see. In one of history's great ironies, scientists today know vastly more than their colleagues a century ago, and possess vastly more data-crunching power, but they are much less confident in the prospects for perfect predictability.

This is a big reason for the "skeptic" half of my "optimistic skeptic" stance. We live in a world where the actions of one nearly powerless man can have ripple effects around the world—ripples that affect us all to varying degrees. A woman living in a Kansas City suburb may think Tunisia is another planet, and her life has no connection to it, but if she were married to an air force navigator who flies out of the nearby Whiteman Air Force Base, she might be surprised to learn that one obscure Tunisian's actions led to protests, that led to riots, that led to the toppling of a dictator, that led to protests in Libya, that led to a civil war, that led to the 2012 NATO intervention, that led to her husband dodging antiaircraft fire over Tripoli. That's an easily traceable connection. Often the connections are harder to spot, but they are all around us, in things like the price we pay at the gas station or the layoffs down the street. In a world where a butterfly in Brazil can make the difference between just another sunny day in Texas and a tornado tearing through a town, it's misguided to think anyone can see very far into the future.[6]

THE OPTIMIST

But it is one thing to recognize the limits on predictability, and quite another to dismiss *all prediction* as an exercise in futility.

Crank up the microscope on a day in the life of that woman living in a Kansas City suburb: At 6:30 in the morning, she drops papers into a briefcase, gets in her car, drives her usual route to work, and parks downtown. As she does every weekday morning, she walks past the statues of lions and into the Greek-inspired office building of the Kansas City Life Insurance Company. At her desk, she works on spreadsheets for a while, participates in a conference call at 10:30, spends a few minutes browsing on the Amazon website, and answers e-mails until 11:50. Then she walks to a little Italian restaurant to have lunch with her sister.

This woman's life is influenced by many unpredictable factors—from the lottery ticket in her purse to the Arab Spring that results in her husband flying missions over Libya to the fact that the price of gas just went up five cents a gallon because there was a coup in some country she's never heard of—but there is as much or more that is quite predictable. Why did she leave home at 6:30? She didn't want to get stuck in rush hour. Or to put that another way, she predicted that traffic would be much heavier later—and she was almost certainly right because rush hour is highly predictable. When she drove, she anticipated other drivers' behavior constantly: they will stop at the intersection when the light is red; they will stay in their lanes and signal before turning. She expected the people who said they would join the 10:30 conference call to do so, and she was right. She arranged to meet her sister at noon at the restaurant because the restaurant's posted hours indicated it would open then, and posted hours are a reliable guide.

We make mundane predictions like these routinely, while others just as routinely make predictions that shape our lives. When the woman turned her computer on, she increased electricity consumption in Kansas City by a bit, as every other worker bee did that morning, and collectively they caused a demand surge, as they do every nonholiday weekday morning around that time. But that didn't cause problems because electricity producers anticipate these surges and vary their output accordingly. When the woman went to Amazon, the website highlighted certain products it thought she would like, a forecast derived from her past purchases and browsing and that of millions of others. We constantly encounter predictive operations like that on the Internet—Google personalizes search results by putting what it thinks you will find most interesting on top—but they operate so smoothly we rarely notice. And then there's the woman's workplace. The Kansas City Life Insurance Company is in the business of forecasting disability and death, and it does a good job. That doesn't mean it knows precisely when I will die, but it does have a good idea of how long someone of my age and profile—sex, income, lifestyle—is likely to live. Kansas City Life was founded in 1895. If its actuaries weren't good forecasters, it would have gone bankrupt long ago.

So much of our reality is this predictable, or more so. I just Googled tomorrow's sunrise and sunset times for Kansas City, Missouri, and got them down to the minute. Those forecasts are reliable, whether they are for tomorrow, the day after, or fifty years from now. The same is true of tides, eclipses, and phases of the moon. All can be predicted from clocklike scientific laws with enough precision to satisfy Laplace's forecasting demon.

Of course each of these pockets of predictability can be abruptly punctured. A good restaurant is very likely to open its doors when it says it will, but it may not, for any number of reasons, from a manager sleeping late, to fire, bankruptcy, pandemic, nuclear war, or a physics experiment accidentally creating a black hole that sucks up the solar system. The same is true of anything else. Even those fifty-year sunrise and sunset forecasts could be off somewhat if, sometime in the next fifty years, a massive space rock bumps Earth off its orbit around the sun. There are no certainties in life—not even death and taxes if we assign a nonzero probability to the invention of technologies that let us upload the contents of our brains into a cloud-computing network and the emergence of a future society so public-spirited and prosperous that the state can be funded with charitable donations.

So is reality clocklike or cloud-like? Is the future predictable or not? These are false dichotomies, the first of many we will encounter. We live in a world of clocks and clouds and a vast jumble of other metaphors. Unpredictability and predictability coexist uneasily in the intricately interlocking systems that make up our bodies, our societies, and the cosmos. How predictable something is depends on what we are trying to predict, how far into the future, and under what circumstances.

Look at Edward Lorenz's field. Weather forecasts are typically quite reliable, under most conditions, looking a few days ahead, but they become increasingly less accurate three, four, and five days out. Much beyond a week, we might as well consult that dart-throwing chimpanzee. So we can't say that weather is predictable or not, only that weather is predictable to some extent under some circumstances—and we must be very careful when we try to be more precise than that. Take something as seemingly simple as the relationship between time and predictability: it is generally true that the further we try to look into the future, the harder it is to see. But there can be prolonged exceptions to the rule. Predicting the continuation of a long bull market in stocks can prove profitable for many years—until it suddenly proves to be your undoing. And predicting that dinosaurs would continue to preside at the top of the food chain was a safe bet for tens of millions of years—until an asteroid set off a cataclysm that opened up ecological niches for a tiny mammal that eventually evolved into a species that tries to predict the future. Laws of physics aside, there are no universal constants, so separating the predictable from the unpredictable is difficult work. There's no way around it.

Meteorologists know that better than anyone. They make large numbers of forecasts and routinely check their accuracy—which is

why we know that one- and two-day forecasts are typically quite accurate while eight-day forecasts are not. With these analyses, meteorologists are able to sharpen their understanding of how weather works
and tweak their models. Then they try again. Forecast, measure, revise. Repeat. It's a never-ending process of incremental improvement
that explains why weather forecasts are good and slowly getting better.
There may be limits to such improvements, however, because weather
is the textbook illustration of nonlinearity. The further out the forecaster tries to look, the more opportunity there is for chaos to flap its
butterfly wings and blow away expectations. Big leaps in computing
power and continued refinement of forecasting models may nudge the
limits a little further into the future but those advances gradually get
harder and the payoffs shrink toward zero. How good can it get? No
one knows. But knowing the current limits is itself a success.

In so many other high-stakes endeavors, forecasters are groping
in the dark. They have no idea how good their forecasts are in the
short, medium, or long term—and no idea how good their forecasts
could become. At best, they have vague hunches. That's because the
forecast-measure-revise procedure operates only within the rarefied
confines of high-tech forecasting, such as the work of macroecono-
mists at central banks or marketing and financial professionals in
big companies or opinion poll analysts like Nate Silver.[7] More often
forecasts are made and then . . . nothing. Accuracy is seldom determined after the fact and is almost never done with sufficient regularity and rigor that conclusions can be drawn. The reason? Mostly it's a
demand-side problem: The consumers of forecasting—governments,
business, and the public—don't demand evidence of accuracy. So
there is no measurement. Which means no revision. And without
revision, there can be no improvement. Imagine a world in which
people love to run, but they have no idea how fast the average person
runs, or how fast the best could run, because runners have never
agreed to basic ground rules—stay on the track, begin the race when

the gun is fired, end it after a specified distance—and there are no independent race officials and timekeepers measuring results. How likely is it that running times are improving in this world? Not very. Are the best runners running as fast as human beings are physically capable? Again, probably not.

"I have been struck by how important measurement is to improving the human condition," Bill Gates wrote. "You can achieve incredible progress if you set a clear goal and find a measure that will drive progress toward that goal. . . . This may seem basic, but it is amazing how often it is not done and how hard it is to get right."[8] He is right about what it takes to drive progress, and it is surprising how rarely it's done in forecasting. Even that simple first step—setting a clear goal—hasn't been taken.

You might think the goal of forecasting is to foresee the future accurately, but that's often not the goal, or at least not the sole goal. Sometimes forecasts are meant to entertain. Think of CNBC's Jim Cramer with his "booyah!" shtick, or John McLaughlin, the host of *The McLaughlin Group*, bellowing at his panelists to predict the likelihood of an event "on a scale from zero to ten, with zero representing zero possibility and ten representing complete metaphysical certitude!" Sometimes forecasts are used to advance political agendas and galvanize action—as activists hope to do when they warn of looming horrors unless we change our ways. There is also dress-to-impress forecasting—which is what banks deliver when they pay a famous pundit to tell wealthy clients about the global economy in 2050. And some forecasts are meant to comfort—by assuring the audience that their beliefs are correct and the future will unfold as expected. Partisans are fond of these forecasts. They are the cognitive equivalent of slipping into a warm bath.

This jumble of goals is seldom acknowledged, which makes it difficult to even start working toward measurement and progress. It's a messy situation, which doesn't seem to be getting better.

And yet this stagnation is a big reason why I am an *optimistic* skeptic. We know that in so much of what people want to predict—politics, economics, finance, business, technology, daily life—predictability exists, to some degree, in some circumstances. But there is so much else we do not know. For scientists, not knowing is exciting. It's an opportunity to discover; the more that is unknown, the greater the opportunity. Thanks to the frankly quite amazing lack of rigor in so many forecasting domains, this opportunity is huge. And to seize it, all we have to do is set a clear goal—accuracy!—and get serious about measuring.

I've been doing that for much of my career. The research that produced the dart-throwing-chimpanzee result was phase one. Phase two started in the summer of 2011, when my research (and life) partner Barbara Mellers and I launched the Good Judgment Project and invited volunteers to sign up and forecast the future. Bill Flack responded. So did a couple of thousand others that first year, and thousands more in the four years that followed. Cumulatively, more than twenty thousand intellectually curious laypeople tried to figure out if protests in Russia would spread, the price of gold would plummet, the Nikkei would close above 9,500, war would erupt on the Korean peninsula, and many other questions about complex, challenging global issues. By varying the experimental conditions, we could gauge which factors improved foresight, by how much, over which time frames, and how good forecasts could become if best practices were layered on each other. Laid out like that, it sounds simple. It wasn't. It was a demanding program that took the talents and hard work of a multidisciplinary team based at the University of California, Berkeley, and the University of Pennsylvania.

Big as it was, the Good Judgment Project (GJP) was only part of a much larger research effort sponsored by the Intelligence Advanced Research Projects Activity (IARPA). Don't be put off by the bland name. IARPA is an agency within the intelligence community that reports to the director of National Intelligence and its job is to support daring research that promises to make American intelligence better at what it does. And a big part of what American intelligence does is forecast global political and economic trends. By one rough estimate, the United States has twenty thousand intelligence analysts assessing everything from minute puzzles to major events such as the likelihood of an Israeli sneak attack on Iranian nuclear facilities or the departure of Greece from the eurozone.[9] How good is all this forecasting? That is not easily answered because the intelligence community, like so many major producers of forecasting, has never been keen on spending money to figure that out. There are various reasons for that reluctance, some more respectable than others, but we'll get into that later. What matters is that this forecasting is critical to national security and yet little can be said with any confidence about how good it is, or even whether it's as good as a multibillion-dollar operation with twenty thousand people should be. To change that, IARPA created a forecasting tournament in which five scientific teams led by top researchers in the field would compete to generate accurate forecasts on the sorts of tough questions intelligence analysts deal with every day. The Good Judgment Project was one of those five teams. Each team would effectively be its own research project, free to improvise whatever methods it thought would work, but required to submit forecasts at 9 a.m. eastern standard time every day from September 2011 to June 2015. By requiring teams to forecast the same questions at the same time, the tournament created a level playing field—and a rich trove of data about what works, how well, and when. Over four years, IARPA posed nearly five hundred questions about world affairs. Time frames were shorter than in my earlier research, with the vast majority of forecasts extending out more than one month and less than one year. In all, we gathered over one million individual judgments about the future.

In year 1, GJP beat the official control group by 60%. In year 2,

we beat the control group by 78%. GJP also beat its university-
affiliated competitors, including the University of Michigan and
MIT, by hefty margins, from 30% to 70%, and even outperformed
professional intelligence analysts with access to classified data. After
two years, GJP was doing so much better than its academic competitors that IARPA dropped the other teams.[10]

I'll delve into details later, but let's note two key conclusions that
emerge from this research. One, foresight is real. Some people—
people like Bill Flack—have it in spades. They aren't gurus or oracles
with the power to peer decades into the future, but they do have a
real, measurable skill at judging how high-stakes events are likely to
unfold three months, six months, a year, or a year and a half in advance. The other conclusion is what makes these superforecasters so
good. It's not really who they are. It is what they do. Foresight isn't a
mysterious gift bestowed at birth. It is the product of particular ways
of thinking, of gathering information, of updating beliefs. These
habits of thought can be learned and cultivated by any intelligent,
thoughtful, determined person. It may not even be all that hard to
get started. One result that particularly surprised me was the effect
of a tutorial covering some basic concepts that we'll explore in this
book and are summarized in the Ten Commandments appendix. It
took only about sixty minutes to read and yet it improved accuracy
by roughly 10% through the entire tournament year. Yes, 10% may
sound modest, but it was achieved at so little cost. And never forget
that even modest improvements in foresight maintained over time
add up. I spoke about that with Aaron Brown, an author, a Wall
Street veteran, and the chief risk manager at AQR Capital Management, a hedge fund with over $100 billion in assets. "It's so hard to
see because it's not dramatic," he said, but if it is sustained "it's the
difference between a consistent winner who's making a living, or the
guy who's going broke all the time."[11] A world-class poker player we
will meet soon could not agree more. The difference between heavy-

weights and amateurs, she said, is that the heavyweights know the difference between a $^{60}/_{40}$ bet and a $^{40}/_{60}$ bet.

And yet, if it's possible to improve foresight simply by measuring, and if the rewards of improved foresight are substantial, why isn't measuring standard practice? A big part of the answer to that question lies in the psychology that convinces us we know things we really don't—things like whether Tom Friedman is an accurate forecaster or not. I'll explore this psychology in chapter 2. For centuries, it hobbled progress in medicine. When physicians finally accepted that their experience and perceptions were not reliable means of determining whether a treatment works, they turned to scientific testing—and medicine finally started to make rapid advances. The same revolution needs to happen in forecasting.

It won't be easy. Chapter 3 examines what it takes to test forecasting as rigorously as modern medicine tests treatments. It's a bigger challenge than it may appear. In the late 1980s I worked out a methodology and conducted what was, at the time, the biggest test of expert political forecasting accuracy ever. One result, delivered many years later, was the punch line that now makes me squirm. But another discovery of that research didn't receive nearly as much attention even though it was far more important: one group of experts had modest but real foresight. What made the difference between the experts with foresight and those who were so hopeless they dragged the average down to the level of a dart-throwing chimp? It wasn't some mystical gift or access to information others didn't have. Nor was it any particular set of beliefs. Indeed, within a quite wide range of views, *what* they thought didn't matter. It was *how* they thought.

Inspired in part by that insight, IARPA created its unprecedented forecasting tournament. Chapter 4 is the story of how that happened—and the discovery of superforecasters. Why are they so good? That question runs through chapters 5 through 9. When you meet them it's hard not to be struck by how smart they are, so you might suspect it's intelligence that makes all the difference. It's not. They're also remarkably numerate. Like Bill Flack, many have advanced degrees in mathematics and science. So is the secret arcane math? No. Even superforecasters who are card-carrying mathematicians rarely use much math. They also tend to be newsjunkies who stay on top of the latest developments and regularly update their forecasts, so you might be tempted to attribute their success to spending endless hours on the job. Yet that too would be a mistake.

Superforecasting does require minimum levels of intelligence, numeracy, and knowledge of the world, but anyone who reads serious books about psychological research probably has those prerequisites. So what is it that elevates forecasting to superforecasting? As with the experts who had real foresight in my earlier research, what matters most is *how* the forecaster thinks. I'll describe this in detail, but broadly speaking, superforecasting demands thinking that is open-minded, careful, curious, and—above all—self-critical. It also demands focus. The kind of thinking that produces superior judgment does not come effortlessly. Only the determined can deliver it reasonably consistently, which is why our analyses have consistently found commitment to self-improvement to be the strongest predictor of performance.

In the final chapters, I'll resolve an apparent contradiction between the demands of good judgment and effective leadership, respond to what I think are the two strongest challenges to my research, and conclude—appropriately for a book about forecasting—with a consideration of what comes next.

A FORECAST ABOUT FORECASTING

But maybe you think this is all hopelessly outdated. After all, we live in an era of dazzlingly powerful computers, incomprehensible algorithms, and Big Data. At its core, the forecasting I study involves subjective judgment: it is people thinking and deciding, nothing more. Isn't the time for such sloppy guesswork drawing to a close?

In 1954, a brilliant psychologist, Paul Meehl wrote a small book that caused a big stir.[12] It reviewed twenty studies showing that well-informed experts predicting outcomes—whether a student would succeed in college or a parolee would be sent back to prison—were not as accurate as simple algorithms that added up objective indicators like ability test scores and records of past conduct. Meehl's claim upset many experts, but subsequent research—now more than two hundred studies—has shown that in most cases statistical algorithms beat subjective judgment, and in the handful of studies where they don't, they usually tie. Given that algorithms are quick and cheap, unlike subjective judgment, a tie supports using the algorithm. The point is now indisputable: when you have a well-validated statistical algorithm, use *it*.

This insight was never a threat to the reign of subjective judgment because we so rarely have well-validated algorithms for the problem at hand. It was just impractical for math to displace plain old thinking—in 1954 and even today.

But spectacular advances in information technology suggest we are approaching a historical discontinuity in humanity's relationship with machines. In 1997 IBM's Deep Blue beat chess champion Garry Kasparov. Now, commercially available chess programs can beat any human. In 2011 IBM's Watson beat *Jeopardy!* champions Ken Jennings and Brad Rutter. That was a vastly tougher computing challenge, but Watson's engineers did it. Today, it's no longer impossible to imagine a forecasting competition in which a supercomputer trounces superforecasters and superpundits alike. After that happens, there will still be human forecasters, but like human *Jeopardy!* contestants, we will only watch them for entertainment.

So I spoke to Watson's chief engineer, David Ferrucci. I was sure that Watson could easily field a question about the present or past like "Which two Russian leaders traded jobs in the last ten years?" But I was curious about his views on how long it will take for Watson or one of its digital descendants to field questions like "Will two top Russian leaders trade jobs in the next ten years?"

In 1965 the polymath Herbert Simon thought we were only twenty years away from a world in which machines could do "any work a man can do," which is the sort of naively optimistic thing people said back then, and one reason why Ferrucci—who has worked in artificial intelligence for thirty years—is more cautious today.[13] Computing is making enormous strides, Ferrucci noted. The ability to spot patterns is growing spectacularly. And machine learning, in combination with burgeoning human-machine interactions that feed the learning process, promises far more fundamental advances to come. "It's going to be one of these exponential curves that we're kind of at the bottom of now," Ferrucci said.

But there is a vast difference between "Which two Russian leaders traded jobs?" and "Will two Russian leaders trade jobs again?" The former is a historical fact. The computer can look it up. The latter requires the computer to make an informed guess about the intentions of Vladimir Putin, the character of Dmitri Medvedev, and the causal dynamics of Russian politics, and then integrate that information into a judgment call. People do that sort of thing all the time, but that doesn't make it easy. It means the human brain is wondrous—because the task is staggeringly hard. Even with computers making galloping advances, the sort of forecasting that superforecasters do is a long way off. And Ferrucci isn't sure we will ever see a human under glass at the Smithsonian with a sign saying "subjective judgment."

Machines may get better at "mimicking human meaning," and thereby better at predicting human behavior, but "there's a difference between mimicking and reflecting meaning and originating meaning," Ferrucci said. That's a space human judgment will always occupy.

In forecasting, as in other fields, we will continue to see human judgment being displaced—to the consternation of white-collar workers—but we will also see more and more syntheses, like "freestyle chess," in which humans with computers compete as teams, the human drawing on the computer's indisputable strengths but also occasionally overriding the computer. The result is a combination that can (sometimes) beat both humans and machines. To reframe the man-versus-machine dichotomy, combinations of Garry Kasparov and Deep Blue may prove more robust than pure-human or pure-machine approaches.

What Ferrucci does see becoming obsolete is the guru model that makes so many policy debates so puerile: "I'll counter your Paul Krugman polemic with my Niall Ferguson counterpolemic, and rebut your Tom Friedman op-ed with my Bret Stephens blog." Ferrucci sees light at the end of this long dark tunnel: "I think it's going to get stranger and stranger" for people to listen to the advice of experts whose views are informed only by their subjective judgment. Human thought is beset by psychological pitfalls, a fact that has only become widely recognized in the last decade or two. "So what I want is that human expert paired with a computer to overcome the human cognitive limitations and biases."[14]

If Ferrucci is right—I suspect he is—we will need to blend computer-based forecasting and subjective judgment in the future. So it's time we got serious about both.

2

Illusions of Knowledge

When the dermatologist saw spots on the back of the patient's hand, he was suspicious and removed a bit of skin. A pathologist confirmed it was a basal cell carcinoma. The patient didn't panic. He too was a physician. He knew this form of cancer seldom spreads. The carcinoma was removed and, as a precaution, the patient arranged to see a big-name specialist.

The specialist discovered a lump in the patient's right armpit, or axilla. How long had it been there? The patient didn't know. The specialist said it should come out. The patient agreed. After all, the specialist was a renowned figure. If he said "take it out," who would disagree? The surgery was booked.

When the anesthesia wore off and the patient awoke, he was surprised to find his whole chest wrapped in bandages. The specialist arrived. His expression was grim. "I must tell you the truth," he began. "Your axilla is full of cancerous tissue. I have done my best to excise it and have removed your pectoralis minor but I may well not have saved your life."[1] That last statement was a modest attempt to soften the blow. As the specialist made all too clear, the patient hadn't long to live.

"For a moment the world seemed to end," the patient later wrote. "After a short period of surprise and shock I turned as far as I could on my side and sobbed unashamedly. I do not remember much about the rest of the day." The next morning, with a clear mind, "I worked out a simple plan of how I would spend my remaining time. . . . A curious feeling of peace came over me when I had completed the plan, and I fell asleep." In the days that followed, visitors came to offer the patient whatever comfort they could. He found it all rather awkward. "It was soon clear that they were more embarrassed than I was," he wrote.[2] He was dying. That was a fact. One had to keep calm and do what one must. There was no use blubbering.

This melancholy moment happened in 1956 but the patient, Archie Cochrane, did not die, which is fortunate because he went on to become a revered figure in medicine. The specialist was wrong. Cochrane didn't have terminal cancer. He didn't have cancer at all, as a pathologist discovered when he examined the tissue removed during surgery. Cochrane was as shocked by his reprieve as by his death sentence. "I had been told that the pathologist had not yet reported," he wrote many years later, "but I never doubted the surgeon's words."[3]

That's the problem. Cochrane didn't doubt the specialist and the specialist didn't doubt his own judgment and so neither man considered the possibility that the diagnosis was wrong and neither thought it wise to wait for the pathologist's report before closing the books on the life of Archie Cochrane. But we shouldn't judge them too harshly. It's human nature. We have all been too quick to make up our minds and too slow to change them. And if we don't examine how we make these mistakes, we will keep making them. This stagnation can go on for years. Or a lifetime. It can even last centuries, as the long and wretched history of medicine illustrates.

BLIND MEN ARGUING

The "long" part is obvious enough. People have been trying to make the sick well for as long as people have been getting sick. But "wretched"? That is less obvious, even for readers familiar with the history of medicine, because "most histories of medicine are strikingly odd," as the British physician and author Druin Burch noted.

"They provide a clear account of what people believed they were doing, but almost none at all of whether they were right."[4] Did the ostrich egg poultices applied by ancient Egyptian physicians actually heal head fractures? In ancient Mesopotamia, did the treatments of the Keeper of the Royal Rectum actually keep royal rectums healthy? What about bloodletting? Everyone from the ancient Greeks to George Washington's doctors swore that it was wonderfully restorative, but did it work? The standard histories are usually mute on these scores, but when we use modern science to judge the efficacy of historical treatments, it becomes depressingly clear that most of the interventions were useless or worse. Until quite recently in historical terms, it was not unusual for a sick person to be better off if there was no physician available because letting an illness take its natural course was less dangerous than what a physician would inflict. And treatments seldom got better, no matter how much time passed. When George Washington fell ill in 1799, his esteemed physicians bled him relentlessly, dosed him with mercury to cause diarrhea, induced vomiting, and raised blood-filled blisters by applying hot cups to the old man's skin. A physician in Aristotle's Athens, or Nero's Rome, or medieval Paris, or Elizabethan London would have nodded at much of that hideous regimen.

Washington died. One might assume that such results would make physicians question their methods but, to be fair, the fact that Washington died proves nothing about the treatments beyond that they failed to prevent his death. It's possible that the treatments helped but not enough to overcome the disease that took Washington's life, or that they didn't help at all, or that the treatments even hastened Washington's death. It's impossible to know which of these conclusions is true merely by observing that one outcome. Even with many such observations, the truth can be difficult or impossible to tease out. There are just too many factors involved, too many possible explanations, too many unknowns. And if physicians are already inclined to think the treatments work—which they are, or they wouldn't prescribe them—all that ambiguity is likely to be read in favor of the happy conclusion that the treatments really are effective. It takes strong evidence and more rigorous experimentation than the "bleed the patient and see if he gets better" variety to overwhelm preconceptions. And that was never done.

Consider Galen, the second-century physician to Roman emperors. No one has influenced more generations of physicians. Galen's writings were the indisputable source of medical authority for more than a thousand years. "It is I, and I alone, who has revealed the true path of medicine," Galen wrote with his usual modesty. And yet Galen never conducted anything resembling a modern experiment. Why should he? Experiments are what people do when they aren't sure what the truth is. And Galen was untroubled by doubt. Each outcome confirmed he was right, no matter how equivocal the evidence might look to someone less wise than the master. "All who drink of this treatment recover in a short time, except those whom it does not help, who all die," he wrote. "It is obvious, therefore, that it fails only in incurable cases."[5]

Galen is an extreme example but he is the sort of figure who pops up repeatedly in the history of medicine. They are men (always men) of strong conviction and a profound trust in their own judgment. They embrace treatments, develop bold theories for why they work, denounce rivals as quacks and charlatans, and spread their insights with evangelical passion. So it went from the ancient Greeks to Galen to Paracelsus to the German Samuel Hahnemann and the American Benjamin Rush. In the nineteenth century, American medicine saw pitched battles between orthodox physicians and a host of charismatic figures with curious new theories like Thomsonianism, which posited that most illness was due to an excess of cold in the body, or the orificial surgery of Edwin Hartley Pratt, whose fundamental insight was that, as one detractor put it, with only modest exaggeration, "the rectum is the focus of existence, contains the essence of life, and performs the functions ordinarily ascribed to the heart and brain."[6] Fringe or mainstream, almost all of it was wrong, with the treatments on offer ranging from the frivolous to the dangerous. Some physicians feared as much but most carried on with business as usual. Ignorance and confidence remained defining features of medicine. As the surgeon and historian Ira Rutkow observed, physicians who furiously debated the merits of various treatments and theories were "like blind men arguing over the colors of the rainbow."[7]

The cure for this plague of certainty came tantalizingly close to discovery in 1747, when a British ship's doctor named James Lind took twelve sailors suffering from scurvy, divided them into pairs, and gave each pair a different treatment: vinegar, cider, sulfuric acid, seawater, a bark paste, and citrus fruit. It was an experiment born of desperation. Scurvy was a mortal threat to sailors on long-distance voyages and not even the confidence of physicians could hide the futility of their treatments. So Lind took six shots in the dark—and one hit. The two sailors given the citrus recovered quickly. But contrary to popular belief, this was not a eureka moment that ushered in the modern era of experimentation. "Lind was behaving in what sounds a modern way, but had no full understanding of what he was doing," noted Druin Burch. "He failed so completely to make sense of his own experiment that even he was left unconvinced of the exceptional benefits of lemons and limes."[8] For years thereafter, sailors kept getting scurvy and doctors kept prescribing worthless medicine.

Not until the twentieth century did the idea of randomized trial experiments, careful measurement, and statistical power take hold. "Is the application of the numerical method to the subject-matter of medicine a trivial and time-wasting ingenuity as some hold, or is it an important stage in the development of our art, as others proclaim it," the *Lancet* asked in 1921. The British statistician Austin Bradford Hill responded emphatically that it was the latter, and laid out a template for modern medical investigation. If patients who were identical in every way were put into two groups, and the groups were treated differently, he wrote, we would know the treatment caused any difference in outcome. It seems simple but is impossible in practice because no two people are exactly alike, not even identical twins, so the experiment will be confounded by the differences among test subjects. The solution lay in statistics: Randomly assigning people to one group or the other would mean whatever differences there are among them should balance out if enough people participated in the experiment. Then we can confidently conclude that the treatment caused any differences in observed outcomes. It isn't perfect. There is no perfection in our messy world. But it beats wise men stroking their chins.

This seems stunningly obvious today. Randomized controlled trials are now routine. Yet it was revolutionary because medicine had never before been scientific. True, it had occasionally reaped the fruits of science like the germ theory of disease and the X-ray. And it dressed up as a science. There were educated men with impressive titles who conducted case studies and reported results in Latin-laden lectures at august universities. But it wasn't scientific.

It was cargo cult science, a term of mockery coined much later by the physicist Richard Feynman to describe what happened after American airbases from World War II were removed from remote South Pacific islands, ending the islanders' only contact with the outside world. The planes had brought wondrous goods. The islanders wanted more. So they "arranged to make things like runways, to put fires along the sides of the runways, to make a wooden hut for a man to sit in, with two wooden pieces on his head like headphones and bars of bamboo sticking out like antennas—he's the controller—and they wait for the planes to land."[9] But the planes never returned. So cargo cult science has the outward form of science but lacks what makes it truly scientific.

What medicine lacked was doubt. "Doubt is not a fearful thing,"

Feynman observed, "but a thing of very great value."[10] It's what propels science forward.

> *When the scientist tells you he does not know the answer, he is an ignorant man. When he tells you he has a hunch about how it is going to work, he is uncertain about it. When he is pretty sure of how it is going to work, and he tells you, "This is the way it's going to work, I'll bet," he still is in some doubt. And it is of paramount importance, in order to make progress, that we recognize this ignorance and this doubt. Because we have the doubt, we then propose looking in new directions for new ideas. The rate of the development of science is not the rate at which you make observations alone but, much more important, the rate at which you create new things to test.*[11]

It was the absence of doubt—and scientific rigor—that made medicine unscientific and caused it to stagnate for so long.

PUTTING MEDICINE TO THE TEST

Unfortunately, this story doesn't end with physicians suddenly slapping themselves on their collective forehead and putting their beliefs to experimental tests. The idea of randomized controlled trials was painfully slow to catch on and it was only after World War II that the first serious trials were attempted. They delivered excellent results. But still the physicians and scientists who promoted the modernization of medicine routinely found that the medical establishment wasn't interested, or was even hostile to their efforts. "Too much that was being done in the name of health care lacked scientific validation," Archie Cochrane complained about medicine in the 1950s and 1960s, and the National Health Service—the British health care system—had "far too little interest in proving and promoting what was effective." Physicians and the institutions they controlled didn't want to let go of the idea that their judgment alone revealed the truth, so they kept doing what they did because they had always done it that way—and they were backed up by respected authority. They didn't need scientific validation. They just knew. Cochrane despised this attitude. He called it "the God complex."

When hospitals created cardiac care units to treat patients recovering from heart attacks, Cochrane proposed a randomized trial to determine whether the new units delivered better results than the old treatment, which was to send the patient home for monitoring and bed rest. Physicians balked. It was obvious the cardiac care units were superior, they said, and denying patients the best care would be unethical. But Cochrane was not a man to back down. As a prison camp physician treating fellow POWs during World War II he often stood up to the authorities. On occasion, he loudly berated trigger-happy German guards. So Cochrane got his trial: some patients, randomly selected, were sent to the cardiac care units while others were sent home for monitoring and bed rest. Partway through the trial, Cochrane met with a group of the cardiologists who had tried to stop his experiment. He told them that he had preliminary results. The difference in outcomes between the two treatments was not statistically significant, he emphasized, but it appeared that patients might do slightly better in the cardiac care units. "They were vociferous in their abuse: 'Archie,' they said, 'we always thought you were unethical. You must stop the trial at once.'" But then Cochrane revealed he had played a little trick. He had reversed the results: home care had done slightly better than the cardiac units. "There was dead silence and I felt rather sick because they were, after all, my medical colleagues."

Unusually high heart disease rates among prisoners drew Cochrane's attention to the justice system, where he encountered the same attitudes among prison wardens, judges, and Home Office officials. What people didn't grasp is that the only alternative to a controlled experiment that delivers real insight is an uncontrolled experiment that produces merely the illusion of insight. Cochrane cited the Thatcher government's "short, sharp, shock" approach to young offenders, which called for brief incarceration in spartan jails governed by strict rules. Did it work? The government had simply implemented it throughout the justice system, making it impossible to answer. If the policy was introduced and crime went down, that might mean the policy worked, or perhaps crime went down for any of a hundred other possible reasons. If crime went up, that might show the policy was useless or even harmful, or it might mean crime would have risen even more but for the beneficial effects of the policy. Naturally, politicians would claim otherwise. Those in power would say it worked; their opponents would say it failed. But nobody would really know. The politicians would be blind men arguing over the colors of the rainbow. If the government had subjected its policy "to a randomized controlled trial then we might, by now, have known its true worth and be some way ahead in our thinking," Cochrane observed. But it hadn't. It had just assumed that its policy would work as expected. This was the same toxic brew of ignorance and confidence that had kept medicine in the dark ages for millennia.

Cochrane's frustration is palpable in his autobiography. Why couldn't people see that intuition alone was no basis for firm conclusions? It was "bewildering."

Yet when this skeptical scientist was told by an eminent physician that his body was riddled with cancer and he should prepare to die, Archie Cochrane meekly acquiesced. He did not think, "That's just one man's subjective judgment, it could be wrong, so I'll wait for the pathologist's report. And why did the surgeon cut out my muscle before hearing from the pathologist, anyway?"[12] Cochrane treated the physician's conclusion as fact and prepared to die.

So there are two riddles. First, there is Cochrane's modest point that much more than intuition is needed before we draw firm conclusions. It is so obviously true. Why did people resist it? Why, specifically, did the specialist not think to wait to hear from the pathologist before removing a swath of Cochrane's flesh? Then there is the puzzle of Cochrane himself. Why did a man who stressed the importance of not rushing to judgment rush to judgment about whether he had terminal cancer?

THINKING ABOUT THINKING

It is natural to identify our thinking with the ideas, images, plans, and feelings that flow through consciousness. What else could it be? If I ask, "Why did you buy that car?" you can trot out reasons: "Good mileage. Cute style. Great price." But you can only share thoughts by introspecting; that is, by turning your attention inward and examining the contents of your mind. And introspection can only capture a tiny fraction of the complex processes whirling inside your head—and behind your decisions.

In describing how we think and decide, modern psychologists often deploy a dual-system model that partitions our mental universe into two domains. System 2 is the familiar realm of conscious thought. It consists of everything we choose to focus on. By contrast, System 1 is largely a stranger to us. It is the realm of automatic perceptual and cognitive operations—like those you are running right now to transform the print on this page into a meaningful sentence or to hold the book while reaching for a glass and taking a sip. We have no awareness of these rapid-fire processes but we could not function without them. We would shut down.

The numbering of the two systems is not arbitrary. System 1 comes first. It is fast and constantly running in the background. If a question is asked and you instantly know the answer, it sprang from

System 1. System 2 is charged with interrogating that answer. Does it stand up to scrutiny? Is it backed by evidence? This process takes time and effort, which is why the standard routine in decision making is this: first System 1 delivers an answer, and only then can System 2 get involved, starting with an examination of what System 1 decided.

Whether System 2 actually *will* get involved is another matter. Try answering this: "A bat and ball together cost $1.10. The bat costs a dollar more than the ball. How much does the ball cost?" If you are like just about everybody who has ever read this famous question, you instantly had an answer: "Ten cents." You didn't think carefully to get that. You didn't calculate anything. It just appeared. For that, you can thank System 1. Quick and easy, no effort required.

But is "ten cents" right? Think about the question carefully.

You probably realized a couple of things. First, conscious thought is demanding. Thinking the problem through requires sustained focus and takes an eternity relative to the snap judgment you got with a quick look. Second, "ten cents" is wrong. It feels right. But it's wrong. In fact, it's obviously wrong—if you give it a sober second thought.

The bat-and-ball question is one item in an ingenious psychological measure, the Cognitive Reflection Test, which has shown that most people—including very smart people—aren't very reflective. They read the question, think "ten cents," and scribble down "ten cents" as their final answer without thinking carefully. So they never discover the mistake, let alone come up with the correct answer (five cents). That is normal human behavior. We tend to go with strong hunches. System 1 follows a primitive psycho-logic: if it feels true, it is.

In the Paleolithic world in which our brains evolved, that's not a bad way of making decisions. Gathering all evidence and mulling it over may be the best way to produce accurate answers, but a hunter-gatherer who consults statistics on lions before deciding whether to worry about the shadow moving in the grass isn't likely to live long enough to bequeath his accuracy-maximizing genes to the next generation. Snap judgments are sometimes essential. As Daniel Kahneman puts it, "System 1 is designed to jump to conclusions from little evidence."[13]

So what about that shadow in the long grass? Should you worry? Well, can you recall a lion emerging from the grass and pouncing on someone? If that memory comes to you easily—it is not the sort of thing people tend to forget—you will conclude lion attacks are common. And then start to worry. Spelling out this process makes it sound ponderous, slow, and calculating but it can happen entirely within System 1—making it automatic, fast, and complete within a few tenths of a second. You see the shadow. Snap! You are frightened—and running. That's the "availability heuristic," one of many System 1 operations—or heuristics—discovered by Daniel Kahneman, his collaborator Amos Tversky, and other researchers in the fast-growing science of judgment and choice.

A defining feature of intuitive judgment is its insensitivity to the quality of the evidence on which the judgment is based. It has to be that way. System 1 can only do its job of delivering strong conclusions at lightning speed if it never pauses to wonder whether the evidence at hand is flawed or inadequate, or if there is better evidence elsewhere. It must treat the available evidence as reliable and sufficient. These tacit assumptions are so vital to System 1 that Kahneman gave them an ungainly but oddly memorable label: WYSIATI (What You See Is All There Is).[14]

Of course, System 1 can't conclude whatever it wants. The human brain demands order. The world must make sense, which means we must be able to explain what we see and think. And we usually can—because we are creative confabulators hardwired to invent stories that impose coherence on the world.

Imagine you're sitting at a table in a research lab, looking at rows of pictures. You pick one, a picture of a shovel. Why are you pointing at that? Of course you can't answer without more information. But if you were actually at that table, with your finger pointing at a picture of a shovel, simply saying "I don't know" would be a lot harder than you might think. Sane people are expected to have sensible-sounding reasons for their actions. It is awkward to tell others, especially white-lab-coated neuroscientists, "I have no idea why—I just am."

In celebrated research, Michael Gazzaniga designed a bizarre situation in which sane people did indeed have no idea why they were doing what they were doing. His test subjects were "split-brain" patients, meaning that the left and right hemispheres of their brains could not communicate with each other because the connection between them, the corpus callosum, had been surgically severed (traditionally as a treatment for severe epilepsy). These people are re-markably normal, but their condition allows researchers to commu-nicate directly with only one hemisphere of their brain—by showing an image to only the left or right field of vision—without sharing the communication with the other hemisphere. It's like talking to two different people. In this case, the left field of vision (which reports to the right hemisphere) was shown a picture of a snowstorm and the person was asked to point to the picture that related to it. So he quite reasonably pointed at the shovel. The right field of vision (which reports to the left hemisphere) was shown an image of a chicken claw—and the person was then asked why his hand was pointed at a shovel. The left hemisphere had no idea why. But the person didn't say "I don't know." Instead, he made up a story: "Oh, that's simple," one patient said. "The chicken claw goes with the chicken, and you need a shovel to clean out the chicken shed."[15]

This compulsion to explain arises with clocklike regularity every time a stock market closes and a journalist says something like "The Dow rose ninety-five points today on news that . . ." A quick check will often reveal that the news that supposedly drove the market came out well after the market had risen. But that minimal level of scrutiny is seldom applied. It's a rare day when a journalist says, "The market rose today for any one of a hundred different reasons, or a mix of them, so no one knows." Instead, like a split-brain patient asked why he is pointing at a picture of a shovel when he has no idea why, the journalist conjures a plausible story from whatever is at hand.

The explanatory urge is mostly a good thing. Indeed, it is the propulsive force behind all human efforts to comprehend reality. The problem is that we move too fast from confusion and uncertainty ("I have no idea why my hand is pointed at a picture of a shovel") to a clear and confident conclusion ("Oh, that's simple") without spending any time in between ("This is one possible explanation but there are others").

In 2011, when a massive car bomb killed eight people and injured over two hundred in Oslo, the capital of Norway, the first reaction was shock. This was Oslo, one of the most peaceful and prosperous cities on the planet. Speculation erupted on the Internet and cable news. It had to be radical Islamists. It was a car bomb intended to kill as many as possible. And the car had been parked outside the office tower where the prime minister works. It *had* to be Islamists. Just like the London, Madrid, and Bali bombings. Just like 9/11. People rushed to Google to see if they could find supporting information. They succeeded: Norway has soldiers in Afghanistan as part of the NATO mission; Norway has a poorly integrated Muslim community; a radical Muslim preacher had been charged with incitement the week before. Then came word that an even more shocking crime had been committed not long after the bombing. It was a mass shooting—dozens dead—at a summer camp for young people run by the ruling Labour Party. Everything fit. These were coordinated attacks by Islamist terrorists. No doubt about it. Whether the terrorists were homegrown or linked to al-Qaeda remained to be seen, but it was obvious the perpetrators had to be extremist Muslims.

As it turned out, there was only one perpetrator. His name is

Anders Breivik. He isn't Muslim. He hates Muslims. Breivik's attacks were aimed at a government that he felt had betrayed Norway with its multiculturalist policies. After Breivik's arrest, many people accused those who had rushed to judgment of Islamophobia, and not without reason, as some of them had seemed all too eager to blame Muslims in general. But given the few facts known at the time, and the history of mass-atrocity terrorism in the preceding decade, it was reasonable to suspect Islamist terrorists. A scientist would describe that as a "plausible hypothesis." But a scientist would have handled that plausible hypothesis very differently.

Like everyone else, scientists have intuitions. Indeed, hunches and flashes of insight—the sense that something is true even if you can't prove it—have been behind countless breakthroughs. The interplay between System 1 and System 2 can be subtle and creative. But scientists are trained to be cautious. They know that no matter how tempting it is to anoint a pet hypothesis as The Truth, alternative explanations must get a hearing. And they must seriously consider the possibility that their initial hunch is wrong. In fact, in science, the best evidence that a hypothesis is true is often an experiment designed to prove the hypothesis is false, but which fails to do so. Scientists must be able to answer the question "What would convince me I am wrong?" If they can't, it's a sign they have grown too attached to their beliefs.

The key is doubt. Scientists can feel just as strongly as anyone else that they know The Truth. But they know they must set that feeling aside and replace it with finely measured degrees of doubt—doubt that can be reduced (although never to zero) by better evidence from better studies.

Such scientific caution runs against the grain of human nature. As the post-Oslo speculation reveals, our natural inclination is to grab on to the first plausible explanation and happily gather supportive evidence without checking its reliability. That is what psychologists call confirmation bias. We rarely seek out evidence that undercuts our first explanation, and when that evidence is shoved under our noses we become motivated skeptics—finding reasons, however tenuous, to belittle it or throw it out entirely.[16] Recall Galen's sublime confidence that his wonderful treatment cured everyone who took it except the "incurable cases" who died. That was pure confirmation bias: "If the patient is cured, it is evidence my treatment works; if the patient dies, it means nothing."

This is a poor way to build an accurate mental model of a complicated world, but it's a superb way to satisfy the brain's desire for order because it yields tidy explanations with no loose ends. Everything is clear, consistent, and settled. And the fact that "it all fits" gives us confidence that we know the truth. "It is wise to take admissions of uncertainty seriously," Daniel Kahneman noted, "but declarations of high confidence mainly tell you that an individual has constructed a coherent story in his mind, not necessarily that the story is true."[17]

BAIT AND SWITCH

When the eminent specialist cut into Archie Cochrane's armpit, he saw tissue that appeared riddled with cancer. Was it? It made sense that it would be. There was the lump in the patient's armpit. The carcinoma on his hand. And years before, Cochrane had been involved in research that had exposed him to X-rays, which was why the first doctor had urged him to see the specialist. It all fit. This was cancer. No doubt about it. And no need to wait for the pathologist's report before removing one of Cochrane's muscles and advising the patient that he hadn't long to live.

Archie Cochrane's skeptical defenses folded because Cochrane found the specialist's story as intuitively compelling as the specialist did. But another mental process was likely at work, as well. Formally, it's called attribute substitution, but I call it *bait and switch*: when faced with a hard question, we often surreptitiously replace it with an easy one. "Should I worry about the shadow in the long grass?" is a hard question. Without more data, it may be unanswerable. So we substitute an easier question: "Can I easily recall a lion attacking someone from the long grass?" That question becomes a proxy for the original question and if the answer is yes to the second question, the answer to the first also becomes yes.

So the availability heuristic—like Kahneman's other heuristics—is essentially a bait-and-switch maneuver. And just as the availability heuristic is usually an unconscious System 1 activity, so too is bait and switch.[18]

Of course we aren't always oblivious to the machinations of our minds. If someone asks about climate change, we may say, "I have no training in climatology and haven't read any of the science. If I tried to answer based on what I know I'd make a mess of it. The knowledgeable people are the climatologists. So I'll substitute 'Do most climatologists think climate change is real?' for 'Is climate change real?'" An ordinary person told by an eminent cancer specialist that she has terminal cancer may engage in the same conscious bait and switch and just accept what the doctor says as true.

But Archie Cochrane was no ordinary fellow. He was a prominent physician. He knew that the pathologist hadn't reported. He knew better than anyone that physicians are often too sure of themselves and that this "God complex" can lead them to make terrible mistakes. And yet he immediately accepted that what the specialist said was the true and final word—because, I suspect, Cochrane unconsciously substituted "Is this the sort of person who should know if I have cancer?" for the question "Do I have cancer?" The answer was "Of course! He is an eminent cancer specialist. He saw the cancerous flesh with his own eyes. This is *exactly* the sort of person who should know whether I have cancer." So Cochrane acquiesced.

I realize I am rocking no one's mental universe by saying that people often jump to judgment. Anyone who has spent time around humans knows that. But that is telling. We *know* we should slow down and think before drawing firm conclusions. And yet, when we are faced with a problem, and a seemingly sensible solution springs to mind, we bypass System 2 and declare, "The answer is ten cents." No one is immune, not even skeptics like Archie Cochrane.

We could call this automatic, nearly effortless mode of thinking about the world the default setting, but that won't do. "Default" suggests we can flip the switch to something else. We can't. Like it or not, System 1 operations keep humming, nonstop, beneath the babbling brook of consciousness.

A better metaphor involves vision. The instant we wake up and look past the tip of our nose, sights and sounds flow to the brain and System 1 is engaged. This perspective is subjective, unique to each of us. Only you can see the world from the tip of your own nose. So let's call it the *tip-of-your-nose perspective.*

BLINKING AND THINKING

As imperfect as the view from the tip of your nose may be, you shouldn't discount it entirely.

Popular books often draw a dichotomy between intuition and analysis—"blink" versus "think"—and pick one or the other as the way to go. I am more of a thinker than a blinker, but blink-think is another false dichotomy. The choice isn't either/or, it is how to blend them in evolving situations. That conclusion is not as inspiring as a simple exhortation to take one path or the other, but it has the advantage of being true, as the pioneering researchers behind both perspectives came to understand.

While Daniel Kahneman and Amos Tversky were documenting

System 1's failings, another psychologist, Gary Klein, was examining decision making among professionals like the commanders of firefighting teams, and discovering that snap judgments can work astonishingly well. One commander told Klein about going to a routine kitchen fire and ordering his men to stand in the living room and hose down the flames. The fire subsided at first but roared back. The commander was baffled. He also noticed the living room was surprisingly hot given the size of the kitchen fire. And why was it so quiet? A fire capable of generating that much heat should make more noise. A vague feeling of unease came over the commander and he ordered everyone out of the house. Just as the firefighters reached the street, the floor in the living room collapsed—because the real source of the fire was in the basement, not the kitchen. How had the commander known they were in terrible danger? He told Klein he had ESP (extrasensory perception), but that was just a story he told himself to cover up the fact that he didn't know how he knew. He just knew—the hallmark of an intuitive judgment.

Drawing such seemingly different conclusions about snap judgments, Kahneman and Klein could have hunkered down and fired off rival polemics. But, like good scientists, they got together to solve the puzzle. "We agree on most of the issues that matter," they concluded in a 2009 paper.[19]

There is nothing mystical about an accurate intuition like the fire commander's. It's pattern recognition. With training or experience, people can encode patterns deep in their memories in vast number and intricate detail—such as the estimated fifty thousand to one hundred thousand chess positions that top players have in their repertoire.[20] If something doesn't fit a pattern—like a kitchen fire giving off more heat than a kitchen fire should—a competent expert senses it immediately. But as we see every time someone spots the Virgin Mary in burnt toast or in mold on a church wall, our pattern-recognition ability comes at the cost of susceptibility to false positives. This, plus the many other ways in which the tip-of-your-nose perspective can generate perceptions that are clear, compelling, and wrong, means intuition can fail as spectacularly as it can work.

Whether intuition generates delusion or insight depends on whether you work in a world full of valid cues you can unconsciously register for future use. "For example, it is very likely that there are early indications that a building is about to collapse in a fire or that an infant will soon show obvious symptoms of infection," Kahneman and Klein wrote. "On the other hand, it is unlikely that there is publicly available information that could be used to predict how well a particular stock will do—if such valid information existed, the price of the stock would already reflect it. Thus, we have more reason to trust the intuition of an experienced fireground commander about the stability of a building, or the intuitions of a nurse about an infant, than to trust the intuitions of a stock broker."[21] Learning the cues is a matter of opportunity and effort. Sometimes learning the cues is easy. "A child does not need thousands of examples to learn to discriminate dogs from cats." But other patterns are much harder to master, like the estimated ten thousand hours of practice it takes to learn those fifty thousand to one hundred thousand chess patterns. "Without those opportunities to learn, a valid intuition can only be due to a lucky accident or to magic," Kahneman and Klein conclude, "and we do not believe in magic."[22]

But there is a catch. As Kahneman and Klein noted, it's often hard to know when there are enough valid cues to make intuition work. And even where it clearly can, caution is advisable. "Often, I cannot explain a certain move, only know that it feels right, and it seems that my intuition is right more often than not," observed the Norwegian prodigy Magnus Carlsen, the world chess champion and the highest-ranked player in history. "If I study a position for an hour then I am usually going in loops and I'm probably not going to come up with something useful. I usually know what I am going to do after 10 seconds; the rest is double-checking."[23] Carlsen respects his intuition, as well he should, but he also does a lot of "double-checking" because he knows that sometimes intuition can let him down and conscious thought can improve his judgment.

That's excellent practice. The tip-of-your-nose perspective can work wonders but it can also go terribly awry, so if you have the time to think before making a big decision, do so—and be prepared to accept that what seems obviously true now may turn out to be false later.

It is hard to argue with advice that feels about as controversial as a fortune-cookie platitude. But tip-of-your-nose illusions are often so convincing that we bypass the advice and go with our gut. Consider a forecast made by Peggy Noonan—the *Wall Street Journal* columnist and former speechwriter for Ronald Reagan—the day before the presidential election of 2012. It will be a Romney victory, Noonan wrote. Her conclusion was based on the big numbers turning out to Romney rallies. The candidate "looks happy and grateful," Noonan observed. And someone who attended a campaign stop had told Noonan about "the intensity and joy of the crowd." Add it up, Noonan concluded, and "the vibrations are right." It's easy to mock Noonan's vibrations. But who among us hasn't felt mistaken certainty that an election, or some other event, was going to break one way or another because it just felt that way? You may not have said "the vibrations are right," but the thinking is the same.[24]

That's the power of the tip-of-your-nose perspective. It is so persuasive that for thousands of years physicians did not doubt their convictions, causing unnecessary suffering on a gargantuan scale. Progress only really began when physicians accepted that the view from the tip of their nose was not enough to determine what works.

All too often, forecasting in the twenty-first century looks too much like nineteenth-century medicine. There are theories, assertions, and arguments. There are famous figures, as confident as they are well compensated. But there is little experimentation, or any-thing that could be called science, so we know much less than most people realize. And we pay the price. Although bad forecasting rarely leads as obviously to harm as does bad medicine, it steers us subtly toward bad decisions and all that flows from them—including mon-etary losses, missed opportunities, unnecessary suffering, even war and death.

Happily, physicians now know the cure for all this. It is a table-spoon of doubt.

3

Keeping Score

When physicians finally learned to doubt themselves, they turned to randomized controlled trials to scientifically test which treatments work. Bringing the rigor of measurement to forecasting might seem easiesr to do: collect forecasts, judge their accuracy, add the numbers. That's it. In no time, we'll know how good Tom Friedman really is.

But it's not nearly so simple. Consider a forecast Steve Ballmer made in 2007, when he was CEO of Microsoft: "There's no chance that the iPhone is going to get any significant market share. No chance."

Ballmer's forecast is infamous. Google "Ballmer" and "worst tech predictions"—or "Bing" it, as Ballmer would prefer—and you will see it enshrined in the forecasting hall of shame, along with such classics as the president of Digital Equipment Corporation declaring in 1977 that "there is no reason anyone would want a computer in their home." And that seems fitting because Ballmer's forecast looks spectacularly wrong. As the author of "The Ten Worst Tech Predictions of All Time" noted in 2013, "the iPhone commands 42% of US smartphone market share and 13.1% worldwide."[1] That's pretty "significant." As another journalist wrote, when Ballmer announced his departure from Microsoft in 2013, "The iPhone alone now generates more revenue than all of Microsoft."[2]

But parse Ballmer's forecast carefully. The key term is "significant market share." What qualifies as "significant"? Ballmer didn't say. And which market was he talking about? North America? The world? And the market for what? Smartphones or mobile phones

in general? All these unanswered questions add up to a big problem. The first step in learning what works in forecasting, and what
doesn't, is to judge forecasts, and to do that we can't make assumptions about what the forecast means. We have to know. There can't
be any ambiguity about whether a forecast is accurate or not and
Ballmer's forecast is ambiguous. Sure, it looks wrong. It feels wrong.
There is a strong case to be made that it *is* wrong. But is it wrong
beyond all reasonable doubt?

I don't blame the reader for thinking this is too lawyerly, a tad
too reminiscent of Bill Clinton's infamous "it depends on what the
meaning of the word 'is' is."[3] After all, Ballmer's meaning seems
plain, even if a literal reading of his words doesn't support that. But
consider his full statement, in context, in an April 2007 interview
with *USA Today*: "There's no chance that the iPhone is going to
get any significant market share. No chance. It's a $500 subsidized
item. They may make a lot of money. But if you actually look at
the 1.3 billion phones that get sold, I'd prefer to have our software
in 60% or 70% or 80% of them, than I would to have 2% or 3%,
which is what Apple might get." That clarifies some things. For one,
Ballmer was clearly referring to the global mobile phone market, so
it's wrong to measure his forecast against US or global smartphone
market share. Using data from the Gartner IT consulting group, I
calculated that the iPhone's share of global mobile phone sales in the
third quarter of 2013 was roughly 6%.[4] That's higher than the "2%
or 3%" Ballmer predicted, but unlike the truncated version so often
quoted, it's not laugh-out-loud wrong. Note also that Ballmer didn't
say the iPhone would be a bust for Apple. Indeed, he said, "They
may make a lot of money." But still there is ambiguity: how much
more than 2% or 3% of the global mobile phone market would the
iPhone have to capture to be deemed "significant"? Ballmer didn't
say. And how much money was he talking about when he said Apple
could earn "a lot of money"? Again, he didn't say.

So how wrong was Steve Ballmer's forecast? His tone was brash and dismissive. In the *USA Today* interview, he seems to scoff at Apple. But his *words* were more nuanced than his tone, and too ambiguous for us to declare with certainty that his forecast was wrong—much less so spectacularly wrong it belongs in the forecasting hall of shame.

It is far from unusual that a forecast that at first looks as clear as a freshly washed window proves too opaque to be conclusively judged right or wrong. Consider the open letter sent to Ben Bernanke, then the chairman of the Federal Reserve, in November 2010. Signed by a long list of economists and commentators, including the Harvard economic historian Niall Ferguson and Amity Shlaes of the Council on Foreign Relations, the letter calls on the Federal Reserve to stop its policy of large-scale asset purchases known as "quantitative easing" because it "risk[s] currency debasement and inflation." The advice was ignored and quantitative easing continued. But in the years that followed, the US dollar wasn't debased and inflation didn't rise. The investor and commentator Barry Ritholtz wrote in 2013 that the signatories had been proved "terribly wrong."[5] Many others agreed. But there was an obvious response: "Wait. It hasn't happened yet. But it will." Ritholtz and the critics might argue that in the context of the 2010 debate, the letter writers expected currency debasement and inflation in the next two or three years if quantitative easing went ahead. Perhaps—but that is not what they wrote. The letter says nothing about the time frame. It wouldn't matter if Ritholtz waited until 2014 or 2015 or 2016. No matter how much time passed, someone could always say, "Just wait. It's coming."[6]

It also isn't clear how much the dollar would have to fall, and inflation rise, to count as "currency debasement and inflation." Worse, the letter says a falling dollar and rising inflation is a "risk." That suggests it's not certain to follow. So if we read the forecast literally, it is saying debasement and inflation may follow, or they may not, which means that if they do not follow, the forecast is not necessarily wrong. That's surely not what the authors intended to communicate, and it's not how people read the statement at the time. But that is what it says.

So here are two forecasts of the sort we routinely encounter. They are serious attempts by smart people to grapple with big issues. Their meaning seems clear. When time passes, their accuracy seems obvious. But it's not. For various reasons, it's impossible to say these forecasts are right or wrong beyond all dispute. The truth is, the truth is elusive.

Judging forecasts is much harder than often supposed, a lesson I learned the hard way—from extensive and exasperating experience.

"A HOLOCAUST . . . WILL OCCUR"

In the early 1980s, many thoughtful people saw mushroom clouds in humanity's future. "If we are honest with ourselves we have to admit that unless we rid ourselves of our nuclear arsenals a holocaust not only might occur but will occur," wrote Jonathan Schell in his influential book *The Fate of the Earth*, "if not today, then tomorrow; if not this year, then the next."[7] Opposition to the arms race brought millions to the streets of cities across the Western world. In June 1982 an estimated seven hundred thousand people marched in New York City in one of the biggest demonstrations in American history.

In 1984, with grants from the Carnegie and MacArthur foundations, the National Research Council—the research arm of the United States National Academy of Sciences—convened a distinguished panel charged with nothing less than "preventing nuclear war." The panelists included three Nobel laureates—the physicist Charles Townes, the economist Kenneth Arrow, and the unclassifiable Herbert Simon—and an array of other luminaries, including the mathematical psychologist Amos Tversky. I was by far the least

impressive member of the panel, a thirty-year-old political psychologist just promoted to associate professor at the University of California, Berkeley. I owed my seat at the table not to a glorious career
of achievement but rather to a quirky research program, which happened to be germane to the panel's mission.

The panel did its due diligence. It invited a range of experts—
intelligence analysts, military officers, government officials, arms
control experts, and Sovietologists—to discuss the issues. They too
were an impressive bunch. Deeply informed, intelligent, articulate.
And pretty confident that they knew what was happening and where
we were heading.

On the basic facts, at least, there was agreement. The long-serving
Soviet leader Leonid Brezhnev had died in 1982 and been replaced
by a frail old man who soon died and was replaced by another, Kon-
stantin Chernenko, who was also expected to die soon. There was
both agreement and disagreement about what would come next. Liberals and conservatives alike largely expected the next Soviet leader
to be another stern Communist Party man. But they disagreed on
why things would work out that way. Liberal experts were sure that
President Ronald Reagan's hard line was strengthening Kremlin
hard-liners, which would bring a neo-Stalinist retrenchment and
worsening relations between the superpowers. Experts of a conservative bent thought that the Soviet system had pretty much perfected
the art of totalitarian self-reproduction, hence the new boss would
be the same as the old boss and the Soviet Union would continue
to threaten world peace by supporting insurgencies and invading its
neighbors. They were equally confident in their views.

The experts were right about Chernenko. He died in March
1985. But then the train of history hit a curve, and as Karl Marx
once quipped, when that happens, the intellectuals fall off.

Within hours of Chernenko's death, the Politburo anointed
Mikhail Gorbachev, an energetic and charismatic fifty-four-year-

old, the next general secretary of the Communist Party of the Soviet Union. Gorbachev changed direction swiftly and sharply. His policies of glasnost (openness) and perestroika (restructuring) liberalized the Soviet Union. Gorbachev also sought to normalize relations with the United States and reverse the arms race. Ronald Reagan responded cautiously, then enthusiastically, and in just a few years the world went from the prospect of nuclear war to a new era in which many people—including the Soviet and American leaders—saw a glimmering chance of eliminating nuclear weapons altogether.

Few experts saw this coming. And yet it wasn't long before most of those who didn't see it coming grew convinced they knew exactly why it had happened, and what was coming next. For liberals, it all made perfect sense. The Soviet economy was crumbling and a new cohort of Soviet leaders was weary of the wasteful struggle with the United States. "We can't go on living this way," Gorbachev said to his wife Raisa the day before his ascension to power.[8] It was bound to happen. So it wasn't all that surprising, when you look at it in the right retrospective light. And no, Reagan didn't deserve credit. If anything, his "evil empire" rhetoric had shored up the Kremlin old guard and delayed the inevitable. For conservatives too the explanation was obvious: Reagan had called the Soviets' bluff by upping the arms-race ante and now Gorbachev was folding. It was all predictable, when you viewed it in the right retrospective light.

My inner cynic started to suspect that no matter what had happened the experts would have been just as adept at downplaying their predictive failures and sketching an arc of history that made it appear they saw it coming all along. After all, the world had just witnessed a huge surprise involving one of the most consequential matters imaginable. If this didn't induce a shiver of doubt, what would? I was not questioning the intelligence or integrity of these experts, many of whom had won big scientific prizes or held high government offices when I was in grade school. But intelligence and integrity are not enough. The national security elites looked a lot like the renowned physicians from the prescientific era. They too overflowed with intelligence and integrity. But tip-of-your-nose delusions can fool anyone, even the best and the brightest—perhaps *especially* the best and the brightest.

JUDGING JUDGMENTS

This got me thinking about expert forecasts. At lunch one day in 1988, my then–Berkeley colleague Daniel Kahneman tossed out a testable idea that proved prescient. He speculated that intelligence and knowledge would improve forecasting but the benefits would taper off fast. People armed with PhDs and decades of experience may be only a tad more accurate than attentive readers of the *New York Times*. Of course Kahneman was just guessing and even Kahneman guesses are just guesses. No one had ever seriously tested the forecasting accuracy of political experts and the more I pondered the challenge, the more I realized why.

Take the problem of timelines. Obviously, a forecast without a time frame is absurd. And yet, forecasters routinely make them, as they did in that letter to Ben Bernanke. They're not being dishonest, at least not usually. Rather, they're relying on a shared implicit understanding, however rough, of the timeline they have in mind. That's why forecasts without timelines don't appear absurd when they are made. But as time passes, memories fade, and tacit time frames that once seemed obvious to all become less so. The result is often a tedious dispute about the "real" meaning of the forecast. Was the event expected this year or next? This decade or next? With no time frame, there is no way to resolve these arguments to everyone's satisfaction—especially when reputations are on the line.

This problem alone renders many everyday forecasts untestable.

Similarly, forecasts often rely on implicit understandings of key terms rather than explicit definitions—like "significant market share" in Steve Ballmer's forecast. This sort of vague verbiage is more the rule than the exception. And it too renders forecasts untestable.

These are among the smaller obstacles to judging forecasts. Probability is a much bigger one.

Some forecasts are easy to judge because they claim unequivocally that something will or won't happen, as in Jonathan Schell's forecast for nuclear war. Either we get rid of nuclear weapons or "a holocaust . . . will occur," Schell wrote. As it turned out, neither superpower scrapped its nuclear arsenal and there was no nuclear war, neither in the year Schell's book appeared nor in the next year. So Schell, read literally, was clearly wrong. But what if Schell had said it was "very likely" there would be nuclear war? Then it would be less clear. Schell might have grossly exaggerated the risk or he might have been exactly right and humanity was lucky to survive the most reckless game of Russian roulette ever played. The only way to settle this definitively would be to rerun history hundreds of times, and if civilization ends in piles of irradiated rubble in most of those reruns, we would know Schell was right. But we can't do that, so we can't know.

But let's imagine we are omnipotent beings and we *can* conduct that experiment. We rerun history hundreds of times and we find that 63% of those reruns end in nuclear war. Was Schell right? Perhaps. But we still can't say with confidence—because we don't know exactly what he meant by "very likely."

That may sound like a semantic quibble. But it is much more than that, as Sherman Kent discovered to his alarm.

In intelligence circles, Sherman Kent is a legend. With a PhD in history, Kent left a faculty position at Yale to join the Research and Analysis Branch of the newly created Coordinator of Information (COI) in 1941. The COI became the Office of Strategic Services (OSS). The OSS became the Central Intelligence Agency (CIA).

By the time Kent retired from the CIA in 1967, he had profoundly shaped how the American intelligence community does what it calls intelligence analysis—the methodical examination of the information collected by spies and surveillance to figure out what it means, and what will happen next.

The key word in Kent's work is *estimate*. As Kent wrote, "estimating is what you do when you do not know."[9] And as Kent emphasized over and over, we never truly know what will happen next. Hence forecasting is all about estimating the likelihood of something happening, which Kent and his colleagues did for many years at the Office of National Estimates—an obscure but extraordinarily influential bureau whose job was to draw on all information available to the CIA, synthesize it, and forecast anything and everything that might help the top officeholders in the US government decide what to do next. Kent and his colleagues were far from perfect. Most notoriously, they published a 1962 estimate that argued the Soviets would not be so foolish as to deploy offensive missiles to Cuba, when, in fact, they already had. But for the most part, their estimates were well regarded because Kent upheld high standards of analytical rigor. In drafting national intelligence estimates, the stakes were high. Every word mattered. Kent weighed each one carefully. But not even Kent's professionalism could stop confusion from seeping in.

In the late 1940s, the Communist government of Yugoslavia broke from the Soviet Union, raising fears the Soviets would invade. In March 1951 National Intelligence Estimate (NIE) 29-51 was published. "Although it is impossible to determine which course of action the Kremlin is likely to adopt," the report concluded, "we believe that the extent of [Eastern European] military and propaganda preparations indicates that an attack on Yugoslavia in 1951 should be considered a serious possibility." By most standards, that is clear, meaningful language. No one suggested otherwise when the estimate was published and read by top officials throughout the government. But a few days later, Kent was chatting with a senior State Department official who casually asked, "By the way, what did you people mean by the expression 'serious possibility'? What kind of odds did you have in mind?" Kent said he was pessimistic. He felt the odds were about 65 to 35 in favor of an attack. The official was startled. He and his colleagues had taken "serious possibility" to mean much lower odds.[10]

Disturbed, Kent went back to his team. They had all agreed to use "serious possibility" in the NIE so Kent asked each person, in turn, what he thought it meant. One analyst said it meant odds of about 80 to 20, or four times more likely than not that there would be an invasion. Another thought it meant odds of 20 to 80—exactly the opposite. Other answers were scattered between those extremes. Kent was floored. A phrase that looked informative was so vague as to be almost useless. Or perhaps it was worse than useless, as it had created dangerous misunderstandings. And what about all the other work they had done? Had they "been seeming to agree on five months' worth of estimative judgments with no real agreement at all?" Kent wrote in a 1964 essay. "Were the NIEs dotted with 'serious possibilities' and other expressions that meant very different things to both producers and readers? What were we really trying to say when we wrote a sentence such as this?"[11]

Kent was right to worry. In 1961, when the CIA was planning to topple the Castro government by landing a small army of Cuban expatriates at the Bay of Pigs, President John F. Kennedy turned to the military for an unbiased assessment. The Joint Chiefs of Staff concluded that the plan had a "fair chance" of success. The man who wrote the words "fair chance" later said he had in mind odds of 3 to 1 against success. But Kennedy was never told precisely what "fair chance" meant and, not unreasonably, he took it to be a much more positive assessment. Of course we can't be sure that if the Chiefs had said "We feel it's 3 to 1 the invasion will fail" that Kennedy would have called it off, but it surely would have made him think harder about authorizing what turned out to be an unmitigated disaster.[12]

Sherman Kent suggested a solution. First, the word "possible" should be reserved for important matters where analysts have to make a judgment but can't reasonably assign any probability. So something that is "possible" has a likelihood ranging from almost zero to almost 100%. Of course that's not helpful, so analysts should narrow the range of their estimates whenever they can. And to avoid confusion, the terms they use should have designated numerical meanings, which Kent set out in a chart.[13]

CERTAINTY	THE GENERAL AREA OF POSSIBILITY
100%	Certain
93% (give or take about 6%)	Almost certain
75% (give or take about 12%)	Probable
50% (give or take about 10%)	Chances about even
30% (give or take about 10%)	Probably not
7% (give or take about 5%)	Almost certainly not
0%	Impossible

So if the National Intelligence Estimate said something is "probable," it would mean a 63% to 87% chance it would happen. Kent's scheme was simple—and it greatly reduced the room for confusion.

But it was never adopted. People liked clarity and precision in principle but when it came time to make clear and precise forecasts they weren't so keen on numbers. Some said it felt unnatural or awkward, which it does when you've spent a lifetime using vague language, but that's a weak argument against change. Others expressed an aesthetic revulsion. Language has its own poetry, they felt, and it's tacky to talk explicitly about numerical odds. It makes you sound like a bookie. Kent wasn't impressed. "I'd rather be a bookie than a goddamn poet," was his legendary response.[14]

A more serious objection—then and now—is that expressing a probability estimate with a number may imply to the reader that it is an objective fact, not the subjective judgment it is. That is a danger. But the answer is not to do away with numbers. It's to inform readers that numbers, just like words, only express estimates—opinions— and nothing more. Similarly, it might be argued that the precision of a number implicitly says "the forecaster knows with exactitude that this number is right." But that's not intended and shouldn't be inferred. Also, bear in mind that words like "serious possibility" suggest the same thing numbers do, the only real difference being that numbers make it explicit, reducing the risk of confusion. And they have another benefit: vague thoughts are easily expressed with vague language but when forecasters are forced to translate terms like "serious possibility" into numbers, they have to think carefully about how they are thinking, a process known as metacognition. Forecasters who practice get better at distinguishing finer degrees of uncertainty, just as artists get better at distinguishing subtler shades of gray.

But a more fundamental obstacle to adopting numbers relates to accountability and what I call the wrong-side-of-maybe fallacy.

If a meteorologist says there is a 70% chance of rain and it doesn't rain, is she wrong? Not necessarily. Implicitly, her forecast also says there is a 30% chance it will *not* rain. So if it doesn't rain, her forecast may have been off, or she may have been exactly right. It's not possible to judge with only that one forecast in hand. The only way to know for sure would be to rerun the day hundreds of times. If it rained in 70% of those reruns, and didn't rain in 30%, she would be bang on. Of course we're not omnipotent beings, so we can't rerun the day—and we can't judge. But people *do* judge. And they always judge the same way: they look at which side of "maybe"—50%—

the probability was on. If the forecast said there was a 70% chance of rain and it rains, people think the forecast was right; if it doesn't rain, they think it was wrong. This simple mistake is extremely common. Even sophisticated thinkers fall for it. In 2012, when the Supreme Court was about to release its long-awaited decision on the constitutionality of Obamacare, prediction markets—markets that let people bet on possible outcomes—pegged the probability of the law being struck down at 75%. When the court upheld the law, the sagacious *New York Times* reporter David Leonhardt declared that "the market—the wisdom of the crowds—was wrong."[15]

The prevalence of this elementary error has a terrible consequence. Consider that if an intelligence agency says there is a 65% chance that an event will happen, it risks being pilloried if it does not—and because the forecast itself says there is a 35% chance it will not happen, that's a big risk. So what's the safe thing to do? Stick with elastic language. Forecasters who use "a fair chance" and "a serious possibility" can even make the wrong-side-of-maybe fallacy work for them: If the event happens, "a fair chance" can retroactively be stretched to mean something considerably bigger than 50%—so the forecaster nailed it. If it doesn't happen, it can be shrunk to something much smaller than 50%—and again the forecaster nailed it. With perverse incentives like these, it's no wonder people prefer rubbery words over firm numbers.

Kent couldn't overcome such political barriers, but as the years passed the case he made for using numbers only grew. Study after study showed that people attach very different meanings to probabilistic language like "could," "might," and "likely." Still the intelligence community resisted. Only after the debacle over Saddam Hussein's supposed weapons of mass destruction, and the wholesale reforms that followed, did it become more acceptable to express probabilities with numbers. When CIA analysts told President Obama they were "70%" or "90%" sure the mystery man in a Pakistani compound was Osama bin Laden, it was a small, posthumous triumph for Sherman Kent. In some other fields, numbers have become standard. "Slight chance of showers" has given way to "30% chance of showers" in weather forecasts. But hopelessly vague language is still so common, particularly in the media, that we rarely notice how vacuous it is. It just slips by.

"I think the debt crisis in Europe is unresolved and may be very close to going critical," the Harvard economic historian and popular commentator Niall Ferguson told an interviewer in January 2012. "The Greek default may be a matter of days away." Was Ferguson right? The popular understanding of "default" involves a complete repudiation of debt, and Greece didn't do that days, months, or years later, but there's also a technical definition of "default," which Greece did shortly after Ferguson's forecast. Which definition was Ferguson using? That's not clear, so while there's reason to think Ferguson was right, we can't be certain. But let's imagine there was no default of any kind. Could we then say Ferguson was wrong? No. He only said Greece "may" default and "may" is a hollow word. It means something is possible but it says nothing about the probability of that possibility. Almost anything "may" happen. I can confidently forecast that the Earth may be attacked by aliens tomorrow. And if it isn't? I'm not wrong. Every "may" is accompanied by an asterisk and the words "or may not" are buried in the fine print. But the interviewer didn't notice the fine print in Ferguson's forecast, so he did not ask him to clarify.[16]

If we are serious about measuring and improving, this won't do. Forecasts must have clearly defined terms and timelines. They must use numbers. And one more thing is essential: we must have lots of forecasts.

We cannot rerun history so we cannot judge one probabilistic forecast—but everything changes when we have *many* probabilistic forecasts. If a meteorologist says there is a 70% chance of rain tomorrow, that forecast cannot be judged, but if she predicts the weather tomorrow, and the day after, and the day after that, for months, her forecasts can be tabulated and her track record determined. If her forecasting is perfect, rain happens 70% of the time when she says there is 70% chance of rain, 30% of the time when she says there is 30% chance of rain, and so on. This is called calibration. It can be plotted on a simple chart. Perfect calibration is captured by the diagonal line on this chart:

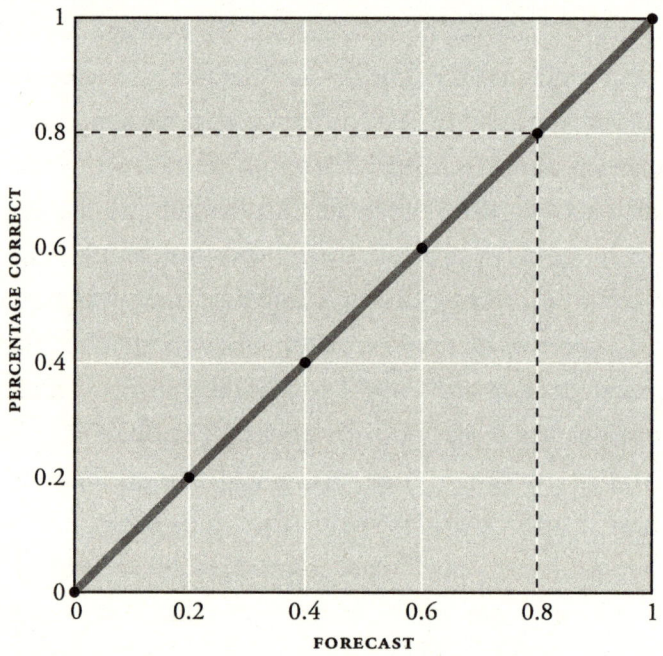

Picture-perfect calibration

If the meteorologist's curve is far above the line, she is underconfident—so things she says are 20% likely actually happen 50% of the time (see opposite page, top). If her curve is far under the line, she is overconfident—so things she says are 80% likely actually happen only 50% of the time (see opposite page, bottom).

This method works well for weather forecasts because there

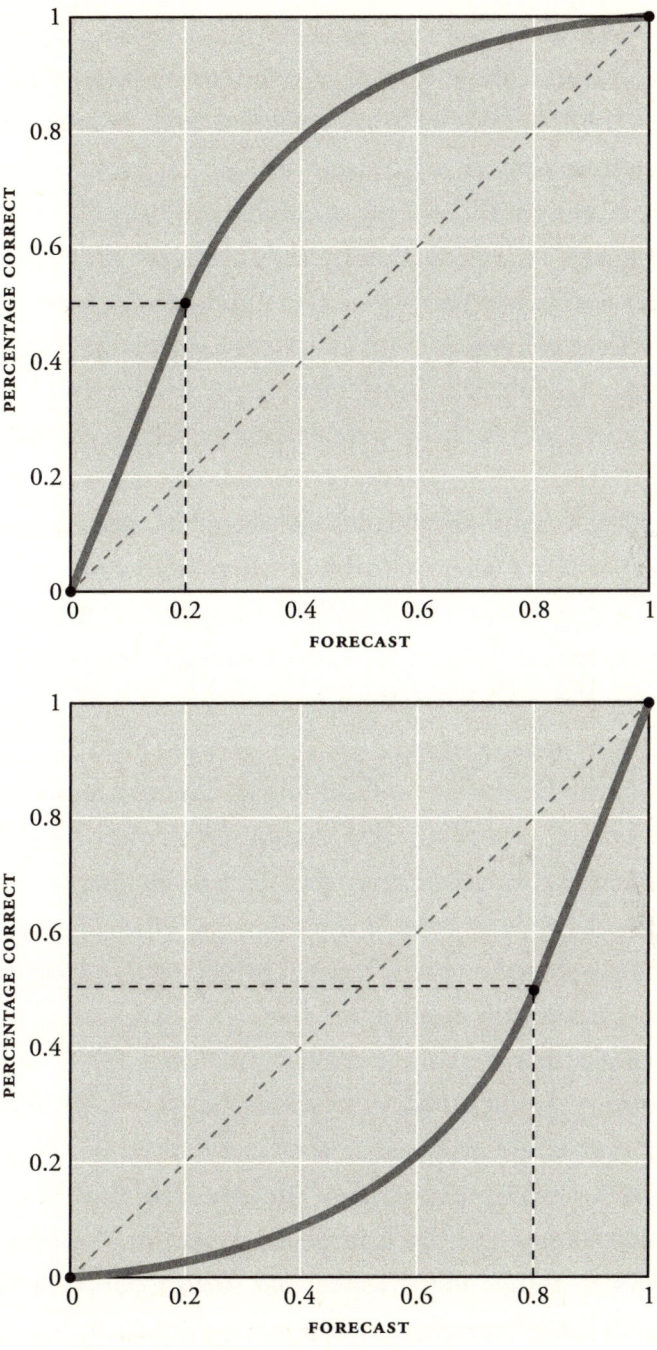

Two ways to be miscalibrated: underconfident (over the line) and overconfident (under the line)

is new weather every day and forecasts stack up fast. But it works less well for events like presidential elections because it would take centuries—undisturbed by wars, plagues, and other shocks that perturb the true underlying causes—to pile up enough forecasts to make the statistics work. A little creativity can help. We could focus on the state level in presidential elections, for example, which would give us fifty results per election, not one. But we still have a problem. The many forecasts required for calibration calculations make it impractical to judge forecasts about rare events, and even with common events it means we must be patient data collectors—and cautious data interpreters.

Important as calibration is, it's not the whole story because "perfect calibration" isn't what we think of when we imagine perfect forecasting accuracy. Perfection is godlike omniscience. It's saying "this will happen" and it does, or "this won't happen" and it doesn't. The technical term for this is "resolution."

The two figures on page 63 show how calibration and resolution capture distinct facets of good judgment. The figure on top represents perfect calibration but poor resolution. It's perfect calibration because when the forecaster says there is a 40% chance something will happen, it happens 40% of the time, and when she says there is a 60% chance something will happen, it happens 60% of the time. But it's poor resolution because the forecaster never strays out of the minor-shades-of-maybe zone between 40% and 60%. The figure on the bottom represents superb calibration *and* resolution. Again, the calibration is superb because forecasts happen as often as they should—40% calls happen 40% of the time. But this time the forecaster is much more decisive and does a great job of assigning high probabilities to things that happen and low probabilities to things that don't.

When we combine calibration and resolution, we get a scoring system that fully captures our sense of what good forecasters should

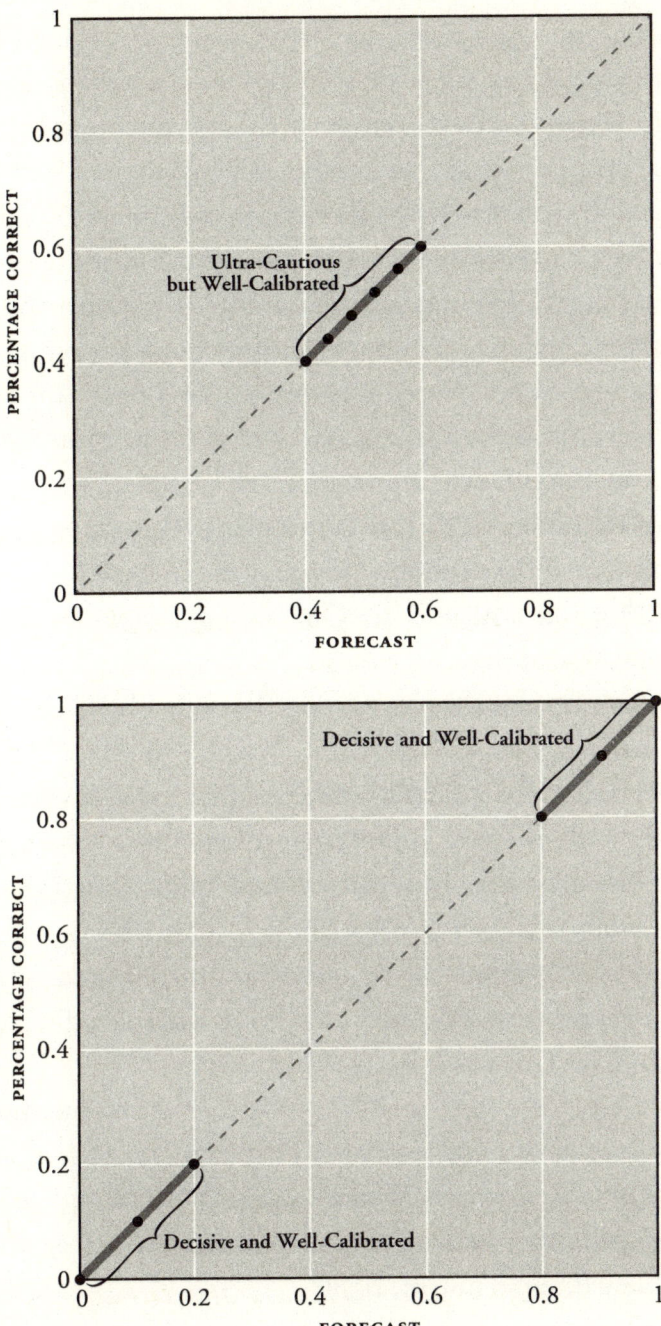

Well-calibrated but cowardly (top); well-calibrated and brave (bottom)

do. Someone who says there is a 70% chance of X should do fairly well if X happens. But someone who says there is a 90% chance of X should do better. And someone bold enough to correctly predict X with 100% confidence gets top marks. But hubris must be punished. The forecaster who says X is a slam dunk should take a big hit if X does not happen. How big a hit is debatable, but it's reasonable to think of it in betting terms. If I say it is 80% likely that the Yankees will beat the Dodgers, and I am willing to put a bet on it, I am offering you 4 to 1 odds. If you take my bet, and put $100 on it, you will pay me $100 if the Yankees win and I will pay you $400 if the Yankees lose. But if I say the probability of a Yankees victory is 90%, I've upped the odds to 9 to 1. If I say a win is 95% likely, I've put the odds at 19 to 1. That's extreme. If you agree to bet $100, I will owe you $1,900 if the Yankees lose. Our scoring system for forecasting should capture that pain.

The math behind this system was developed by Glenn W. Brier in 1950, hence results are called Brier scores. In effect, Brier scores measure the distance between what you forecast and what actually happened. So Brier scores are like golf scores: lower is better. Perfection is 0. A hedged fifty-fifty call, or random guessing in the aggregate, will produce a Brier score of 0.5. A forecast that is wrong to the greatest possible extent—saying there is a 100% chance that something will happen and it doesn't, every time—scores a disastrous 2.0, as far from The Truth as it is possible to get.[17]

So we've come a long way. We have forecasting questions with clearly defined terms and timelines. We have lots of forecasts with numbers, and the math to calculate scores. We have squeezed out as much ambiguity as appears humanly possible. We're ready to march into the New Enlightenment, right?

THE MEANING OF THE MATH

Not quite. Remember that the whole point of this exercise is to judge the accuracy of forecasts so we can then figure out what works in forecasting and what doesn't. To do that, we have to interpret the meaning of the Brier scores, which requires two more things: benchmarks and comparability.

Let's suppose we discover that you have a Brier score of 0.2. That's far from godlike omniscience (0) but a lot better than chimp-like guessing (0.5), so it falls in the range of what one might expect from, say, a human being. But we can say much more than that. What a Brier score means depends on what's being forecast. For instance, it's quite easy to imagine circumstances where a Brier score of 0.2 would be disappointing. Consider the weather in Phoenix, Arizona. Each June, it gets very hot and sunny. A forecaster who followed a mindless rule like, "always assign 100% to hot and sunny" could get a Brier score close to 0, leaving 0.2 in the dust. Here, the right test of skill would be whether a forecaster can do better than mindlessly predicting no change. This is an underappreciated point. For example, after the 2012 presidential election, Nate Silver, Princeton's Sam Wang, and other poll aggregators were hailed for correctly predicting all fifty state outcomes, but almost no one noted that a crude, across-the-board prediction of "no change"—if a state went Democratic or Republican in 2008, it will do the same in 2012—would have scored forty-eight out of fifty, which suggests that the many excited exclamations of "He called all fifty states!" we heard at the time were a tad overwrought. Fortunately, poll aggregators are pros: they know that improving predictions tends to be a game of inches.

Another key benchmark is other forecasters. Who can beat everyone else? Who can beat the consensus forecast? How do they pull it off? Answering these questions requires comparing Brier scores, which, in turn, requires a level playing field. Forecasting the weather in Phoenix is just plain easier than forecasting the weather in Spring-field, Missouri, where weather is notoriously variable, so comparing the Brier scores of a Phoenix meteorologist with those of a Spring-field meteorologist would be unfair. A 0.2 Brier score in Springfield could be a sign that you are a world-class meteorologist. It's a simple point, with a big implication: dredging up old forecasts from news-papers will seldom yield apples-to-apples comparisons because, out-side of tournaments, real-world forecasters seldom predict exactly the same developments over exactly the same time period.

Add it all up and we are ready to roll. Like Archie Cochrane and other pioneers of evidence-based medicine, we must run carefully crafted experiments. Assemble forecasters. Ask them large numbers of questions with precise time frames and unambiguous language. Require that forecasts be expressed using numerical probability scales. And wait for time to pass. If the researchers have done their jobs, the results will be clear. The data can be analyzed and the key questions—How good are the forecasters? Who are the best? What sets them apart?—can be answered.

EXPERT POLITICAL JUDGMENT

That's what I set out to do in the mid-1980s, but I ran into rough spots early on. Despite my all but begging the highest-profile pun-dits to take part, none would participate. Nonetheless, I managed to recruit 284 serious professionals, card-carrying experts whose liveli-hoods involved analyzing political and economic trends and events. Some were academics working in universities or think tanks. Others worked for branches of the US government, or for international or-ganizations such as the World Bank and the International Mone-tary Fund, or for the media. A small number were quite famous, others well known in their professional communities, some early in their careers and at that point quite obscure. But I still had to guarantee anonymity because even experts who were not in the Tom Friedman–elite class were reluctant to risk their reputations for zero professional payoff. Anonymity also ensured that participants would make their best guesses, uninfluenced by fear of embarrassment. The effects of public competition would have to wait for a future study.

The first questions put to the experts were about themselves. Age? (The average was forty-three.) Relevant work experience? (The average was 12.2 years.) Education? (Almost all had postgraduate training; half had PhDs.) We also asked about their ideological leanings and preferred approaches to solving political problems.

Forecast questions covered time frames that ranged from one to five to ten years out, and tapped into diverse topics drawn from the news of the day: political and economic, domestic and international. They were asked about whatever topics experts could be found expounding on in the media and halls of power, which meant our experts would sometimes be asked to forecast in their zone of expertise, but more often not—which let us compare the accuracy of true subject-matter experts with that of smart, well-informed laypeople. In total, our experts made roughly twenty-eight thousand predictions.

Asking questions took years. Then came the waiting, a test of patience for even the tenured. I began the experiment when Mikhail Gorbachev and the Soviet Politburo were key players shaping the fate of the world; by the time I started to write up the results, the USSR existed only on historical maps and Gorbachev was doing commercials for Pizza Hut. The final results appeared in 2005—twenty-one years, six presidential elections, and three wars after I sat on the National Research Council panel that got me thinking about forecasting. I published them in the academic treatise *Expert Political Judgment: How Good Is It? How Can We Know?* To keep things simple, I'll call this whole research program "EPJ."

AND THE RESULTS . . .

If you didn't know the punch line of EPJ before you read this book, you do now: the average expert was roughly as accurate as a dart-throwing chimpanzee. But as students are warned in introductory statistics classes, averages can obscure. Hence the old joke about statisticians sleeping with their feet in an oven and their head in a freezer because the average temperature is comfortable.

In the EPJ results, there were two statistically distinguishable groups of experts. The first failed to do better than random guessing, and in their longer-range forecasts even managed to lose to the chimp. The second group beat the chimp, though not by a wide margin, and they still had plenty of reason to be humble. Indeed, they only barely beat simple algorithms like "always predict no change" or "predict the recent rate of change." Still, however modest their foresight was, they had some.

So why did one group do better than the other? It wasn't whether they had PhDs or access to classified information. Nor was it *what they thought*—whether they were liberals or conservatives, optimists or pessimists. The critical factor was *how they thought.*

One group tended to organize their thinking around Big Ideas, although they didn't agree on which Big Ideas were true or false. Some were environmental doomsters ("We're running out of everything"); others were cornucopian boomsters ("We can find cost-effective substitutes for everything"). Some were socialists (who favored state control of the commanding heights of the economy); others were free-market fundamentalists (who wanted to minimize regulation). As ideologically diverse as they were, they were united by the fact that their thinking was so ideological. They sought to squeeze complex problems into the preferred cause-effect templates and treated what did not fit as irrelevant distractions. Allergic to wishy-washy answers, they kept pushing their analyses to the limit (and then some), using terms like "furthermore" and "moreover" while piling up reasons why they were right and others wrong. As a result, they were unusually confident and likelier to declare things "impossible" or "certain." Committed to their conclusions, they were reluctant to change their minds even when their predictions clearly failed. They would tell us, "Just wait."

The other group consisted of more pragmatic experts who drew on many analytical tools, with the choice of tool hinging on the particular problem they faced. These experts gathered as much information from as many sources as they could. When thinking, they often shifted mental gears, sprinkling their speech with transition markers such as "however," "but," "although," and "on the other hand." They talked about possibilities and probabilities, not certainties. And while no one likes to say "I was wrong," these experts more readily admitted it and changed their minds.

Decades ago, the philosopher Isaiah Berlin wrote a much-acclaimed but rarely read essay that compared the styles of thinking of great authors through the ages. To organize his observations, he drew on a scrap of 2,500-year-old Greek poetry attributed to the warrior-poet Archilochus: "The fox knows many things but the hedgehog knows one big thing." No one will ever know whether Archilochus was on the side of the fox or the hedgehog but Berlin favored foxes. I felt no need to take sides. I just liked the metaphor because it captured something deep in my data. I dubbed the Big Idea experts "hedgehogs" and the more eclectic experts "foxes."

Foxes beat hedgehogs. And the foxes didn't just win by acting like chickens, playing it safe with 60% and 70% forecasts where hedgehogs boldly went with 90% and 100%. Foxes beat hedgehogs on *both* calibration and resolution. Foxes had real foresight. Hedgehogs didn't.

How did hedgehogs manage to do slightly worse than random guessing? To answer that question, let's meet a prototypic hedgehog.[18]

Larry Kudlow hosted a business talk show on CNBC and is a widely published pundit, but he got his start as an economist in the Reagan administration and later worked with Art Laffer, the economist whose theories were the cornerstone of Ronald Reagan's economic policies. Kudlow's one Big Idea is supply-side economics. When President George W. Bush followed the supply-side prescription by enacting substantial tax cuts, Kudlow was certain an economic boom of equal magnitude would follow. He dubbed it "the Bush boom." Reality fell short: growth and job creation were positive but somewhat disappointing relative to the long-term average and particularly in comparison to that of the Clinton era, which began with a substantial tax hike. But Kudlow stuck to his guns and insisted, year after year, that the "Bush boom" was happening as forecast, even if commentators hadn't noticed. He called it "the biggest story never told." In December 2007, months after the first rumblings of the financial crisis had been felt, the economy looked shaky, and many observers worried a recession was coming, or had even arrived, Kudlow was optimistic. "There is no recession," he wrote. "In fact, we are about to enter the seventh consecutive year of the Bush boom."[19]

The National Bureau of Economic Research later designated December 2007 as the official start of the Great Recession of 2007–9. As the months passed, the economy weakened and worries grew, but Kudlow did not budge. There is no recession and there will be no recession, he insisted. When the White House said the same in April 2008, Kudlow wrote, "President George W. Bush may turn out to be the top economic forecaster in the country."[20] Through the spring and into summer, the economy worsened but Kudlow denied it. "We are in a mental recession, not an actual recession,"[21] he wrote, a theme he kept repeating until September 15, when Lehman Brothers filed for bankruptcy, Wall Street was thrown into chaos, the global financial system froze, and people the world over felt like passengers in a plunging jet, eyes wide, fingers digging into armrests.

How could Kudlow be so consistently wrong? Like all of us, hedgehog forecasters first see things from the tip-of-your-nose perspective. That's natural enough. But the hedgehog also "knows one big thing," the Big Idea he uses over and over when trying to figure out what will happen next. Think of that Big Idea like a pair of glasses that the hedgehog never takes off. The hedgehog sees everything through those glasses. And they aren't ordinary glasses. They're green-tinted glasses—like the glasses that visitors to the Emerald City were required to wear in L. Frank Baum's *The Wonderful Wizard of Oz*. Now, wearing green-tinted glasses may sometimes be helpful, in that they accentuate something real that might otherwise be overlooked. Maybe there is just a trace of green in a tablecloth that a naked eye might miss, or a subtle shade of green in running water. But far more often, green-tinted glasses distort reality. Everywhere you look, you see green, whether it's there or not. And very often, it's not. The Emerald City wasn't even emerald in the fable. People only thought it was because they were forced to wear green-tinted glasses! So the hedgehog's one Big Idea doesn't improve his foresight. It distorts it. And more information doesn't help because it's all seen through the same tinted glasses. It may increase the hedgehog's confidence, but not his accuracy. That's a bad combination. The predictable result? When hedgehogs in the EPJ research made forecasts on the subjects they knew the most about—their own specialties—their accuracy declined. The American economy is Larry Kudlow's beat, but in 2008, when it was increasingly obvious that it was in trouble, he didn't see what others did. He couldn't. Everything looked green to him.

Not that being wrong hurt Kudlow's career. In January 2009, with the American economy in a crisis worse than any since the Great

Depression, Kudlow's new show, *The Kudlow Report*, premiered on CNBC. That too is consistent with the EPJ data, which revealed an inverse correlation between fame and accuracy: the more famous an expert was, the less accurate he was. That's not because editors, producers, and the public go looking for bad forecasters. They go looking for hedgehogs, who just happen to be bad forecasters. Animated by a Big Idea, hedgehogs tell tight, simple, clear stories that grab and hold audiences. As anyone who has done media training knows, the first rule is "keep it simple, stupid." Better still, hedgehogs are confident. With their one-perspective analysis, hedgehogs can pile up reasons why they are right—"furthermore," "moreover"—without considering other perspectives and the pesky doubts and caveats they raise. And so, as EPJ showed, hedgehogs are likelier to say something definitely will or won't happen. For many audiences, that's satisfying. People tend to find uncertainty disturbing and "maybe" underscores uncertainty with a bright red crayon. The simplicity and confidence of the hedgehog impairs foresight, but it calms nerves—which is good for the careers of hedgehogs.

Foxes don't fare so well in the media. They're less confident, less likely to say something is "certain" or "impossible," and are likelier to settle on shades of "maybe." And their stories are complex, full of "howevers" and "on the other hands," because they look at problems one way, then another, and another. This aggregation of many perspectives is bad TV. But it's good forecasting. Indeed, it's essential.

DRAGONFLY EYE

In 1906 the legendary British scientist Sir Francis Galton went to a country fair and watched as hundreds of people individually guessed the weight that a live ox would be after it was "slaughtered and dressed." Their average guess—their collective judgment—was

1,197 pounds, one pound short of the correct answer, 1,198 pounds. It was the earliest demonstration of a phenomenon popularized by— and now named for—James Surowiecki's bestseller *The Wisdom of Crowds.* Aggregating the judgment of many consistently beats the accuracy of the average member of the group, and is often as startlingly accurate as Galton's weight-guessers. The collective judgment isn't always more accurate than any individual guess, however. In fact, in any group there are likely to be individuals who beat the group. But those bull's-eye guesses typically say more about the power of luck—chimps who throw a lot of darts will get occasional bull's-eyes—than about the skill of the guesser. That becomes clear when the exercise is repeated many times. There will be individuals who beat the group in each repetition, but they will tend to be *different* individuals. Beating the average consistently requires rare skill.

Some reverently call it the miracle of aggregation but it is easy to demystify. The key is recognizing that useful information is often dispersed widely, with one person possessing a scrap, another holding a more important piece, a third having a few bits, and so on. When Galton watched people guessing the weight of the doomed ox, he was watching them translate whatever information they had into a number. When a butcher looked at the ox, he contributed the information he possessed thanks to years of training and experience. When a man who regularly bought meat at the butcher's store made his guess, he added a little more. A third person, who remembered how much the ox weighed at last year's fair, did the same. And so it went. Hundreds of people added valid information, creating a collective pool far greater than any one of them possessed. Of course they also contributed myths and mistakes, creating a pool of misleading clues as big as the pool of useful clues. But there was an important difference between the two pools. All the valid information pointed in one direction—toward 1,198 pounds—but the errors had different sources and pointed in different directions. Some suggested the correct answer was higher, some lower. So they canceled each other out. With valid information piling up and errors nullifying themselves, the net result was an astonishingly accurate estimate.

How well aggregation works depends on what you are aggregating. Aggregating the judgments of many people who know nothing produces a lot of nothing. Aggregating the judgments of people who know a little is better, and if there are enough of them, it can produce impressive results, but aggregating the judgments of an equal number of people who know lots about lots of different things is most effective because the collective pool of information becomes much bigger. Aggregations of aggregations can also yield impressive results. A well-conducted opinion survey aggregates a lot of information about voter intentions, but combining surveys—a "poll of polls"—turns many information pools into one big pool. That's the core of what Nate Silver, Sam Wang, and other statisticians did in the presidential election of 2012. And a poll of polls can be further aggregated with other data sources. PollyVote is a project of an academic consortium that forecasts presidential elections by aggregating diverse sources, including election polls, the judgments of a panel of political experts, and quantitative models developed by political scientists. In operation since the 1990s, it has a strong record, often sticking with the eventual winner when the polls turn and the experts change their minds.

Now look at how foxes approach forecasting. They deploy not one analytical idea but many and seek out information not from one source but many. Then they synthesize it all into a single conclusion. In a word, they aggregate. They may be individuals working alone, but what they do is, in principle, no different from what Galton's crowd did. They integrate perspectives and the information contained within them. The only real difference is that the process occurs within one skull.

But doing this sort of inside-your-head aggregation can be challenging. Consider a guess-the-number game in which players must guess a number between 0 and 100. The person whose guess comes closest to two-thirds of the average guess of all contestants wins. That's it. And imagine there is a prize: the reader who comes closest to the correct answer wins a pair of business-class tickets for a flight between London and New York.

The *Financial Times* actually held this contest in 1997, at the urging of Richard Thaler, a pioneer of behavioral economics. If I were reading the *Financial Times* in 1997, how would I win those tickets? I might start by thinking that because anyone can guess anything between 0 and 100 the guesses will be scattered randomly. That would make the average guess 50. And two-thirds of 50 is 33. So I should guess 33. At this point, I'm feeling pretty pleased with myself. I'm sure I've nailed it. But before I say "final answer," I pause, think about the other contestants, and it dawns on me that they went through the same thought process as I did. Which means they all guessed 33 too. Which means the average guess is not 50. It's 33. And two-thirds of 33 is 22. So my first conclusion was actually wrong. I should guess 22.

Now I'm feeling very clever indeed. But wait! The other contestants also thought about the other contestants, just as I did. Which means they would have all guessed 22. Which means the average guess is actually 22. And two-thirds of 22 is about 15. So I should . . . See where this is going? Because the contestants are aware of each other, and aware that they are aware, the number is going to keep shrinking until it hits the point where it can no longer shrink. That point is 0. So that's my final answer. And I will surely win. My logic is airtight. And I happen to be one of those highly educated people who is familiar with game theory, so I know 0 is called the Nash equilibrium solution. QED. The only question is who will come with me to London.

Guess what? I'm wrong.

In the actual contest, many people did work all the way down to 0, but 0 was not the right answer. It wasn't even close to right. The average guess of all the contestants was 18.91, so the winning guess was 13. How did I get this so wrong? It wasn't my logic, which was sound. I failed because I only looked at the problem from one perspective—the perspective of logic.

Who are the other contestants? Are they *all* the sort of people who would think about this carefully, spot the logic, and pursue it relentlessly to the final answer of 0? If they were Vulcans, certainly. But they are humans. Maybe we can assume that *Financial Times* readers are a tad smarter than the general public, and better puzzle solvers, but they can't all be perfectly rational. Surely some of them will be cognitively lazy and fail to realize that the other contestants are working through the problem just as they are. They will settle on 33 as their final answer. Maybe some others will spot the logic and get to 22, but they may not keep thinking, so they will stop there. And that's just what happened—33 and 22 were popular answers. And because I did not think about the problem from this different perspective, and factor it into my own judgment, I was wrong.

What I should have done is look at the problem from both perspectives—the perspectives of both logic and psycho-logic—and combine what I saw. And this merging of perspectives need not be limited to two. In Thaler's guess-the-number game we might easily imagine a third perspective and use it to further improve our judgment. The first perspective is that of the rational Vulcan. The second is that of the sometimes rational but a little lazy human. A third perspective would be that of contestants who identified the first two perspectives and aggregated them to make their guess. In the original *Star Trek* TV series, Mr. Spock was the unflappably logical Vulcan, Dr. McCoy was the hot-headed human, and Captain Kirk was the synthesis of the two. In the guess-the-number game, Spock's answer would have been 0, McCoy's would have been 33—or maybe 22—and Captain Kirk would have considered them both. So we could call this the Captain Kirk perspective. If there are only a few Captain Kirks among the contestants, their responses may not shift the math much. But if there are more, their sophisticated thinking may make a significant difference and it would improve our answer, at least a little, if we could factor that third perspective into our own judgment. It would not be easy. This is getting complicated and the gradations of judgment required—should the final guess be 10 or 11 or 12?—are fine-grained. But sometimes these fine distinctions are the difference between good and great, as we will see later with the superforecasters.

And there is no reason to stop at three or four perspectives, although in the guess-the-number game that's about as far as it is practical to go. In other contexts, a fourth, fifth, and sixth perspective can further sharpen a judgment. In theory, there is no limit. So the best metaphor for this process is the vision of the dragonfly.

Like us, dragonflies have two eyes, but theirs are constructed very differently. Each eye is an enormous, bulging sphere, the surface of which is covered with tiny lenses. Depending on the species, there may be as many as thirty thousand of these lenses on a single eye, each one occupying a physical space slightly different from those of the adjacent lenses, giving it a unique perspective. Information from these thousands of unique perspectives flows into the dragonfly's brain where it is synthesized into vision so superb that the dragonfly can see in almost every direction simultaneously, with the clarity and precision it needs to pick off flying insects at high speed.

A fox with the bulging eyes of a dragonfly is an ugly mixed metaphor but it captures a key reason why the foresight of foxes is superior to that of hedgehogs with their green-tinted glasses. Foxes aggregate perspectives.

Unfortunately, aggregation doesn't come to us naturally. The tip-of-your-nose perspective insists that it sees reality objectively and correctly, so there is no need to consult other perspectives. All too often we agree. We don't consider alternative views—even when it's clear that we should.

This is painfully obvious at a poker table. Even weak players know, in principle, that seeing through the eyes of opponents is critical. She raised the bet $20? What does that tell me about her thinking—and the cards she has? Each bet is another clue to what your opponent is holding, or wants you to think she is holding, and the only way to piece it together is to imagine yourself in her seat. Good perspective-takers can make a lot of money. So you might suppose that anyone who takes poker seriously would get good at it, quickly, or take up another hobby. And yet they so often don't.

"Here's a very simple example," says Annie Duke, an elite professional poker player, winner of the World Series of Poker, and a former PhD-level student of psychology. "Everyone who plays poker knows you can either fold, call, or raise [a bet]. So what will happen is that when a player who isn't an expert sees another player raise, they automatically assume that that player is strong, as if the size of the bet is somehow correlated at one with the strength of the other person's hand." This is a mistake. Duke teaches poker and to get her students to see like dragonflies she walks them through a game situation. A hand is dealt. You like your cards. In the first of several rounds of betting, you wager a certain amount. The other player immediately raises your bet substantially. Now, what do you think the other player has? Duke has taught thousands of students "and universally, they say 'I think they have a really strong hand.'" So then she asks them to imagine the same situation, except they're playing against her. The cards are dealt. Their hand is more than strong— it's unbeatable. Duke makes her bet. Now, what will you do? Will you raise her bet? "And they say to me, 'Well, no.'" If they raise,

Duke may conclude their hand is strong and fold. They don't want to scare her off. They want Duke to stay in for each of the rounds of betting so they can expand the pot as much as possible before they scoop it up. So they won't raise. They'll only call. Duke then walks them through the same hypothetical with a hand that is beatable but still very strong. Will you raise? No. How about a little weaker hand that is still a likely winner? No raise. "They would never raise with any of these really great hands because they don't want to chase me away." Then Duke asks them: Why did you assume that an opponent who raises the bet has a strong hand if you would not raise with the same strong hand? "And it's not until I walk them through the exercise," Duke says, that people realize they failed to truly look at the table from the perspective of their opponent.

If Duke's students were all vacationing retirees trying poker for the first time, this would only tell us that dilettantes tend to be naive. But "these are people who have played enough poker, and are passionate about the game, and consider themselves good enough, that they're paying a thousand dollars for a seminar with me," Duke says. "And they don't understand this basic concept."[22]

Stepping outside ourselves and really getting a different view of reality is a struggle. But foxes are likelier to give it a try. Whether by virtue of temperament or habit or conscious effort, they tend to engage in the hard work of consulting other perspectives.

But remember the old reflexivity-paradox joke. There are two types of people in the world: those who think there are two types and those who don't. I'm of the second type. My fox/hedgehog model is not a dichotomy. It is a spectrum. In EPJ, my analyses extended to what I called "hybrids"—"fox-hedgehogs," who are foxes a little closer to the hedgehog end of the spectrum, and "hedgehog-foxes," who are hedgehogs with a little foxiness. But even expanding the categories to four doesn't capture people's styles of thinking. People can and do think differently in different circumstances—cool and calculating at work, perhaps, but intuitive and impulsive when shopping. And our thinking habits are not immutable. Sometimes they evolve without our awareness of the change. But we can also, with effort, choose to shift gears from one mode to another.[23]

No model captures the richness of human nature. Models are supposed to simplify things, which is why even the best are flawed. But they're necessary. Our minds are full of models. We couldn't function without them. And we often function pretty well because some of our models are decent approximations of reality. "All models are wrong," the statistician George Box observed, "but some are useful." The fox/hedgehog model is a starting point, not the end.

Forget the dart-throwing-chimp punch line. What matters is that EPJ found modest but real foresight, and the critical ingredient was the style of thinking. The next step was figuring out how to advance that insight.

4

Superforecasters

"We judge that Iraq has continued its weapons of mass destruction (WMD) programs in defiance of UN resolutions and restrictions. Baghdad has chemical and biological weapons as well as missiles with ranges in excess of UN restrictions; if left unchecked, it probably will have a nuclear weapon during this decade."[1]

The language is flat but that opening was a grabber when it was released to the public in October 2002. Terrorists had committed the 9/11 atrocities thirteen months earlier. The United States had invaded Afghanistan to oust the Taliban, who had harbored Osama bin Laden. Then the administration of George W. Bush turned its attention to Saddam Hussein's Iraq: suggesting that Iraq had ties to al-Qaeda, that Iraq was behind 9/11, that Iraq was a menace to other countries in the Middle East and the oil that flowed from the region, that Iraq had not destroyed its WMDs as required by the United Nations, that it was building up its stockpiles and was becoming more dangerous by the day. Saddam Hussein had, or would soon have, the ability to hit Europe, the White House claimed, and even the United States. Critics responded that the administration had long ago decided to invade Iraq and was exaggerating the threat by using vivid language—"We don't want the smoking gun to be a mushroom cloud," in Condoleezza Rice's words—to gin up support for its war.[2] That was when National Intelligence Estimate 2002-16HC was released.

National Intelligence Estimates are the consensus view of the Central Intelligence Agency, the National Security Agency, the

Defense Intelligence Agency, and thirteen other agencies. Collectively, these agencies are known as the intelligence community, or IC.

The exact numbers are classified, but by one rough estimate the IC has a budget of more than $50 billion and employs one hundred thousand people. Of these, twenty thousand are intelligence analysts, whose job is not to collect information but to make sense of what is collected and judge its implications for national security.[3] And this fantastically elaborate, expensive, and experienced intelligence apparatus concluded in October 2002 that the key claims of the Bush administration about Iraqi WMDs were correct. Many people found that persuasive. The job of intelligence is to speak truth to power, not to tell the politicians temporarily in charge what they want to hear, so, for them, the NIE settled the matter. It was now a fact that Saddam Hussein had active WMD programs churning out deadly weapons—and the threat was growing. What to do about these facts was another question, but only those blinded by politics would deny them. Even caustic critics of the Bush administration—people like Tom Friedman, who derisively called them "Bushies"—were convinced Saddam Hussein was hiding something, somewhere.

We now know that these "facts" were false. After invading in 2003, the United States turned Iraq upside down looking for WMDs but found nothing. It was one of the worst—arguably *the* worst—intelligence failure in modern history. The IC was humiliated. There were condemnations in the media, official investigations, and the familiar ritual of intelligence officials sitting in hearings, faces sweaty, expressions grim, as congressional committees took turns tearing into them.

What went wrong? One explanation was that the IC had caved to White House bullying. The intelligence had been politicized. But official investigations rejected that claim. So did Robert Jervis, a fact I find more compelling because Jervis has a four-decade track record of insightful, nonpartisan scholarship about intelligence. Jervis is the author of *Why Intelligence Fails*, which meticulously dissects both the failure of the IC to foresee the Iranian revolution in 1979—Jervis conducted a postmortem for the CIA that was classified for decades—and the false alarm on Saddam Hussein's WMDs. In the latter case, the IC's conclusion was sincere, Jervis decided. And it was reasonable.

"But the conclusion wasn't reasonable," you may think. "It was wrong!" That reaction is totally understandable—but it too is wrong. Remember, the question is not "Was the IC's judgment correct?" It is "Was the IC's judgment reasonable?" Answering that question requires putting ourselves in the position of the people making the judgment at the time, which means looking at only the information available then, and that evidence was sufficient to lead virtually every major intelligence agency on the planet to suspect, with varying confidence, that Saddam was hiding something—not because they had glimpsed what he was hiding but because Saddam was acting like someone who was hiding something. What other explanation could there be for playing a game of hide-and-seek with UN arms inspectors that risks triggering an invasion and your own downfall?

But few things are harder than mental time travel. Even for historians, putting yourself in the position of someone at the time—and not being swayed by your knowledge of what happened later—is a struggle. So the question "Was the IC's judgment reasonable?" is challenging. But it's a snap to answer "Was the IC's judgment correct?" As I noted in chapter 2, a situation like that tempts us with a bait and switch: replace the tough question with the easy one, answer it, and then sincerely believe that we have answered the tough question.

This particular bait and switch—replacing "Was it a good decision?" with "Did it have a good outcome?"—is both popular and pernicious. Savvy poker players see this mistake as a beginner's blunder. A novice may overestimate the probability that the next card will win her the hand, bet big, get lucky, and win, but winning doesn't retroactively make her foolish bet wise. Conversely, a pro may correctly see that there is a high probability of winning the hand, bet big, get unlucky, and lose, but that doesn't mean her bet was unwise. Good poker players, investors, and executives all understand this. If they don't, they can't remain good at what they do—because they will draw false lessons from experience, making their judgment worse over time.

So it's not oxymoronic to conclude, as Robert Jervis did, that the intelligence community's conclusion was both reasonable and wrong. But—and this is key—Jervis did *not* let the intelligence community off the hook. "There were not only errors but correctable ones," he wrote about the IC's analysis. "Analysis could and should have been better." Would that have made a difference? In a sense, no. "The result would have been to make the intelligence assessments less certain rather than to reach a fundamentally different conclusion." So the IC still would have concluded that Saddam had WMDs, they just would have been much less confident in that conclusion. That may sound like a gentle criticism. In fact, it's devastating, because a less-confident conclusion from the IC may have made a huge difference: If some in Congress had set the bar at "beyond a reasonable doubt" for supporting the invasion, then a 60% or 70% estimate that Saddam was churning out weapons of mass destruction would not have satisfied them. The congressional resolution authorizing the use of force might not have passed and the United States might not have invaded. Stakes rarely get much higher than thousands of lives and trillions of dollars.[4]

But NIE 2002-16HC didn't say 60% or 70%. It said, "Iraq has . . ." "Baghdad has . . ." Statements like these admit no possibility of surprise. They are the equivalent of "The sun rises in the east and sets in the west." At a White House briefing on December 12, 2002, the CIA director, George Tenet, used the phrase "slam dunk." He later protested that the quote had been taken out of context, but that doesn't matter here because "slam dunk" did indeed sum up the IC's attitude. And that was unusual. Intelligence analysis always involves uncertainty, often big dollops of it. Analysts know that. Yet on Iraqi WMDs, the IC fell prey to hubris. As a result, it wasn't merely wrong. It was wrong when it said it couldn't be wrong. Post-mortems even revealed that the IC had never seriously explored the *idea* that it could be wrong. "There were no 'red teams' to attack the prevailing views, no analyses from devil's advocates, no papers that provided competing possibilities," Jervis wrote. "Most strikingly, no one proposed a view close to the one we now believe to be true." As the presidential investigation of the debacle tartly noted, "failing to conclude that Saddam had ended his banned weapons program is one thing—not even considering it as a possibility is another."[5]

The IC is a huge bureaucracy that responds slowly even to the shock of major failures. Jervis told me that after he finished his post-mortem on the 1979 failure to foresee the Iranian revolution—the biggest geopolitical disaster of that era—"I saw the head of the [CIA] office of political analysis, and she said, 'I know you haven't heard anything from us, and that must confirm all your concerns, but we're going to have this big meeting and analysis and discussion with you.' And that is the end of the story. It never happened." The shock of the WMD failure was different. The bureaucracy was shaken to its foundation. "They took that to heart," Jervis said.[6]

In 2006 the Intelligence Advanced Research Projects Activity (IARPA) was created. Its mission is to fund cutting-edge research with the potential to make the intelligence community smarter and more effective. As its name suggests, IARPA was modeled after DARPA, the famous defense agency whose military-related research has had a huge influence on the modern world. DARPA's work even contributed to the invention of the Internet.

In 2008 the Office of the Director of National Intelligence—which sits atop the entire network of sixteen intelligence agencies—asked the National Research Council to form a committee. The task was to synthesize research on good judgment and help the IC put that research to good use. By Washington's standards, it was a bold (or rash) thing to do. It's not every day that a bureaucracy pays one of the world's most respected scientific institutions to produce an objective report that might conclude that the bureaucracy is clueless.

Distinguished scientists from a range of disciplines sat on the committee, which was chaired by the psychologist Baruch Fischhoff. I was in the room too, probably because of the controversy I stirred up with the "Can you beat the dart-throwing chimp?" challenge in my 2005 book *Expert Political Judgment.* Two years later, we delivered a report that was 100% Archie Cochrane: don't believe until you test. "The IC should not rely on analytical methods that violate well-documented behavioral principles or that have no evidence of efficacy beyond their intuitive appeal," the report noted. The IC should "rigorously test current and proposed methods under conditions that are as realistic as possible. Such an evidence-based approach to analysis will promote the continuous learning needed to keep the IC smarter and more agile than the nation's adversaries."[7]

It's a simple idea but, as was true in medicine for so long, it is routinely overlooked. For example, the CIA gives its analysts a manual written by Richards Heuer, a former analyst, that lays out relevant insights from psychology, including biases that can trip up an analyst's thinking. It's fine work. And it makes sense that giving analysts a basic grasp of psychology will help them avoid cognitive traps and thus help produce better judgments. But does it? No one knows. It has never been tested. Some analysts think the training is so intuitively compelling that it doesn't need to be tested. Sound familiar?

Even the $50 billion question—How accurate are the forecasts of intelligence analysts?—can't be answered. Of course, some think they know. Senior officials may claim that the IC is right 80% or 90% of the time. But these are just guesses. Like nineteenth-century physicians who were sure that their treatments cured patients 80%

or 90% of the time, they may be right, or close to right, or very wrong. Absent accuracy metrics, there is no meaningful way to hold intelligence analysts accountable for accuracy.

Note the word *meaningful* in that last sentence. When the director of National Intelligence is dragged into Congress for a blown call, that is accountability for accuracy. It may be ill informed or capricious, and serve no purpose beyond political grandstanding, but it is accountability. By contrast, *meaningful* accountability requires more than getting upset when something goes awry. It requires systematic tracking of accuracy—for all the reasons laid out earlier. But the intelligence community's forecasts have never been systematically assessed.

What there is instead is accountability for process: Intelligence analysts are told what they are expected to do when researching, thinking, and judging, and then held accountable to those standards. Did you consider alternative hypotheses? Did you look for contrary evidence? It's sensible stuff, but the point of making forecasts is not to tick all the boxes on the "how to make forecasts" checklist. It is to foresee what's coming. To have accountability for process but not accuracy is like ensuring that physicians wash their hands, examine the patient, and consider all the symptoms, but never checking to see whether the treatment works.

The intelligence community is not alone in operating this way. The list of organizations that produce or buy forecasts without bothering to check for accuracy is astonishing. But thanks to the shock of the Iraqi WMD debacle, and the prodding of the National Research Council report, and the efforts of some dedicated civil servants, the IC decided to do something about it. Or more precisely, IARPA decided.

The Intelligence Advanced Research Projects Activity is an agency few outside the intelligence community have heard of, and for good reason. IARPA doesn't have spies doing cloak-and-dagger work, or analysts who interpret information. Its job is to identify and support high-risk, high-payoff research with the potential to improve the IC's capabilities. That makes IARPA similar to DARPA, but DARPA is much more famous because it's bigger, has been around longer, and often funds whiz-bang technology. Most intelligence research isn't so exotic and yet it can be just as important to national security.

In the summer of 2010, two IARPA officials, Jason Matheny and Steve Rieber, visited Berkeley. Barbara Mellers and I met them at a hotel with a tourist-trap view of San Francisco, where they gave us news as pleasant as the vista. They planned to act on the key recommendation in the National Research Council report—a recommendation I had confidently predicted would gather dust. IARPA would sponsor a massive tournament to see who could invent the best methods of making the sorts of forecasts that intelligence analysts make every day. Will the president of Tunisia flee to a cushy exile in the next month? Will an outbreak of H5N1 in China kill more than ten in the next six months? Will the euro fall below $1.20 in the next twelve months?

IARPA was looking for questions in the Goldilocks zone of difficulty, neither so easy that any attentive reader of the *New York Times* could get them right nor so hard that no one on the planet could. IARPA saw this Goldilocks zone as the best place both for finding new forecasting talent and for testing new methods of cultivating talent. The proposed tournament would be, by design, quite different from my earlier EPJ tournament: their longest questions would usually be shorter than my shortest questions. IARPA didn't want to waste money pushing people to do what we now know to be pretty much impossible. Human visual systems will never be able to read the bottom line off Snellen eye-exam charts one hundred meters away—and exercising your eye muscles from now until eternity won't change that. And as EPJ and other studies have shown, human cognitive systems will never be able to forecast turning points in the lives of individuals or nations several years into the future—and heroic searches for superforecasters won't change that.

IARPA's plan was to create tournament-style incentives for top researchers to generate accurate probability estimates for Goldilocks-zone questions.[8] The research teams would compete against one another and an independent control group. Teams had to beat the combined forecast—the "wisdom of the crowd"—of the control group, and by margins we all saw as intimidating. In the first year, IARPA wanted teams to beat that standard by 20%—and it wanted that margin of victory to grow to 50% by the fourth year.

But that was only part of IARPA's plan. Within each team, researchers could run Archie Cochrane–style experiments to assess what really works against internal control groups. Researchers might think, for example, that giving forecasters a basic training exercise would improve their accuracy. But if they simply trained all forecasters, what would it prove? If forecasters' accuracy rose, it might be because the training worked. Or maybe the questions got easier. Or maybe the forecasters just got lucky. If accuracy fell, it might be because the training was counterproductive or perhaps accuracy would have declined even more but for the training. There would be no way to know. Recognize the problem? It's the one physicians faced throughout the history of medicine. Archie Cochrane saw the solution: Quit pretending you know things you don't and start running experiments. Give the training to one randomly chosen group of forecasters but not another. Keep all else constant. Compare results. If the trainees become more accurate, while the untrained don't, the training worked.

The research possibilities were limited only by imagination, but to exploit them we needed a lot of forecasters. My colleagues and I put the word out through blogs and professional networks: Do you want to forecast the world's future? Here's your chance, and you won't even have to leave home, just spend a little time each day thinking about political-economic puzzles and make your best guesses. Our recruitment efforts were rewarded. In the first year, several thousand volunteers signed up and roughly 3,200 passed through our initial gauntlet of psychometric tests and started forecasting. We called our research team and program the Good Judgment Project.

A project on this scale costs many millions of dollars a year. But that's not what made it bureaucratically gutsy for IARPA to do this. After all, the intelligence community's annual budget is around $50 billion, which is more than most countries' annual gross domestic product. Next to that mountain of cash, the cost of the IARPA tournament was an anthill. No, what made it gutsy was what it could reveal.

Here's one possible revelation: Imagine you get a couple of hundred ordinary people to forecast geopolitical events. You see how often they revise their forecasts and how accurate those forecasts prove to be and use that information to identify the forty or so who are the best. Then you have everyone make lots more forecasts. This time, you calculate the average forecast of the whole group—"the wisdom of the crowd"—but with extra weight given to those forty top forecasters. Then you give the forecast a final tweak: You "extremize" it, meaning you push it closer to 100% or zero. If the forecast is 70% you might bump it up to, say, 85%. If it's 30%, you might reduce it to 15%.[9]

Now imagine that the forecasts you produce this way beat those of every other group and method available, often by large margins. Your forecasts even beat those of professional intelligence analysts inside the government who have access to classified information—by margins that remain classified.

Think how shocking it would be to the intelligence professionals who have spent their lives forecasting geopolitical events—to be beaten by a few hundred ordinary people and some simple algorithms.

It actually happened. What I've described is the method we used to win IARPA's tournament. There is nothing dazzlingly innovative about it. Even the extremizing tweak is based on a pretty simple insight: When you combine the judgments of a large group of people to calculate the "wisdom of the crowd" you collect all the relevant information that is dispersed among all those people. But none of those people has access to all that information. One person knows only some of it, another knows some more, and so on. What would happen if every one of those people were given *all* the information? They would become more confident—raising their forecasts closer to 100% or zero. If you *then* calculated the "wisdom of the crowd" it too would be more extreme. Of course it's impossible to give every person all the relevant information—so we extremize to simulate what would happen if we could.

Thanks to IARPA, we now know a few hundred ordinary people and some simple math can not only compete with professionals supported by a multibillion-dollar apparatus but also beat them.[10]

And that's just one of the unsettling revelations IARPA's decision made possible. What if the tournament discovered ordinary people who could—without the assistance of any algorithmic magic—beat the IC? Imagine how threatening that would be.

With his gray beard, thinning hair, and glasses, Doug Lorch doesn't look like a threat to anyone. He looks like a computer programmer, which he was, for IBM. He is retired now. He lives in a quiet neighborhood in Santa Barbara with his wife, an artist who paints lovely watercolors. His Facebook avatar is a duck. Doug likes to drive his little red convertible Miata around the sunny streets, enjoying the California breeze, but that can only occupy so many hours in the day. Doug has no special expertise in international affairs, but he has a healthy curiosity about what's happening. He reads the *New York Times*. He can find Kazakhstan on a map. So he volunteered for the Good Judgment Project. Once a day, for an hour or so, his dining room table became his forecasting center, where he opened his laptop, read the news, and tried to anticipate the fate of the world.

In the first year, Doug answered 104 questions like "Will Serbia be officially granted European Union candidacy by 31 December 2011?" and "Will the London Gold Market Fixing price of gold (USD per ounce) exceed $1,850 on 30 September 2011?" That's a lot of forecasting, but it understates what Doug did.

In my EPJ research, I had asked experts to make only one forecast per question and scored it later. By contrast, the IARPA tournament encouraged forecasters to update their forecasts in real time. So if a question with a closing date six months in the future opened, a forecaster could make her initial judgment—say, a 60% chance the event will happen by the six-month deadline—then read something in the news the next day that convinces her to move her forecast to 75%. For scoring purposes, those will later be counted as separate forecasts. If a week passes without her making any changes to the forecast, her forecast stays at 75% for those seven days. She may then spot some new information that convinces her to lower her forecast to 70%, which is where the forecast will stay until she changes it again. The process goes on like this until six months pass and the question closes. At this point, all of her forecasts are rolled into the calculation that produces the final Brier score for this one question. And that's just one question. Over four years, nearly five hundred questions about international affairs were asked of thousands of GJP's forecasters, generating well over one million judgments about the future. But even at the individual level, the numbers quickly added up. In year 1 alone, Doug Lorch made roughly one thousand separate forecasts.

Doug's accuracy was as impressive as his volume. At the end of the first year, Doug's overall Brier score was 0.22, putting him in fifth spot among the 2,800 competitors in the Good Judgment Project. Remember that the Brier score measures the gap between forecasts and reality, where 2.0 is the result if your forecasts are the perfect opposite of reality, 0.5 is what you would get by random guessing, and 0 is the center of the bull's-eye. So 0.22 is prima facie impressive, given the difficulty of the questions. Consider this one, which was first asked on January 9, 2011: "Will Italy restructure or default on its debt by 31 December 2011?" We now know the correct answer is no. To get a 0.22, Doug's average judgment across the eleven-month duration of the question had to be no at roughly 68% confidence—not bad given the wave of financial panics rocking the eurozone during this period. And Doug had to be that accurate, on average, on all the questions.

In year 2, Doug joined a superforecaster team and did even better, with a final Brier score of 0.14, making him the best forecaster of the 2,800 GJP volunteers. He also beat by 40% a prediction market in which traders bought and sold futures contracts on the outcomes of the same questions. He was the only person to beat the extremizing algorithm. And Doug not only beat the control group's "wisdom of the crowd," he surpassed it by more than 60%, meaning that he single-handedly exceeded the fourth-year performance target that IARPA set for multimillion-dollar research programs that were free to use every trick in the forecasting textbook for improving accuracy.

By any mortal standard, Doug Lorch did astonishingly well. The only way to make Doug look unimpressive would be to compare him to godlike omniscience—a Brier score of 0—which would be like belittling Tiger Woods in his prime for failing to hit holes in one.

That made Doug Lorch a threat. This is a man with no applicable experience or education, and no access to classified information. The only payment he received was the $250 Amazon gift certificate that all volunteers got at the end of each season. Doug Lorch was simply a retiree who, rather than collect stamps, or play golf, or build model airplanes, made forecasts, and he was so good at it that there wasn't a lot of room for an experienced intelligence analyst with a salary, a security clearance, and a desk in CIA headquarters to do better. Someone might ask why the United States spends billions of dollars every year on geopolitical forecasting when it could give Doug a gift certificate and let him do it.

Of course if Doug Lorch were a uniquely gifted oracle, he would pose little threat to the status quo. There is only so much forecasting one man can do. But Doug isn't unique. We have already met Bill Flack, the retired Department of Agriculture employee from Nebraska. There were 58 others among the 2,800 volunteers who scored at the top of the charts in year 1. They were our first class of superforecasters. At the end of year 1, their collective Brier score was 0.25, compared with 0.37 for all the other forecasters—and that gap grew in later years so that by the end of the four-year tournament, superforecasters had outperformed regulars by over 60%. Another gauge of how good superforecasters were is how much further they could see into the future. Across all four years of the tournament, superforecasters looking out three hundred days were more accurate than regular forecasters looking out one hundred days. In other words, regular forecasters needed to triple their foresight to see as far as superforecasters.

How much do performance differentials of these magnitudes matter? Let's arbitrarily say that the Brier score of the average regular forecaster is equivalent to 20/100 vision. An optometrist gives that forecaster glasses that improve his eyesight to 20/40. That's a 60% improvement. How much does it matter? Twenty/forty is not even close to hawkeyed vision. But look at the Snellen charts on page 95. The change from 20/100 to 20/40 results in a decent grasp of the letters on rows two through five and a much-improved ability to catch baseballs, recognize friends on the street, read the fine print in contracts, and avoid head-on collisions. Cumulatively, that's life changing.

Now, remember that these superforecasters are amateurs forecasting global events in their spare time with whatever information they can dig up. Yet they have somehow managed to set the performance bar so high that even the professionals have struggled to get over it, let alone clear it with enough room to justify their offices, salaries, and pensions. Of course it would be wonderful to have a direct comparison between superforecasters and intelligence analysts, but such a thing would be closely guarded. However, in November 2013, the *Washington Post* editor David Ignatius reported that "a participant in the project" had told him that the superforecasters "performed about 30 percent better than the average for intelligence community analysts who could read intercepts and other secret data."[11]

IARPA knew this could happen when it bankrolled the tournament, which is why a decision like that is so unusual. Testing may obviously be in the interest of an organization, but organizations consist of people who have interests of their own, most notably preserving and enhancing a comfortable status quo. Just as famous, well-remunerated pundits are loath to put their reputations at risk by having their accuracy publicly tested, so too are the power players inside organizations unlikely to try forecasting tournaments if it means putting their own judgment to the test. Bob in the CEO suite does not want to hear, much less let others hear, that Dave in the mail room is better at forecasting the company's business trends than he is.

And yet, IARPA did just that: it put the intelligence community's mission ahead of the interests of the people inside the intelligence community—at least ahead of those insiders who didn't want to rock the bureaucratic boat.

RESISTING GRAVITY—BUT FOR HOW LONG?

The purpose of laying out an argument as I have done here is to convince the reader, but I hope you're not convinced about these superforecasters—yet.

Imagine that I asked each of my 2,800 volunteers to predict whether a coin I am about to toss will land heads or tails. They do. I then flip the coin and record who got it right. I repeat this procedure 104 times (the number of forecasts made in the first year of the tournament). The results would look like a classic bell curve.

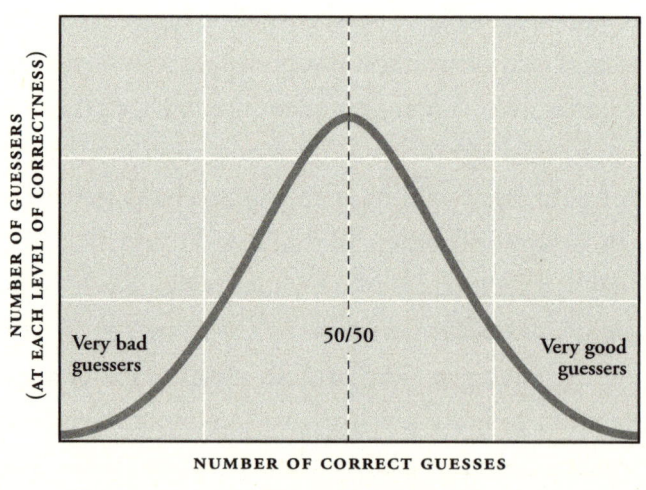

Coin-toss game

The great majority of my forecasters will have accurately predicted the coin toss about 50% of the time, and they can be found in the middle of the curve. But a few will get quite different results. Some will mostly be wrong (far left of the curve); others mostly right (far right of the curve). What do these extreme results tell us about the skill of the people who got them? Unless you believe in ESP, the answer is nothing. There is no skill involved. Someone who correctly calls a coin toss isn't demonstrating coin-flipping forecasting ability whether he does it one time or a hundred. It's all luck. Of course it takes a lot of luck to correctly call 70% of 104 coin tosses, and if you have only one person making calls it's extremely unlikely. But if you have 2,800 coin-toss callers, the unlikely becomes quite likely.

This is not complicated stuff. But it's easy to misinterpret randomness. We don't have an intuitive feel for it. Randomness is invisible from the tip-of-your-nose perspective. We can only see it if we step outside ourselves.

The psychologist Ellen Langer has shown how poorly we grasp randomness in a series of experiments. In one, she asked Yale students to watch someone flip a coin thirty times and predict whether it would come up heads or tails. The students could not see the actual flipping but they were told the results of each toss. The results, however, were rigged: all students got a total of fifteen right and fifteen wrong, but some students got a string of hits early while others started with a string of misses. Langer then asked the students how well they thought they would do if the experiment were repeated. Students who started off with a string of hits had a higher opinion of their skill and thought they would shine again. Langer called this the "illusion of control," but it is also an "illusion of prediction." And think about the context. These are students at an elite university who know their intelligence is being tested with an activity that is the very symbol of randomness. As Langer wrote, you would expect them to be "super-rational." Yet the first pattern they encountered fooled them into sincerely believing that they could predict entirely random outcomes.[12]

Outside Yale labs, delusions of this sort are routine. Watch business news on television, where talking heads are often introduced with a reference to one of their dramatic forecasting successes: "Pedro Ziff called the crash of 2008!" The point is to make them credible so we'll want to hear their next forecast. But even if we assume these statements are true accounts of what the person forecast—they often are not—they tell us next to nothing about the guest's accuracy, as viewers would know if they applied a little System 2 thought. Even a dart-throwing chimp will hit the occasional bull's-eye if he throws enough darts, and anyone can easily "predict" the next stock market crash by incessantly warning that the stock market is about to crash. And yet many people take these hollow claims seriously.

A variant of this fallacy is to single out an extraordinarily successful person, show that it was extremely unlikely that the person could do what he or she did, and conclude that luck could not be the explanation. This often happens in news coverage of Wall Street. Someone beats the market six or seven years in a row, journalists profile the great investor, calculate how unlikely it is to get such results by luck alone, and triumphantly announce that it's proof of skill. The mistake? They ignore how many other people were trying to do what the great man did. If it's many thousands, the odds of *someone* getting that lucky shoot up. Think of a lottery winner. It is fantastically unlikely that one particular ticket will win a major lottery, often one in many millions, but we don't conclude that lottery winners are highly skilled ticket-pickers—because we know there are millions of tickets sold, which makes it highly likely that someone, somewhere, will win.

A similar mistake can be found by rummaging through remaindered business books: a corporation or executive is on a roll, going from success to success, piling up money and fawning profiles in magazines. What comes next? Inevitably, it's a book recounting the successes and assuring readers that they can reap similar successes simply by doing whatever the corporation or executive did. These stories may be true—or fairy tales. It's impossible to know. These books seldom provide solid evidence that the highlighted qualities or actions caused happy outcomes, much less that someone who replicates them will get similarly happy outcomes. And they rarely acknowledge that factors beyond the hero's control—luck—may have played a role in the happy outcomes.[13]

Lest I add to this unfortunate genre, I should say unequivocally that the evidence presented so far does not establish that the super-forecasters are super, much less that if readers retire to Santa Barbara and drive a little red convertible they can forecast as accurately as Doug Lorch. So what should we make of Doug and the others? Are they superforecasters or superlucky?

Don't answer yet. It is another of those pesky false dichotomies that buzz, like mosquitoes, around efforts to judge judgment. Most things in life involve skill *and* luck, in varying proportions. The mix may be almost all luck and a little skill, or almost all skill and a little luck, or it could be one of a thousand other possible variations. That complexity makes it hard to figure out what to chalk up to skill and what to luck—a subject probed in depth by Michael Mauboussin, a global financial strategist, in his book *The Success Equation*. But as Mauboussin noted, there is an elegant rule of thumb that applies to athletes and CEOs, stock analysts and superforecasters. It involves "regression to the mean."

Some statistical concepts are both easy to understand and easy to forget. Regression to the mean is one of them. Let's say the average height of men is five feet eight inches. Now imagine a man who is six feet tall and then picture his adult son. Your initial System 1 hunch may be that the son is also six feet. That's possible, but unlikely. To see why, we have to engage in some strenuous System 2 reasoning. Imagine that we knew everyone's height and computed the correlation between the heights of fathers and sons. We would find a strong but imperfect relationship, a correlation of about 0.5, as captured by the line running through the data points in the chart below. It tells us that when the father is six feet, we should make a compromise prediction based on both the father's height and the population average. Our best guess for the son is five feet ten. The son's height has regressed toward the mean by two inches, halfway between the population average and the father's height.[14]

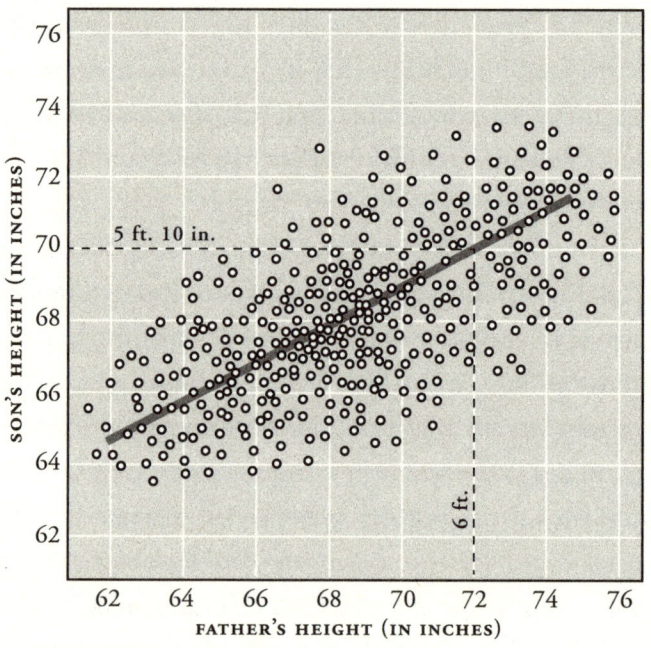

Best prediction of heights of sons from heights of fathers, assuming a 0.5 correlation between the two variables

But as I said, regression to the mean is as easy to forget as it is to understand. Say you suffer from chronic back pain. Not all days are the same. Some days, you feel fine; others, you feel some pain but not a lot; and occasionally it's awful. Of course it's when you have one of those awful days that you are most likely to seek help by visiting a homeopath or some other dispenser of medical treatments unsupported by solid scientific evidence. The next day you wake up and . . . you feel better! The treatment works! The placebo effect may have helped, but you probably would have felt better the next day even if you had received no treatment at all—thanks to regression to the mean, a fact that won't occur to you unless you stop and think carefully, instead of going with the tip-of-your-nose conclusion. This modest little mistake is responsible for many of the things people believe but shouldn't.

Keep regression to the mean in mind, however, and it becomes a valuable tool. Imagine that we had our 2,800 volunteers predict the outcome of 104 coin tosses a second time. The distribution would again look like a bell curve, with most people clustered around 50% and tiny numbers correctly predicting almost none or almost all. But *who* gets the amazingly good results this time? Most likely it will be different people from last time. The correlation across rounds will be close to zero, and your best prediction for any given forecaster will be the average accuracy rate of 50%—in other words, total regression to the mean.

To make the point unmistakable, imagine that we ask *only* those who got amazingly good results in the first round to do the exercise again. Thanks to regression to the mean, it's likely that most will do worse the second time. And the decline will be biggest for the luckiest. Those who got 90% right should expect a rapid descent to 50%. Of course it's possible that a few people will again get nine or ten right, but the fact that everyone else is rapidly regressing to the mean should make us hesitate before we declare them coin-toss gurus. Make them do the exercise again. Eventually their luck will run out.

So regression to the mean is an indispensable tool for testing the role of luck in performance: Mauboussin notes that slow regression is more often seen in activities dominated by skill, while faster regression is more associated with chance.[15]

To illustrate, imagine two people in the IARPA tournament,

Frank and Nancy. In year 1, Frank does horribly but Nancy is out-standing. On the bell curve below, Frank is ranked in the bottom 1% and Nancy in the top 99%. If their results were caused entirely by luck—like coin flipping—then in year 2 we would expect both Frank and Nancy to regress all the way back to 50%. If their results were equal parts luck and skill, we would expect halfway regression: Frank should rise to around 25% (between 1% and 50%) and Nancy fall to around 75% (between 50% and 99%). If their results were entirely decided by skill, there would be no regression: Frank would be just as awful in year 2 and Nancy would be just as spectacular.

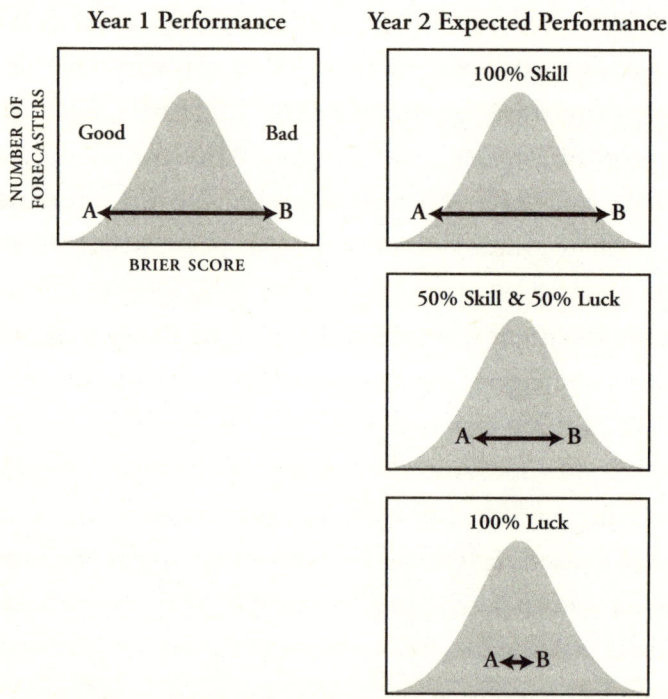

Amount of luck in tournament determines amount of regression to the mean from one year to the next.

So how did superforecasters hold up across years? That's the key question. And the answer is phenomenally well. For instance, in

years 2 and 3 we saw the opposite of regression to the mean: the superforecasters as a whole, including Doug Lorch, actually increased
their lead over all other forecasters.

But that result should make attentive readers suspicious. It suggests there was little or *no* luck behind the superforecasters' results.
Given the nature of what they were predicting—and the irreducible
uncertainty that lurks in some questions—I deeply doubt this possibility. Some questions were resolved by quirky last-minute events
that no one, this side of God, could have foreseen. One such question
asked whether there would be a fatal confrontation between vessels
on the East China Sea. The answer turned out to be yes when, just
before the closing date for the question, an angry Chinese fishing boat
captain stabbed a South Korean coast guard officer who had seized
his boat for a border violation. Other questions pivoted on complex
interactions among systems of variables. Take the price of oil, long
a graveyard topic for forecasting reputations.[16] The number of factors that can drive the price up or down is huge—from frackers in
the United States to jihadists in Libya to battery designers in Silicon
Valley—and the number of factors that can influence those factors
is even bigger. Many of these causal ties are also nonlinear, which, as
Edward Lorenz showed, means even something as tiny as a butterfly's
wing flaps can make a dramatic difference to what happens.

So we have a mystery. If chance is playing a significant role, why
aren't we observing significant regression of superforecasters as a
whole toward the overall mean? An offsetting process must be pushing up superforecasters' performance numbers. And it's not hard to
guess what that was: after year 1, when the first cohort of superforecasters was identified, we congratulated them, anointed them
"super," and put them on teams with fellow superforecasters. Instead
of regressing toward the mean, their scores got even better. This suggests that being recognized as "super" and placed on teams of intellectually stimulating colleagues improved their performance enough

to erase the regression to the mean we would otherwise have seen. In years 3 and 4, we harvested fresh crops of superforecasters and put them to work in elite teams. That gave us more apples-to-apples comparisons. The new cohorts continued to do as well or better than they did in the previous year, again contrary to the regression hypothesis.

But, as Wall Streeters well know, mortals can only defy the laws of statistical gravity for so long. The consistency in performance of superforecasters as a group should not mask the inevitable turnover among some top performers over time. The correlation between how well individuals do from one year to the next is about 0.65, modestly higher than that between the heights of fathers and sons. So we should still expect considerable regression toward the mean. And we observe just that. Each year, roughly 30% of the individual superforecasters fall from the ranks of the top 2% next year. But that also implies a good deal of consistency over time: 70% of superforecasters remain superforecasters. The chances of such consistency arising among coin-flip guessers (where the year-to-year correlation is 0) is less than 1 in 100,000,000, but the chances of such consistency arising among forecasters (where year-to-year correlation is 0.65) is far higher, about 1 in 3.[17]

All of this suggests two key conclusions. One, we should not treat the superstars of any given year as infallible, not even Doug Lorch. Luck plays a role and it is only to be expected that the superstars will occasionally have a bad year and produce ordinary results—just as superstar athletes occasionally look less than stellar.

But more basically, and more hopefully, we can conclude that the superforecasters were not just lucky. Mostly, their results reflected skill.

Which raises the big question: Why are superforecasters so good?

5

Supersmart?

In 2008 Sanford "Sandy" Sillman was diagnosed with multiple sclerosis. It wasn't life threatening, but it was debilitating. It made him weak and easily exhausted. He had back and hip pain. Walking was difficult. Even typing became a struggle. By 2011, he recalled, "I could see the writing on the wall." He would soon have to give up his job as an atmospheric scientist.

Sandy was fifty-seven. He knew that the loss of his work would leave a void in his life and he would need something to keep him busy at a pace he could manage. So when he read about a forecasting tournament recruiting volunteers, he signed up and started making forecasts for the Good Judgment Project. "When people stop working, they feel a bit lost and a bit worthless," he told me in an e-mail he dictated using software that translates voice to text. "I thought GJP might be good as a 'transition project' for me—not so much pressure or importance as work, but still something that counted, and also keeping my mind alive."

And what a mind it is. Sandy has a bachelor of arts degree, with a double major in math and physics, from Brown University, plus a master of science degree from MIT's technology and policy program, along with a second master's degree, in applied mathematics, from Harvard—and a PhD in applied physics from Harvard. After earning his doctorate, he became an atmospheric research scientist at the University of Michigan, where his work—published under such daunting titles as "Effects of Additional Nonmethane Volatile Organic Compounds, Organic Nitrates, and Direct Emissions of

Oxygenated Organic Species on Global Tropospheric Chemistry"—
won him awards and honors. And his intelligence isn't confined to
math and science. He's a voracious reader, and not only in English.
He's fluent in French, thanks to school and time as a visiting scholar
in Switzerland. He added Russian to his repertoire because his wife
is Russian, and he can speak and read Italian because "I actually
decided when I was 12 that I wanted to learn Italian and started
just doing it on my own." He also speaks Spanish, but Sandy thinks
that's so close to Italian it shouldn't count as another language.

Unfortunately, Sandy's forecast for his health proved accurate.
In 2012 he went on disability leave—although, as he wrote in a
typically gentle and gracious note to colleagues at the University of
Michigan, "I prefer to view it as the equivalent of early retirement."

More happily, a remarkable number of Sandy's other forecasts
proved accurate as well. In year 1 of the tournament, after being randomly assigned to a control condition that had him forecasting by
himself, Sandy finished with a Brier score of 0.19. That put him in
a tie for overall champion—beating out roughly 2,800 others, most
of whom worked in more stimulating conditions. Sandy was thrilled.
"It is a bit nonprofessional to say so, but of course it is very exciting.
You feel great. You 'tingle' a bit. The only thing like it was when I
was in high school and placed first in a math competition. I suppose
I am still a high schooler at heart."[1] When we put together our first
list of superforecasters, Sandy's name was at the top.

It's hard not to suspect that Sandy's remarkable mind explains
his remarkable results. And that the same is true of the other superforecasters.

Two years into the research, we hosted a gathering of superforecasters in the conference room atop Huntsman Hall at the Wharton
School, and it was obvious from the chatter alone that these were
very sharp people who follow the news closely, particularly the elite
media. They love books too. When I asked Joshua Frankel what he

reads for fun, the young Brooklyn filmmaker rattled off the names of highbrow authors like Thomas Pynchon, thought for a moment, and added that he'd recently read a biography of the German rocket scientist Wernher von Braun and various histories of New York, although Frankel was careful to note that the books about New York are also for his work: he is producing an opera about the legendary clash between Robert Moses, New York's great urban planner, and the free-spirited antiplanner Jane Jacobs. Frankel is not someone to tangle with on *Jeopardy!*

Are superforecasters better simply because they are more knowledgeable and intelligent than others? That would be flattering for them but deflating for the rest of us. Knowledge is something we can all increase, but only slowly. People who haven't stayed mentally active have little hope of catching up to lifelong learners. Intelligence feels like an even more daunting obstacle. There are believers in cognitive enhancement pills and computer puzzles who may someday be vindicated, but most people feel that adult intelligence is relatively fixed, a function of how well you did in the DNA lottery at conception and the lottery for loving, wealthy families at birth. If superforecasting is a job for three-standard-deviation MENSA-certified geniuses—the top 1%—then the vast majority of us can never qualify. So why bother trying?

The idea that knowledge and intelligence drive foresight is plausible, but as Archie Cochrane showed so well, plausibility is not enough. We must put the hypothesis to the test. Thanks to project coleader Barbara Mellers, and the volunteers who endured a grueling battery of psychological tests before they started forecasting, we had the data to do that.[2]

To gauge fluid intelligence, or raw crunching power, volunteers had to figure out puzzles like the one on page 108, where the goal is to fill in the missing space at the lower right. Solving it requires identifying the rules generating patterns in the row (each row must have a distinctive symbol in the center of its figures) and each column (each column must contain all three shapes). The correct answer is the second figure in the second row.[3]

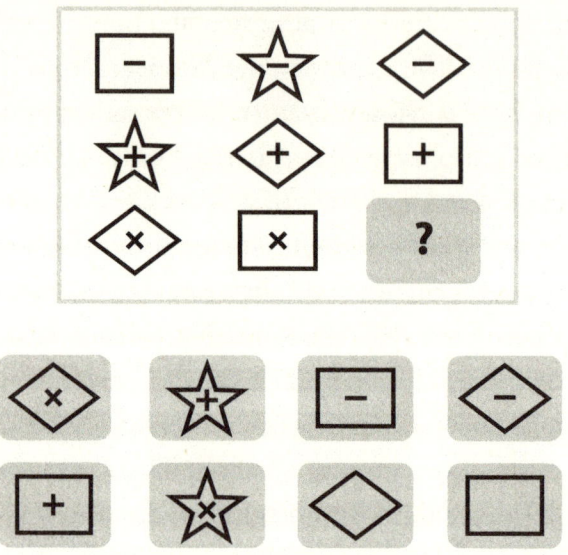

Fluid intelligence as inductive spatial reasoning

High-powered pattern recognition skills won't get you far, though, if you don't know where to look for patterns in the real world. So we measured crystallized intelligence—knowledge—using some U.S.-centric questions like "How many Justices sit on the Supreme Court?" and more global questions like "Which nations are permanent members of the UN Security Council?"

Before we get to the results, bear in mind that several thousand people volunteered for the GJP in the first year and the 2,800 who were motivated enough to work through all the testing and make forecasts were far from a randomly selected sample. That matters. Random selection ensures a sample is representative of the population from which it's drawn. Lacking that, we can't assume our volunteers reflected the population at large, in the United States or anywhere. After all, our 2,800 volunteers were people who had read about the forecasting tournament on a blog or in an article and thought to themselves, "Yes, I'd like to spend a good-size chunk of my precious free time analyzing Nigerian politics, Greek bonds, Chinese military expenditures, Russian oil and gas production, and other complex geopolitical matters. I'd like to do that for the better part of a year. And I'd like to do it for no material gain other than a $250 gift certificate." We can be quite confident these are not average people. So to understand the role of intelligence and knowledge in superforecaster success, we have to go a step further. We must compare the superforecasters' intelligence and knowledge not only with that of other forecasters, but with that of the general population of the United States.

What did we find? Regular forecasters scored higher on intelligence and knowledge tests than about 70% of the population. Superforecasters did better, placing higher than about 80% of the population.

Note three things. First, the big jumps in intelligence and knowledge are from the public to the forecasters, not from forecasters to superforecasters. Second, although superforecasters are well above average, they did not score off-the-charts high and most fall well short of so-called genius territory, a problematic concept often arbitrarily defined as the top 1%, or an IQ of 135 and up.

So it seems intelligence and knowledge help but they add little beyond a certain threshold—so superforecasting does not require a Harvard PhD and the ability to speak five languages. I find that conclusion satisfying because it squares nicely with the hunch Daniel Kahneman shared with me all those years ago, when I started this research—that high-powered subject-matter experts would not be much better forecasters than attentive readers of the *New York Times*. It should also satisfy the reader. If you've made it this far, you've probably got the right stuff.

But having the requisite intelligence and knowledge is not enough. Many clever and informed forecasters in the tournament fell far short of superforecaster accuracy. And history is replete with brilliant people who made forecasts that proved considerably less than prescient. Robert McNamara—defense secretary under Presidents Kennedy and Johnson—was famously dubbed one of "the best and the brightest," but he and his colleagues escalated the war in Vietnam in the firm belief that if South Vietnam were lost to the Communists all of Southeast Asia would follow, and American security would be imperiled. Their certainty wasn't based on any serious analysis. In fact, no serious analysis of this critical forecast was conducted until 1967—years *after* the decisions to escalate had been made.[4]

"The foundations of our decision making were gravely flawed," McNamara wrote in his autobiography. "We failed to analyze our assumptions critically, then or later."[5]

Ultimately, it's not the crunching power that counts. It's how you use it.

FERMI-IZE

Here's a question that definitely was not asked in the forecasting tournament: How many piano tuners are there in Chicago?

Don't even think about letting Google find the answer for you. The Italian American physicist Enrico Fermi—a central figure in the invention of the atomic bomb—concocted this little brainteaser decades before the invention of the Internet. And Fermi's students did not have the Chicago yellow pages at hand. They had nothing. And yet Fermi expected them to come up with a reasonably accurate estimate.

Outside Fermi's classroom, most people would frown, roll their eyes, scratch an ear, and sigh. "Well, maybe"—long pause—and they would offer a number. How did they arrive at that number? Ask them and they would shrug and say nothing more informative than "It seems about right." The number came out of a black box. They had no idea how it was generated.

Fermi knew people could do much better and the key was to break down the question with more questions like "What would have to be true for this to happen?" Here, we can break the question down by asking, "What information would allow me to answer the question?"

So what would we need to know to calculate the number of piano tuners in Chicago? Well, the number of piano tuners depends on how much piano-tuning work there is and how much work it takes to employ one piano tuner. So I could nail this question if I knew four facts:

1. The number of pianos in Chicago
2. How often pianos are tuned each year
3. How long it takes to tune a piano
4. How many hours a year the average piano tuner works

With the first three facts, I can figure out the total amount of piano-tuning work in Chicago. Then I can divide it by the last and, just like that, I'll have a pretty good sense of how many piano tuners there are in Chicago.

But I don't have *any* of that information! So you may think I've wasted my time by exchanging one question I can't answer for four.

Not so. What Fermi understood is that by breaking down the question, we can better separate the knowable and the unknowable. So guessing—pulling a number out of the black box—isn't eliminated. But we have brought our guessing process out into the light of day where we can inspect it. And the net result tends to be a more accurate estimate than whatever number happened to pop out of the black box when we first read the question.

Of course, all this means we have to overcome our deep-rooted fear of looking dumb. Fermi-izing dares us to be wrong. In that spirit, I'll take my best shot at each of the four items:

1. How many pianos are there in Chicago? I have no idea. But just as I broke down the first question, I can break this down by asking what I would need to know in order to answer it.

   a. How many *people* are there in Chicago? I'm not sure, but I do know Chicago is the third-largest American city after New York and Los Angeles. And I think LA has 4 million people or so. That's helpful. To narrow this down, Fermi would advise setting a confidence interval—a range that you are 90% sure contains the right answer. So I'm pretty sure Chicago has more than, say, 1.5 million people. And I'm pretty sure it has fewer than 3.5 million people. But where is the correct answer within that range? I'm not sure. So I'll take the midpoint and guess that Chicago has 2.5 million people.

   b. What percentage of people own a piano? Pianos are too expensive for most families—and most who can afford one don't really want one. So I'll put it at one in one hundred. That's mostly a black-box guess but it's the best I can do.

   c. How many institutions—schools, concert halls, bars—own pianos? Again, I don't know. But many would, and some, like music schools, would own many pianos. I'll again make a black-box guess and say that it's enough to double the per person number of pianos to roughly two in one hundred.

   d. With those guesses, I can do some simple math and conclude that there are fifty thousand pianos in Chicago.

2. How often are pianos tuned? Maybe once a year. That strikes me as reasonable. Why? I don't know. It's another black-box guess.

3. How long does it take to tune a piano? I'll say two hours. Again, it's a black-box guess.

4. How many hours a year does the average piano tuner work? This one I can break down.

 a. The standard American workweek is 40 hours, minus two weeks of vacation. I don't see any reason why piano tuners would be different. So I'll multiply 40 hours by 50 weeks to come up with 2,000 hours a year.

 b. But piano tuners have to spend some of that time traveling between pianos, so I should reduce my total by that much. How much time do they spend between jobs? I'll guess 20% of their work hours. So I conclude that the average piano tuner works 1,600 hours a year.

Now I'll assemble my guesses to make a final calculation: If 50,000 pianos need tuning once a year, and it takes 2 hours to tune one piano, that's 100,000 total piano-tuning hours. Divide that by the annual number of hours worked by one piano tuner and you get 62.5 piano tuners in Chicago.

So I will estimate that there are sixty-three piano tuners in Chicago.

How close am I? Many people have taken a crack at Fermi's classic puzzler over the years, including the psychologist Daniel Levitin, whose presentation I've adapted here.[6] Levitin found eighty-three listings for piano tuners in the Chicago yellow pages, but many were duplicates, such as businesses with more than one phone number. So the precise number isn't certain. But my estimate, which rests on a lot of crude guesswork, looks suprisingly close to the mark.

Fermi was renowned for his estimates. With little or no information at his disposal, he would often do back-of-the-envelope calculations like this to come up with a number that subsequent measurement revealed to be impressively accurate. In many physics and engineering faculties, Fermi estimates or Fermi problems—strange tests like "estimate the number of square inches of pizza consumed by all the students at the University of Maryland during one semester"—are part of the curriculum.

I shared Levitin's discussion of Fermi estimation with a group of superforecasters and it drew a chorus of approval. Sandy Sillman told me Fermi estimation was so critical to his job as a scientist working with atmospheric models that it became "a part of my natural way of thinking."

That's a huge advantage for a forecaster, as we shall see.[7]

A MURDER MYSTERY

On October 12, 2004, Yasser Arafat, the seventy-five-year-old leader of the Palestine Liberation Organization, became severely ill with vomiting and abdominal pain. Over the next three weeks, his condition worsened. On October 29, he was flown to a hospital in France. He fell into a coma. Decades earlier, before adopting the role of statesman, Arafat had directed bombings and shootings and survived many Israeli attempts on his life, but on November 11, 2004, the man who was once a seemingly indestructible enemy of Israel was pronounced dead. What killed him was uncertain. But even before he died there was speculation that he had been poisoned.

In July 2012 researchers at Switzerland's Lausanne University Institute of Radiation Physics announced that they had tested some of Arafat's belongings and discovered unnaturally high levels of polonium-210. That was ominous. Polonium-210 is a radioactive element that can be deadly if ingested. In 2006 Alexander Litvinenko—a former Russian spy living in London and a prominent critic of Vladimir Putin—was murdered with polonium-210.

That August, Arafat's widow gave permission for his body to be exhumed and tested by two separate agencies, in Switzerland and France. So IARPA asked tournament forecasters the following question: "Will either the French or Swiss inquiries find elevated levels of polonium in the remains of Yasser Arafat's body?"

On its face, this was a tough question, a *CSI: Jerusalem* murder mystery, with all the byzantine complexities of the Israeli-Palestinian conflict in the background. How would the average person tackle it? They would probably start with the hunch that came to them the moment they read the question.

The strength of the hunch would depend on the person. Someone who knew only a little about Arafat and the long Israeli-Palestinian conflict might only experience a whisper. But for someone who is well-informed and passionate about politics in that volatile region it would be more like a shout. "Israel would never do that!" they might feel. Or "Of course Israel did it!" That hunch is the tip-of-your-nose perspective. It sprang out of a black box. How exactly it was generated by the person who experiences it I cannot say. But turning it into a forecast is easy. How strongly do you feel? If the hunch is "Israel would never do that!" make your forecast 5% or zero. If it's "Of course Israel did it!" forecast 95% or 100% and you're done. If you're more ambivalent, choose something closer to 50%. When TV pundits make quick volleys of forecasts, this is pretty much all they do.

That's no way to make accurate forecasts. If the tip-of-your-nose perspective contains an error, you won't catch it—just as you won't catch it if you blurt out "Ten cents!" on the Cognitive Reflection Test.

And there is a mistake here. Did you catch it?

Read the question again: "Will either the French or Swiss inquiries find elevated levels of polonium in the remains of Yasser Arafat's body?" Neither "Israel would never do that!" nor "Of course Israel did it!" is actually responsive to that question. They answer a different question: "Did Israel poison Yasser Arafat?" System 1 pulled a classic bait and switch: the hard question that was actually asked was replaced by the easy question that wasn't.

That trap could have been avoided. The key is to *Fermi-ize*.

Bill Flack lives in Kearney, Nebraska, smack in the middle of the Midwest and a planet away from the Middle East. He has no expertise in the Israeli-Palestinian conflict, to say the least. But he didn't need any to get off to a great start on this question.

Thinking like Fermi, Bill unpacked the question by asking himself "What would it take for the answer to be yes? What would it take for it to be no?" He realized that the first step of his analysis had nothing to do with politics. Polonium decays quickly. For the answer to be yes, scientists would have to be able to detect polonium on the remains of a man dead for years. Could they? A teammate had posted a link to the Swiss team's report on the testing of Arafat's possessions, so Bill read it, familiarized himself with the science of polonium testing, and was satisfied that they could do it. Only *then* did he move on to the next stage of the analysis.

Again, Bill asked himself how Arafat's remains could have been contaminated with enough polonium to trigger a positive result. Obviously, "Israel poisoned Arafat" was one way. But because Bill carefully broke the question down, he realized there were others. Arafat had many Palestinian enemies. They could have poisoned him. It was also possible that there had been "intentional postmortem contamination by some Palestinian faction looking to give the appearance that Israel had done a Litvinenko on Arafat,"[8] Bill told me later. These alternatives mattered because each additional way Arafat's body could have been contaminated with polonium increased the probability that it was. Bill also noted that only one of the two European teams had to get a positive result for the correct answer to the question to be yes, another factor that nudged the needle in that direction.

This was only the beginning, but thanks to Bill's Fermi-style analysis he had already avoided the bait-and-switch tiger trap and laid out a road map for subsequent analysis. He was off to a terrific start.

OUTSIDE FIRST

So what's the next step? Most people who knew better than to draw a conclusion based on their gut feeling about Israel's culpability would think now is the time to roll up their sleeves and dig into the complex politics surrounding Arafat at the time of his death.

But it's too soon for that. To illustrate why, I'm going to ask you a question about the Renzetti family.

The Renzettis live in a small house at 84 Chestnut Avenue. Frank Renzetti is forty-four and works as a bookkeeper for a moving company. Mary Renzetti is thirty-five and works part-time at a day care. They have one child, Tommy, who is five. Frank's widowed mother, Camila, also lives with the family.

My question: How likely is it that the Renzettis have a pet?

To answer that, most people would zero in on the family's details. "Renzetti is an Italian name," someone might think. "So are 'Frank' and 'Camila.' That may mean Frank grew up with lots of brothers and sisters, but he's only got one child. He probably wants to have a big family but he can't afford it. So it would make sense that he compensated a little by getting a pet." Someone else might think, "People get pets for kids and the Renzettis only have one child, and Tommy isn't old enough to take care of a pet. So it seems unlikely." This sort of storytelling can be very compelling, particularly when the available details are much richer than what I've provided here.

But superforecasters wouldn't bother with any of that, at least not at first. The first thing they would do is find out what percentage of American households own a pet.

Statisticians call that the base rate—how common something is within a broader class. Daniel Kahneman has a much more evocative visual term for it. He calls it the "outside view"—in contrast to the "inside view," which is the specifics of the particular case. A few minutes with Google tells me about 62% of American households own pets. That's the outside view here. Starting with the outside view means I will start by estimating that there is a 62% chance the Renzettis have a pet. Then I will turn to the inside view—all those details about the Renzettis—and use them to adjust that initial 62% up or down.

It's natural to be drawn to the inside view. It's usually concrete and filled with engaging detail we can use to craft a story about what's going on. The outside view is typically abstract, bare, and doesn't lend itself so readily to storytelling. So even smart, accomplished people routinely fail to consider the outside view. The *Wall Street Journal* columnist and former Reagan speechwriter Peggy Noonan once predicted trouble for the Democrats because polls had found that George W. Bush's approval rating, which had been rock-bottom at the end of his term, had rebounded to 47% four years after leaving office, equal to President Obama's. Noonan found that astonishing—and deeply meaningful.[9] But if she had considered the outside view she would have discovered that presidential approval *always* rises after a president leaves office. Even Richard Nixon's number went up. So Bush's improved standing wasn't surprising in the least—which strongly suggests the meaning she drew from it was illusory.

Superforecasters don't make that mistake. If Bill Flack were asked whether, in the next twelve months, there would be an armed clash between China and Vietnam over some border dispute, he wouldn't immediately delve into the particulars of that border dispute and the current state of China-Vietnam relations. He would instead look at how often there have been armed clashes in the past. "Say we get hostile conduct between China and Vietnam every five years," Bill says. "I'll use a five-year recurrence model to predict the future." In any given year, then, the outside view would suggest to Bill there is a 20% chance of a clash. Having established that, Bill would look at the situation today and adjust that number up or down.

It's often possible to find different outside views. In the Renzetti problem, the pet ownership rate of American households is one outside view. But it can be refined. Single-family detached homes like 84 Chestnut Avenue are more pet-friendly living environments than apartment buildings or condos. So we could narrow the lens and use the pet ownership rate of American single-family detached homes— let's say it's 73%—as our outside view. That second outside view more closely matches the particular case we're interested in, so 73% would probably be a better bet as our starting point.

Of course I've made this easy for myself by offering examples where the outside view is obvious. But what is the outside view in the Arafat-polonium question? That's tough. It's not as if dead Middle Eastern leaders are routinely exhumed to investigate suspicions of poisoning—so there's no way we're going to be able to do a quick Google search and find that poison is detected in 73% of cases like this. But that doesn't mean we should skip the outside view and go straight to the inside.

Let's think about this Fermi-style. Here we have a famous person who is dead. Major investigative bodies think there is enough reason for suspicion that they are exhuming the body. Under those circumstances, how often would the investigation turn up evidence of poisoning? I don't know and there is no way to find out. But I do know there is at least a prima facie case that persuades courts and medical investigators that this is worth looking into. It has to be considerably above zero. So let's say it's at least 20%. But the probability can't be 100% because if it were that clear and certain the evidence would have been uncovered before burial. So let's say the probability cannot be higher than 80%. That's a big range. The midpoint is 50%. So that outside view can serve as our starting point.

You may wonder why the outside view should come first. After all, you could dive into the inside view and draw conclusions, then turn to the outside view. Wouldn't that work as well? Unfortunately, no, it probably wouldn't. The reason is a basic psychological concept called anchoring.

When we make estimates, we tend to start with some number and adjust. The number we start with is called the anchor. It's important because we typically underadjust, which means a bad anchor can easily produce a bad estimate. And it's astonishingly easy to settle on a bad anchor. In classic experiments, Daniel Kahneman and Amos Tversky showed you could influence people's judgment merely by exposing them to a number—any number, even one that is obviously meaningless, like one randomly selected by the spin of a wheel.[10] So a forecaster who starts by diving into the inside view risks being swayed by a number that may have little or no meaning. But if she starts with the outside view, her analysis will begin with an anchor that is meaningful. And a better anchor is a distinct advantage.

THE INSIDE VIEW

You've Fermi-ized the question, consulted the outside view, and now, finally, you can delve into the inside view. In the case of the Arafat-polonium question, that means digging into Middle Eastern politics and history. And there's a lot of that. So you fill a small library with books and settle in for six months of reading. Right?

Wrong. Such diligence would be admirable, but it would also be misguided. If you aimlessly examine one tree, then another, and another, you will quickly become lost in the forest. A good exploration of the inside view does not involve wandering around, soaking up any and all information and hoping that insight somehow emerges. It is targeted and purposeful: it is an investigation, not an amble.[11]

Again, Fermi-ization is key. When Bill Flack Fermi-ized the Arafat-polonium question, he realized there were several pathways to a "yes" answer: Israel could have poisoned Arafat; Arafat's Palestinian enemies could have poisoned him; or Arafat's remains could have been contaminated after his death to make it look like a poisoning. Hypotheses like these are the ideal framework for investigating the inside view.

Start with the first hypothesis: Israel poisoned Yasser Arafat with polonium. What would it take for that to be true?

1. Israel had, or could obtain, polonium.
2. Israel wanted Arafat dead badly enough to take a big risk.
3. Israel had the ability to poison Arafat with polonium.

Each of these elements could then be researched—looking for evidence pro and con—to get a sense of how likely they are to be true, and therefore how likely the hypothesis is to be true. Then it's on to the next hypothesis. And the next.

This sounds like detective work because it is—or to be precise, it is detective work as real investigators do it, not the detectives on TV shows. It's methodical, slow, and demanding. But it works far better than wandering aimlessly in a forest of information.

THESIS, ANTITHESIS, SYNTHESIS

So you have an outside view and an inside view. Now they have to be merged, just as your brain merges the different perspectives of your two eyeballs into a single vision.

David Rogg, a superforecaster and semiretired software engineer living in Virginia, did that when he tackled a question about terrorism in Europe. It was early 2015, shortly after terrorists had murdered eleven people at the Paris satirical magazine *Charlie Hebdo*. IARPA asked: "Will there be an attack carried out by Islamist militants in France, the UK, Germany, the Netherlands, Denmark, Spain, Portugal, or Italy between 21 January and 31 March 2015?"

At a moment when the media was awash with information about Islamist terrorism and Muslim communities in Europe, it was tempting to rush to the inside view. David knew better. First, he found a list of Islamist terror attacks on Wikipedia. Then he counted the number of attacks in the specified countries over the previous five years. There were six. "So I calculate the base rate as 1.2/year," he wrote in the GJP forum.

Having established the outside view, David switched to the inside view. In the previous several years, the Islamic State of Iraq and Syria (ISIS) movement had surged to prominence. Hundreds of European Muslims had enlisted. And ISIS had repeatedly threatened Europe with terror attacks. David decided that this changed the situation so significantly that the data from 2010 and earlier years were no longer relevant. So he dropped 2010 from his calculation. That raised the base rate to 1.5, "which I suspect is still low" given the level of ISIS recruitment and threats. But David also noted that security measures had been sharply increased after the *Charlie Hebdo* attack, which would decrease the likelihood of attack. Balancing these two factors, David decided, "I'll only raise it by, say, 1/5, to 1.8 [attacks per year]."

There were 69 days left in the forecast period. So David divided 69 by 365. Then he multiplied by 1.8. Result: 0.34. So he concluded that there is a 34% chance the answer to IARPA's question would be yes.[12]

It was a textbook merger of outside and inside views. But David wasn't saying "34%, final answer," like a contestant on *Who Wants to Be a Millionaire?* Remember, he shared his analysis on a GJP forum. Why? Because he wanted to know what his teammates were thinking. In other words, he was looking for more perspectives.

Coming up with an outside view, an inside view, and a synthesis of the two isn't the end. It's a good beginning. Superforecasters constantly look for other views they can synthesize into their own.

There are many different ways to obtain new perspectives. What do other forecasters think? What outside and inside views have they come up with? What are experts saying? You can even train *yourself* to generate different perspectives.

When Bill Flack makes a judgment, he often explains his thinking to his teammates, as David Rogg did, and he asks them to critique it. In part, he does that because he hopes they'll spot flaws and offer their own perspectives. But writing his judgment down is also a way of distancing himself from it, so he can step back and scrutinize it: "It's an auto-feedback thing," he says. "Do I agree with this? Are there holes in this? Should I be looking for something else to fill this in? Would I be convinced by this if I were somebody else?"

That is a very smart move. Researchers have found that merely asking people to assume their initial judgment is wrong, to seriously consider why that might be, and then make another judgment, produces a second estimate which, when combined with the first, improves accuracy almost as much as getting a second estimate from another person.[13] The same effect was produced simply by letting several weeks pass before asking people to make a second estimate. This approach, built on the "wisdom of the crowd" concept, has been called "the crowd within." The billionaire financier George Soros exemplifies it. A key part of his success, he has often said, is his mental habit of stepping back from himself so he can judge his own thinking and offer a different perspective—to himself.[14]

There is an even simpler way of getting another perspective on a question: tweak its wording. Imagine a question like "Will the South African government grant the Dalai Lama a visa within six months?" The naive forecaster will go looking for evidence that suggests the Dalai Lama will get his visa while neglecting to look for evidence that suggests he won't. The more sophisticated forecaster knows about confirmation bias and will seek out evidence that cuts both ways. But if you are constantly thinking the question is "Will he get his visa?" your mental playing field is tilted in one direction and you may unwittingly slide into confirmation bias: "This is South Africa! Black government officials suffered under apartheid. Of course they will give a visa to Tibet's own Nelson Mandela." To check that tendency, turn the question on its head and ask, "Will the South African government *deny* the Dalai Lama for six months?" That tiny wording change encourages you to lean in the opposite direction and look for reasons why it would deny the visa—a desire not to anger its biggest trading partner being a rather big one.

DRAGONFLY FORECASTING

Outside views, inside view, other outside and inside views, second opinions from yourself . . . that's a lot of perspectives—and inevitably a lot of dissonant information. David Rogg's neat synthesis of contrary outside and inside views made it look easy, but it's not. And the difficulty only mounts as the number of perspectives being synthesized increases.

The commentary that superforecasters post on GJP forums is rife with "on the one hand/on the other" dialectical banter. And superforecasters have more than two hands. "On the one hand, Saudi Arabia runs few risks in letting oil prices remain low because it has large financial reserves," wrote a superforecaster trying to decide if the Saudis would agree to OPEC production cuts in November 2014. "On the other hand, Saudi Arabia needs higher prices to support higher social spending to buy obedience to the monarchy. Yet on the third hand, the Saudis may believe they can't control the drivers of the price dive, like the drilling frenzy in North America and falling global demand. So they may see production cuts as futile. Net answer: Feels no-ish, 80%." (As it turned out, the Saudis did not support production cuts—much to the shock of many experts.)[15]

That is "dragonfly eye" in operation. And yes, it is mentally demanding. Superforecasters pursue point-counterpoint discussions routinely, and they keep at them long past the point where most people would succumb to migraines. They are the polar opposite of the people who blurt out "Ten cents!" on the Cognitive Reflection Test—which is why, to the surprise of no one, they did superbly on the CRT. Forget the old advice to think twice. Superforecasters often think thrice—and sometimes they are just warming up to do a deeper-dive analysis.

Yet these are ordinary people. Forecasting is their hobby. Their only reward is a gift certificate and bragging rights on Facebook. Why do they put so much into it? One answer is it's fun. "Need for cognition" is the psychological term for the tendency to engage in and enjoy hard mental slogs. People high in need for cognition are the sort who like crosswords and Sudoku puzzles, the harder, the better—and superforecasters score high in need-for-cognition tests.

An element of personality is also likely involved. In personality psychology, one of the "Big Five" traits is "openness to experience," which has various dimensions, including preference for variety and intellectual curiosity. It's unmistakable in many superforecasters. Most people who are not from Ghana would find a question like "Who will win the presidential election in Ghana?" pointless. They wouldn't know where to start, or why to bother. But when I put that hypothetical question to Doug Lorch and asked for his reaction, he simply said, "Well, here's an opportunity to learn something about Ghana."[16]

But ultimately, as with intelligence, this has less to do with traits someone possesses and more to do with behavior. A brilliant puzzle solver may have the raw material for forecasting, but if he doesn't also have an appetite for questioning basic, emotionally charged beliefs he will often be at a disadvantage relative to a less intelligent person who has a greater capacity for self-critical thinking. It's not the raw crunching power you have that matters most. It's what you do with it.

Look at Doug Lorch. His natural inclination is obvious. But he doesn't assume it will see him through. He cultivates it. Doug knows that when people read for pleasure they naturally gravitate to the like-minded. So he created a database containing hundreds of information sources—from the *New York Times* to obscure blogs—that are tagged by their ideological orientation, subject matter, and geographical origin, then wrote a program that selects what he should read next using criteria that emphasize diversity. Thanks to Doug's simple invention, he is sure to constantly encounter different perspectives. Doug is not merely open-minded. He is *actively* open-minded.

Active open-mindedness (AOM) is a concept coined by the psychologist Jonathan Baron, who has an office next to mine at the University of Pennsylvania. Baron's test for AOM asks whether you agree or disagree with statements like:

People should take into consideration evidence that goes against their beliefs.

It is more useful to pay attention to those who disagree with you than to pay attention to those who agree.

Changing your mind is a sign of weakness.

Intuition is the best guide in making decisions.

It is important to persevere in your beliefs even when evidence is brought to bear against them.

Quite predictably, superforecasters score highly on Baron's test. But more important, superforecasters illustrate the concept. They walk the talk.

For superforecasters, beliefs are hypotheses to be tested, not treasures to be guarded. It would be facile to reduce superforecasting to a bumper-sticker slogan, but if I had to, that would be it.

6

Superquants?

We live in the era of Big Data. Vast, proliferating information-technology networks churn out staggering quantities of information that can be analyzed by data scientists armed with powerful computers and arcane math. Order and meaning are extracted. Reality is seen and foreseen like never before. And most of us—let's be honest with ourselves—don't have the dimmest idea how data scientists do what they do. We find it a little intimidating, if not dazzling. As the scientist and science fiction writer Arthur C. Clarke famously observed, "Any sufficiently advanced technology is indistinguishable from magic."

As an assistant professor of mathematics at Cornell, Lionel Levine is one of the magicians. His résumé lists an AB in math from Harvard, a PhD in math from Berkeley, a string of prestigious grants and fellowships, and a longer string of papers with occult titles like "Scaling Limits for Internal Aggregation Models with Multiple Sources." As one expects of math wizards, he is young. He graduated from Harvard the same year the intelligence community decided it was 100% certain that Saddam Hussein had weapons of mass destruction.

Levine is also a superforecaster. And while he is an extreme case, he underscores a central feature of superforecasters: they have a way with numbers. Most aced a brief test of basic numeracy that asked questions like, "The chance of getting a viral infection is 0.05%. Out of 10,000 people, about how many of them are expected to get infected?" (The answer is 5.) And numeracy is just as evident on their résumés. Many have backgrounds in math, science, or computer programming. Even Joshua Frankel, the Brooklyn filmmaker now living in the world of the arts, attended a New York high school that specialized in math and science, and his first job after graduating from college involved the creation of visual effects using computer animation. I have yet to find a superforecaster who isn't comfortable with numbers and most are more than capable of putting them to practical use. And they do, occasionally. When Bill Flack is asked to forecast something like currency exchange rates he will go into historical changes in the rate and build a Monte Carlo model based on that. That's basic stuff for the cognoscenti. It is as obscure as ancient Aramaic for everyone else.

On Wall Street, math wizards are called quants, and the math they use can get a lot more esoteric than Monte Carlo models. Given superforecasters' affinity for data it would be reasonable to suspect that it explains their superb results. An algorithmic sleight of hand, a whispered statistical spell, and presto! A startlingly accurate forecast! Numbers people might like that conclusion but for those who haven't done any calculus since high school, and are now in a cold sweat because they just read the word *calculus*, it would put a moat and a castle wall between them and superforecasting.

There is no moat and no castle wall. While superforecasters do occasionally deploy their own explicit math models, or consult other people's, that's rare. The great majority of their forecasts are simply the product of careful thought and nuanced judgment. "I can think of a couple of questions where a little bit of math was useful," Lionel Levine recalled about his own forecasting, but otherwise he relies on subjective judgment. "It's all, you know, balancing, finding relevant information and deciding how relevant is this really? How much should it really affect my forecast?" Not using math is even a point of pride for the math professor. People would just assume that his forecasting success was thanks to math, he said, "so I kind of, in a contrarian way, set out to prove that I can be a good forecaster without using any."[1]

But the fact that superforecasters are almost uniformly highly numerate people is not mere coincidence. Superior numeracy *does* help superforecasters, but not because it lets them tap into arcane math models that divine the future. The truth is simpler, subtler, and much more interesting.

WHERE'S OSAMA?

Early in 2011, the attention of the US intelligence community was riveted on a peculiar compound. Its high walls encircled a cluster of buildings, which was normal in this wealthy neighborhood of the Pakistani city of Abbottabad. But the compound's occupants were unknown and clearly wanted to stay that way. That was unusual. And there were bits and strands of evidence that collectively suggested this was the residence of Osama bin Laden. That was approaching unique.

Had they finally located the terrorist mastermind almost a decade after the 9/11 attacks? Everyone knows the answer to that question now. But the analysts did not then. Each had to make a difficult judgment that could lead to the launch of a military assault inside a volatile nation armed with nuclear weapons. Those judgments, and their consequences, would later be dramatized in the movie *Zero Dark Thirty*.

"I'm about to go look the president in the eye and what I'd like to know, no fucking bullshit, is where everyone stands on this thing," says the actor James Gandolfini, playing CIA Director Leon Panetta in *Zero Dark Thirty*. He sits at the head of a conference table and glares. "Now, very simply. Is he there or is he not fucking there?"

The deputy director answers first. "We don't deal in certainty," he says. "We deal in probability. I'd say there's a sixty percent probability he's there."

The fictional Panetta points to the next person.

"I concur," he says. "Sixty percent."

"I'm at eighty percent," the next in line says. "Their OPSEC [operational security] convinces me."

"You guys ever agree on anything?" Panetta asks.

So it goes around the table, from one person to the next. Sixty percent, one says. Eighty percent. Sixty percent. Panetta leans back in his chair and sighs. "This is a clusterfuck, isn't it?"

Let's pause the movie here. What does the fictional Leon Panetta want more than anything? Agreement. He wants each person to come to the same conclusion so he can be sure that that conclusion is correct, or at least the best available. Most people in that position would feel the same way. Agreement is reassuring. Disagreement is . . . well, we may not use the same colorful description as the fictional Leon Panetta, but most would share the sentiment.

But the fictional Leon Panetta is wrong. The people at the table were asked to independently judge a difficult problem and tell the CIA director what they sincerely believed. Even if they all looked at the same evidence—and there's likely to be some variation—it is unlikely they would all reach precisely the same conclusion. They are different people. They have different educations, training, experiences, and personalities. A smart executive will not expect universal agreement, and will treat its appearance as a warning flag that groupthink has taken hold. An array of judgments is welcome proof that the people around the table are actually thinking for themselves and offering their unique perspectives. The fictional Leon Panetta should have been delighted when he heard different judgments from different people. It was "the wisdom of the crowd," gift wrapped. All he had to do was synthesize the judgments. A simple averaging would be a good start. Or he could do a weighted averaging—so that those whose judgment he most respects get more say in the collective conclusion. Either way, it is dragonfly eye at work.

I asked the real Leon Panetta about this famous scene and he confirmed that something like it did happen. "A lot of these people were intelligence analysts, people who had been involved in operations for a period of time. There was a lot of experience in that room," he recalled. But not a lot of agreement. Judgments varied "from people that thought the chances were as low as thirty to forty percent to people that thought it was ninety percent and above, and it varied everywhere in between." But the real Leon Panetta—a former congressman, chief of staff to President Clinton, and secretary of defense to President Obama—had a completely different reaction to that diversity than the fictional Leon Panetta. He welcomed it. "I encourage the people around me not to tell me what they thought I wanted to hear but what they believed, and to be honest," Panetta said.[2] When he was chief of staff to the president, he considered obtaining and presenting diverse views to be a critical part of his job. The real and fictional Leon Panettas are a study in contrasts.

Now let's press Play on the movie again.

After the fictional Leon Panetta expresses disgust with the lack of consensus, Maya, the hero of *Zero Dark Thirty*, gets her chance. She has been sitting at the back of the room, steaming. "A hundred percent, he's there," she declares. "OK, fine, ninety-five percent because I know certainty freaks you guys out. But it's a hundred!" The fictional Panetta is impressed. While others mewl about uncertainty, Maya has the blunt force of a battering ram. After the compound was discovered, she was so sure bin Laden was there she wanted it bombed to rubble immediately. When weeks went by without any attack, she scrawled the number of days that had passed on the window of her superior. We watched her stomp up and write "21" in big red digits, circling it for emphasis. Later, she wrote 98, 99, 100—and underscored it in thick Magic Marker. We felt her frustration. Maya is right. Bin Laden is there. Ignore the others.

The fictional Panetta is with Maya and the audience. The others wouldn't commit themselves to a yes or no, he tells an aide later, because they are "cowed." Probabilities are for weaklings.

Press Pause again. Think about how the fictional Leon Panetta thinks. He sees only two options: yes, bin Laden is there; no, he is not. There are only two settings on his mental dial. There is no maybe, let alone settings for degrees of maybe. Judging by how that scene in *Zero Dark Thirty* plays out, the filmmakers respect that. They are betting the audience will too. Is Osama bin Laden there? Yes or no? This is "no fucking bullshit" thinking. That's how Maya thinks. And she's right.

Or so it seems until you engage System 2 and think twice. In reality, Maya is unreasonable. Given the evidence at hand, it was likely that the man in the compound was bin Laden. One could even argue it was highly probable. But 100%? Absolutely certain? No chance whatsoever that it is not him? No. The man in the compound could have been a different terrorist. Or a drug trafficker, an Afghan warlord, an arms dealer, or maybe a wealthy Pakistani businessman suffering from paranoid schizophrenia. Even if the likelihood of each alternative being true were tiny, they would easily add up to 1%, 2%, 5%, or more—so we can't be 100% certain that it is Osama bin Laden. Do such fine-grained distinctions matter? Well, the intelligence community was once so sure Saddam Hussein had weapons of mass destruction that they did not explore the possibility that he did not. Yes, they matter.

Of course, as Maya was stomping about, there was an objective truth. Bin Laden was there. So Maya's claim was correct but it was more extreme than the evidence could support, meaning she was "right but unreasonable"—the mirror image of the "wrong but reasonable" position the intelligence community would have been in if it had scaled back the "slam dunk" to a 60% or 70% chance that Saddam Hussein had WMDs. The final outcome—happy for Maya, unhappy for the IC—doesn't change that.

The real Leon Panetta understands process-outcome paradoxes like this. And he is much less keen on certainty than the fictional Leon Panetta. "Nothing is one hundred percent," he said several times during our interview.

The real Leon Panetta thinks like a superforecaster.[3]

THE THIRD SETTING

A similar scene plays out in a book written by the journalist Mark Bowden. Only this time the man at the head of the table isn't a fictional Leon Panetta. It's the real Barack Obama.

Sitting in the White House's legendary Situation Room, Obama listened as an array of CIA officers expressed their opinions on the identity of the man in the mysterious Pakistani compound. The CIA's team leader told the president he was almost sure it was bin Laden. "He put his confidence level at 95%," Mark Bowden wrote in *The Finish: The Killing of Osama bin Laden*, Bowden's account of the decision making behind one of the most famous commando raids in history. A second CIA officer agreed with the first. But others were less sanguine. "Four senior officers at the Directorate of National Intelligence had reviewed the case and written out their own opinions," Bowden recounted. "Most seemed to place their confidence level at about 80%. Some were as low as 40 or even 30%." Another officer said he was 60% confident it was bin Laden in the compound.

"OK, this is a probability thing," the president said in response, according to Bowden's account.

Bowden editorializes: "Ever since the agency's erroneous call, a decade earlier, that Saddam Hussein was hiding weapons of mass destruction, a finding that had kicked off a long and very costly war, the CIA had instituted an almost comically elaborate process for weighing certainty. . . . It was like trying to contrive a mathematical formula for good judgment." Bowden was clearly not impressed by the CIA's use of numbers and probabilities. Neither was Barack Obama, according to Bowden. "What you ended up with, as the president was finding, and as he would later explain to me, was not more certainty but more confusion."

Bowden reported that Obama told him in a later interview, "In this situation, what you started to get was probabilities that disguised uncertainty as opposed to actually providing you with useful information." Bowden then wrote that "Obama had no trouble admitting it to himself. If he acted on this, he was going to be taking a gamble, pure and simple. A big gamble."

After listening to the widely ranging opinions, Obama addressed the room. " 'This is fifty-fifty,' he said. That silenced everyone. 'Look guys, this is a flip of the coin. I can't base this decision on the notion that we have any greater certainty than that.' "[4]

Bowden clearly admires Obama's conclusion. Should he?

The information Bowden provides is sketchy but it appears that the median estimate of the CIA officers—the "wisdom of the crowd"—was around 70%. And yet Obama declares the reality to be "fifty-fifty." What does he mean by that? We have to be careful here because there are actually several possibilities.

One is that Obama means it literally. He heard an array of views and settled on 50% as the probability closest to the mark. If so, he's misguided. The collective judgment is higher than that and based on Bowden's account he has no reasonable basis for thinking 50% is more accurate. It's a number plucked out of the air.

But as researchers have shown, people who use "50%" or "fifty-fifty" often do *not* mean it literally. They mean "I'm not sure" or "it's uncertain"—or more simply "maybe."[5] Given the context, I suspect that's what Obama had in mind.

If so, that may have been reasonable. Obama was an executive making a critical decision. He may well have felt that he would order the strike if there was *any* significant possibility that bin Laden was in the compound. It didn't matter whether the probability was 90%, 70%, or perhaps even 30%. So rather than waste time trying to nail down a number, he cut the discussion short and moved on.[6]

Of course I don't know if that was Obama's thinking. And there is another possible explanation—one that is much less defensible.

Like the fictional Leon Panetta, Obama may have been bothered by the wide variation in estimates. The disagreement made him think they were unreliable. So he retreated to what probability theorists call the ignorance prior, the state of knowledge you are in before you know whether the coin will land heads or tails or, in this case, whether Osama will be in the master bedroom when the Navy SEALs come knocking. And that was a mistake because it meant Obama did not make full use of the information available at the table.[7] But unlike that of the fictional Leon Panetta, Obama's mental dial didn't have just two settings. It had a third: maybe. So that's where he settled.

Bowden's account reminded me of an offhand remark that Amos Tversky made some thirty years ago, when we served on that National Research Council committee charged with preventing nuclear war. In dealing with probabilities, he said, most people only have three settings: "gonna happen," "not gonna happen," and "maybe." Amos had an impish sense of humor. He also appreciated the absurdity of an academic committee on a mission to save the world. So I am 98% sure he was joking. And 99% sure his joke captures a basic truth about human judgment.

PROBABILITY FOR THE STONE AGE

Human beings have coped with uncertainty for as long as we have been recognizably human. And for almost all that time we didn't have access to statistical models of uncertainty because they didn't exist. It was remarkably late in history—arguably as late as the 1713 publication of Jakob Bernoulli's *Ars Conjectandi*—before the best minds started to think seriously about probability.

Before that, people had no choice but to rely on the tip-of-your-nose perspective. You see a shadow moving in the long grass. Should you worry about lions? You try to think of an example of a lion attacking from the long grass. If the example comes to mind easily, run! As we saw in chapter 2, that's your System 1 at work. If the response is strong enough, it can produce a binary conclusion: "Yes, it's a lion," or "No, it's not a lion." But if it's weaker, it can produce an unsettling middle possibility: "Maybe it's a lion." What the tip-of-your-nose perspective will not deliver is a judgment so fine grained that it can distinguish between, say, a 60% chance that it is a lion and an 80% chance. That takes slow, conscious, careful thought. Of course, when you were dealing with the pressing existential problems our ancestors faced, it was rarely necessary to make such fine distinctions. It may not even have been desirable. A three-setting dial gives quick, clear directions. Is that a lion? YES = run! MAYBE = stay alert! NO = relax. The ability to distinguish between a 60% probability and an 80% probability would add little. In fact, a more fine-grained analysis could slow you down—and get you killed.

In this light, the preference for two- and three-setting mental dials makes sense. And lots of research underscores the point. A parent willing to pay something to reduce her child's risk of contracting a serious disease from 10% to 5% may be willing to pay two to three times as much to reduce the risk from 5% to 0%. Why is a decline from 5% to 0% so much more valuable than a decline from 10% to

5%? Because it delivers more than a 5% reduction in risk. It delivers certainty. Both 0% and 100% weigh far more heavily in our minds than the mathematical models of economists say they should.[8] Again, this is not surprising if you think about the world in which our brain evolved. There was always at least a tiny chance a lion was lurking in the vicinity. Or a snake. Or someone who covets your hut and is carrying a club. Or any of the countless other threats people faced. But our ancestors couldn't maintain a state of constant alert. The cognitive cost would have been too great. They needed worry-free zones. The solution? Ignore small chances and use the two-setting dial as much as possible. Either it is a lion or it isn't. Only when something undeniably falls between those two settings—only when we are compelled—do we turn the mental dial to maybe.[9]

Harry Truman once joked that he wanted to hear from a one-armed economist because he was sick of hearing "on the one hand . . . on the other . . ."—a joke that bears more than a passing resemblance to Tversky's. We want answers. A confident yes or no is satisfying in a way that maybe never is, a fact that helps to explain why the media so often turn to hedgehogs who are sure they know what is coming no matter how bad their forecasting records may be. Of course it's not always wrong to prefer a confident judgment. All else being equal, our answers to questions like "Does France have more people than Italy?" are likelier to be right when we are confident they are right than when we are not. Confidence and accuracy are positively correlated. But research shows we exaggerate the size of the correlation. For instance, people trust more confident financial advisers over those who are less confident even when their track records are identical. And people equate confidence and competence, which makes the forecaster who says something has a middling probability of happening less worthy of respect. As one study noted, people "took such judgments as indications the forecasters were either generally incompetent, ignorant of the facts in a given case, or lazy, unwilling to expend the effort required to gather information that would justify greater confidence."[10]

This sort of primal thinking goes a long way to explaining why so many people have a poor grasp of probability. Some of it can be chalked up to simple ignorance and misunderstanding—like people who think that "a 70% chance of rain in Los Angeles" means "it will rain 70% of the day but not the other 30%" or "it will rain in 70% of Los Angeles but not the other 30%" or "70% of forecasters think it will rain but 30% don't." But there is something much more fundamental underlying mistakes like these. To grasp the meaning of "a 70% chance of rain tomorrow" we have to understand that rain may or may not happen, and that over 100 days on which we forecast chances of rain, if our forecasts are good, it should rain on 70% of them and be dry on the rest. Nothing could be further removed from our natural inclination to think "It will rain" or "It won't rain"—or, if you insist, "Maybe it will rain."[11]

The deeply counterintuitive nature of probability explains why even very sophisticated people often make elementary mistakes. When David Leonhardt claimed a prediction market's forecast was wrong because it had said there was a 75% chance a law would be struck down, and it wasn't, I was pretty sure that if someone had pointed out his error to him he would have slapped his forehead and said, "Of course!" I had that suspicion confirmed later, when Leonhardt wrote an excellent column about exactly this trap: If a forecaster says there is a 74% chance the Republicans will win control of the Senate in an upcoming election, Leonhardt warned readers, do not conclude the forecast was wrong if the party doesn't take the Senate because "a 74 percent chance it will" also means "a 26 percent chance it won't."[12]

The confusion caused by the three-setting mental dial is pervasive. Robert Rubin, the former Treasury secretary, told me how he and his then-deputy Larry Summers would often be frustrated when

they briefed top policy makers in the White House and Congress because people would treat an 80% probability that something would
happen as a certainty that it would. "You almost had to pound the
table, to say 'yes there's a high probability but this also might not happen,'" Rubin said. "But the way people think, they seem to translate
a high probability into 'this *will* happen.'" And yet, if we were to take
these presumably educated, accomplished people out of that context,
sit them down in a classroom, and tell them that the statement "There
is an 80% chance that something will happen" means there is a 20%
chance it won't, they would surely roll their eyes and say, "That's obvious." But outside of a classroom, away from abstractions, when dealing with real issues, these educated, accomplished people reverted to
the intuitive. Only when the probabilities were closer to even did they
easily grasp that the outcome may or may not happen, Rubin said. "If
you say something is 60/40, people kind of get the idea."[13]

Amos Tversky died, far too young, in 1996. But that would have
made him smile.

PROBABILITY FOR THE INFORMATION AGE

Scientists come at probability in a radically different way.

They relish uncertainty, or at least accept it, because in scientific
models of reality, certainty is illusory. Leon Panetta may not be a scientist, but he captured that insight perfectly when he said, "Nothing
is one hundred percent."

That may be a little surprising. "Most people would identify science with certainty," wrote the mathematician and statistician William Byers. "Certainty, they feel, is a state of affairs with no downside,
so the most desirable situation would be one of absolute certainty.
Scientific results and theories seem to promise such certainty."[14] In the
popular mind, scientists generate facts and chisel them into granite

tablets. This collection of facts is what we call "science." As the work of accumulating facts proceeds, uncertainty is pushed back. The ultimate goal of science is uncertainty's total eradication.

But that is a very nineteenth-century view of science. One of twentieth-century science's great accomplishments has been to show that uncertainty is an ineradicable element of reality. "Uncertainty is real," Byers writes. "It is the dream of total certainty that is an illusion."[15] This is true both at the margin of scientific knowledge and at what currently appears to be its core. Scientific facts that look as solid as rock to one generation of scientists can be crushed to dust beneath the advances of the next.[16] All scientific knowledge is tentative. Nothing is chiseled in granite.

In practice, of course, scientists do use the language of certainty, but only because it is cumbersome whenever you assert a fact to say "although we have a substantial body of evidence to support this conclusion, and we hold it with a high degree of confidence, it remains possible, albeit extremely improbable, that new evidence or arguments may compel us to revise our view of this matter." But there is always supposed to be an invisible asterisk when scientists say "this is true"—because nothing is certain. (And, yes, that is true of my work too, including everything in this book. Sorry about that.)

If nothing is certain, it follows that the two- and three-setting mental dials are fatally flawed. Yes and no express certainty. They have to go. The only setting that remains is maybe—the one setting people intuitively want to avoid.

Of course a one-setting mental dial would be useless. Is that a lion? Maybe. Will they find polonium in Yasser Arafat's remains? Maybe. Is the man in the mysterious compound Osama bin Laden? Maybe. So "maybe" has to be subdivided into degrees of probability. One way to do that is with vague terms like "probably" and "unlikely," but as we have seen that introduces dangerous ambiguity, which is why scientists prefer numbers. And those numbers should be as finely subdivided as forecasters can manage. That might mean 10%, 20%, 30% . . . or 10%, 15%, 20% . . . or 10%, 11%, 12%. The finer grained the better, as long as the granularity captures real distinctions—meaning that if outcomes you say have an 11% chance of happening really do occur 1% less often than 12% outcomes and 1% more often than 10% outcomes. This complex mental dial is the basis of probabilistic thinking.

Robert Rubin is a probabilistic thinker. As a student at Harvard, he heard a lecture in which a philosophy professor argued there is no provable certainty and "it just clicked with everything I'd sort of thought," he told me. It became the axiom that guided his thinking through twenty-six years at Goldman Sachs, as an adviser to President Bill Clinton, and as secretary of the Treasury. It's in the title of his autobiography: *In an Uncertain World*. By rejecting certainty, everything became a matter of probability for Rubin, and he wanted as much precision as possible. "One of the first times I met with him, he asked me if a bill would make it through Congress, and I said 'absolutely,'" a young Treasury aide told the journalist Jacob Weisberg. "He didn't like that one bit. Now I say the probability is 60%—and we can argue over whether it's 59 or 60%."[17]

During his tenure in the Clinton administration—a golden era of soaring stocks and Rubinomics—Rubin was praised lavishly. After the crash of 2008, Rubin was criticized with equal vigor, but whether Rubin is a hero or a villain, or something in between, isn't my domain of expertise. What's interesting to me is how so many people reacted when Rubin's probabilistic thinking was laid out in a 1998 *New York Times* feature story. They found it startlingly counterintuitive, challenging. Professionals pinned Rubin's thoughts on thinking to cubicle walls alongside inspirational messages and photos of their kids. "People in all kinds of circumstances have told me it affected them," he recounted in 2003. That reaction bemused Rubin. He thought he had said nothing surprising. But when he expanded on the theme in his autobiography the reaction was the same. More than a decade later, "I still have people come to me when I speak at panels or things and say 'I have a copy of the book, can you sign it?' or 'It was really important to me and interesting because of this discussion of probabilities,'" Rubin says. "I can't say why what seems obvious to me seems to a lot of people to be insightful."[18]

Probabilistic thinking and the two- and three-setting mental dials that come more naturally to us are like fish and birds—they are fundamentally different creatures. Each rests on different assumptions about reality and how to cope with it. And each can seem surpassingly strange to someone accustomed to thinking the other way.

UNCERTAIN SUPERS

Robert Rubin would not have to "pound the table" to make superforecasters understand that an 80% chance of something happening implies a 20% chance it won't. Thanks in part to their superior numeracy, superforecasters, like scientists and mathematicians, tend to be probabilistic thinkers.

An awareness of irreducible uncertainty is the core of probabilistic thinking, but it's a tricky thing to measure. To do that, we took advantage of a distinction that philosophers have proposed between "epistemic" and "aleatory" uncertainty. Epistemic uncertainty is something you don't know but is, at least in theory, knowable. If you wanted to predict the workings of a mystery machine, skilled engineers could, in theory, pry it open and figure it out. Mastering mechanisms is a prototypical clocklike forecasting challenge. Aleatory uncertainty is something you not only don't know; it is unknowable. No matter how much you want to know whether it will rain in Philadelphia one year from now, no matter how many great meteorologists you consult, you can't outguess the seasonal averages.

You are dealing with an intractably cloud-like problem, with uncertainty that it is impossible, even in theory, to eliminate. Aleatory uncertainty ensures life will always have surprises, regardless of how carefully we plan. Superforecasters grasp this deep truth better than most. When they sense that a question is loaded with irreducible uncertainty—say, a currency-market question—they have learned to be cautious, keeping their initial estimates inside the shades-of-maybe zone between 35% and 65% and moving out tentatively. They know the "cloudier" the outlook, the harder it is to beat that dart-throwing chimpanzee.[19]

Another nugget of evidence comes from the phrase "fifty-fifty." To careful probabilistic thinkers, 50% is just one in a huge range of settings, so they are no likelier to use it than 49% or 51%. Forecasters who use a three-setting mental dial are much likelier to use 50% when they are asked to make probabilistic judgments because they use it as a stand-in for maybe. Hence, we should expect frequent users of 50% to be less accurate. And that's exactly what the tournament data show.[20]

I once asked Brian Labatte, a superforecaster from Montreal, what he liked to read. Both fiction and nonfiction, he said. How much of each, I asked? "I would say 70% . . ."—a long pause—"no, 65/35 nonfiction to fiction."[21] That's remarkably precise for a casual conversation. Even when making formal forecasts in the IARPA tournament, ordinary forecasters were not usually that precise. Instead, they tended to stick to the tens, meaning they might say something was 30% likely, or 40%, but not 35%, much less 37%. Superforecasters were much more granular. Fully one-third of their forecasts used the single percentage point scale, meaning they would think carefully and decide that the chance of something happening was, say, 3% rather than 4%. Like the Treasury aide taught to think in fine-grained probabilities by his boss, Robert Rubin, superforecasters try to be so precise that they sometimes debate differences that most of us see as inconsequential—whether the correct probability is 5% or 1%, or whether it is a fraction of 1% close enough to zero to justify rounding down. These are not debates about how many angels can dance on the head of a pin because sometimes precision on that scale matters. It means moving from a world in which a threat or an opportunity is extremely improbable but possible to one in which it is categorically impossible—which matters if the consequences of the improbable happening are great enough. Imagine an Ebola outbreak. Or funding the next Google.

Now, I have urged the reader to be skeptical and a skeptic may have doubts about this. It's easy to impress people by stroking your chin and declaring "There is a 73% probability Apple's stock will finish the year 24% above where it started." Toss in a few technical terms most people don't understand—"stochastic" this, "regression" that—and you can use people's justified respect for math and science to get them nodding along. This is granularity as bafflegab. It is unfortunately common. So how can we know that the granularity we see among superforecasters is meaningful? How can we be sure that when Brian Labatte makes an initial estimate of 70% but then stops himself and adjusts it to 65% the change is likely to produce a more accurate estimate? The answer lies in the tournament data. Barbara Mellers has shown that granularity predicts accuracy: the average forecaster who sticks with the tens—20%, 30%, 40%—is less accurate than the finer-grained forecaster who uses fives—20%, 25%, 30%—and still less accurate than the even finer-grained forecaster who uses ones—20%, 21%, 22%. As a further test, she rounded forecasts to make them less granular, so a forecast at the greatest granularity possible in the tournament, single percentage points, would be rounded to the nearest five, and then the nearest ten. This way, all of the forecasts were made one level less granular. She then recalculated Brier scores and discovered that superforecasters lost accuracy in response to even the smallest-scale rounding, to the nearest

0.05, whereas regular forecasters lost little even from rounding four times as large, to the nearest 0.2.[22]

Brian Labatte's granularity isn't bafflegab. It is precision—and a key reason why he is a superforecaster.

Most people never attempt to be as precise as Brian, preferring to stick with what they know, which is the two- or three-setting mental model. That is a serious mistake. As the legendary investor Charlie Munger sagely observed, "If you don't get this elementary, but mildly unnatural, mathematics of elementary probability into your repertoire, then you go through a long life like a one-legged man in an ass-kicking contest."[23]

Even very sophisticated people and organizations don't push themselves to Brian's level. To take just one example, the National Intelligence Council (NIC)—which produces the National Intelligence Estimates that inform ultrasensitive decisions like whether to invade Iraq or negotiate with Iran—asks its analysts to make judgments on a five- or seven-degree scale.

Remote	Unlikely	Even chance	Probably, likely	Almost certainly

Remote	Very unlikely	Unlikely	Even chance	Probably, likely	Very likely	Almost certainly

Degree of granularity inside the intelligence community

That's a big improvement on a two- or three-setting dial—but it still falls short of what the most committed superforecasters can achieve on many questions. I have known people who served on the

NIC, and I suspect they are selling themselves short. The NIC—or any other organization with top-flight people—could get similar results if they valued and encouraged it. And they should.[24]

The reward, remember, is a clearer perception of the future. And that's invaluable in the ass-kicking contest of life.

BUT WHAT DOES IT ALL MEAN?

In the Kurt Vonnegut classic *Slaughterhouse-Five*, an American prisoner of war muttered something a guard did not like. "The guard knew English, and he hauled the American out of ranks, knocked him down," Vonnegut wrote.

> *The American was astonished. He stood up shakily, spitting blood. He'd had two teeth knocked out. He had meant no harm by what he'd said, evidently, had no idea that the guard would hear and understand. "Why me?" he asked the guard.*
>
> *The guard shoved him back in ranks. "Vy you? Vy anybody?" he said.*

Vonnegut drums this theme relentlessly. "Why me?" moans Billy Pilgrim when he is abducted by aliens. "That is a very Earthling question to ask, Mr. Pilgrim," the aliens respond. "Why you? Why us for that matter? Why anything?"[25] Only the naive ask "Why?" Those who see reality more clearly don't bother.

It's a trenchant insight. When something unlikely and important happens it's deeply human to ask "Why?"

The religious message that whatever happens, even tragedy, is a meaningful part of a divine plan is ancient, and however one feels about religion there's no question that this sort of thinking can be consoling and help people endure the otherwise unendurable. Oprah

Winfrey, a woman who overcame adversity to achieve stupendous success, personifies and promotes the idea. Using secular language, she said in a commencement address at Harvard University that "there is no such thing as failure. Failure is just life trying to move us in another direction. . . . Learn from every mistake because every experience, encounter, and particularly your mistakes are there to teach you and force you into being who you are." Everything happens for a reason. Everything has a purpose. In the final episode of her landmark TV show, Winfrey made essentially the same point in explicitly religious language: "I understand the manifestation of grace and God, so I know there are no coincidences. There are none. Only divine order here."[26]

Religion is not the only way to satisfy the yearning for meaning. Psychologists find that many atheists also see meaning in the significant events in their lives, and a majority of atheists said they believe in fate, defined as the view that "events happen for a reason and that there is an underlying order to life that determines how events turn out."[27] Meaning is a basic human need. As much research shows, the ability to find it is a marker of a healthy, resilient mind. Among survivors of the 9/11 attacks, for example, those who saw meaning in the atrocity were less likely to suffer post-traumatic stress responses.[28]

But as psychologically beneficial as this thinking may be, it sits uneasily with a scientific worldview. Science doesn't tackle "why" questions about the purpose of life. It sticks to "how" questions that focus on causation and probabilities. Snow building up on the side of a mountain may slip and start an avalanche, or it may not. Until it happens, or it doesn't, it could go either way. It is not predetermined by God or fate or anything else. It is not "meant to be." It has no meaning. "Maybe" suggests that, contra Einstein, God *does* play dice with the cosmos. Thus, probabilistic thinking and divine-order thinking are in tension. Like oil and water, chance and fate do not mix. And to the extent that we allow our thoughts to move in the direction of fate, we undermine our ability to think probabilistically.

Most people tend to prefer fate. With the psychologist Laura Kray and other colleagues, I tested the effect of counterfactual thinking, which is thinking about how something might have turned out differently than it actually did.[29] In one experiment, students at Northwestern University wrote a short essay explaining how they chose to go to Northwestern. Half of them were then asked to list ways that "things could have turned out differently." Finally, all of them rated how strongly they agreed with three statements: "My decision to come to Northwestern defines who I am," "Coming to Northwestern has added meaning to my life," and "My decision to come to Northwestern was one of the most significant choices of my life." As expected, students who had engaged in counterfactual thinking— imagining the different choices they might have made—imbued their decision to come to Northwestern with more meaning. A second experiment asked participants to think of a close friend. Again, imagining how things might have turned out differently caused people to imbue the relationship with deeper significance. A third experiment asked people to identify a turning point in their lives. Half were asked to describe only the facts: what happened, when it happened, who was involved, what they were thinking and feeling. The other half were asked to describe how their lives would be now if the turning point had not occurred. All participants then judged the degree to which the turning point was "a product of fate." As expected, those who had contemplated alternative paths in life saw the path taken as meant to be.

Think about the love of your life and the countless events that had to happen as they did to bring the two of you together. If you had studied that night rather than gone to the party. Or your spouse had walked a bit faster and not missed that train. Or you had accepted your friend's invitation to go out of town that weekend. The what-ifs stretch over the horizon. Once, it was vanishingly unlikely that you two would meet. And yet, you did. What do you make of that? Most people don't think "Wow, what luck!" Instead, they take the sheer improbability of it happening, and the fact it happened, as proof it was *meant* to happen.

Something strikingly similar happens on a cosmic scale. Think of the Big Bang, the dominant scientific explanation for the origin of the universe. Big Bang theory tells us how finely tuned the laws of nature need to be for stars, planets, and life to arise. Even tiny deviations and we would not exist. Most people don't respond to that observation by saying "Wow, we were lucky!"—or by wondering whether billions of Big Bangs generated billions of parallel universes, a few of which turned out by chance to be life friendly. Some physicists think this way. But most of us suspect that something—perhaps God—was behind it. It was *meant* to be.

Natural as such thinking may be, it is problematic. Lay out the tangled chain of reasoning in a straight line and you see this: "The probability that I would meet the love of my life was tiny. But it happened. So it was meant to be. Therefore the probability that it would happen was 100%." This is beyond dubious. It's incoherent. Logic and psycho-logic are in tension.

A probabilistic thinker will be less distracted by "why" questions and focus on "how." This is no semantic quibble. "Why?" directs us to metaphysics; "How?" sticks with physics. The probabilistic thinker would say, "Yes, it was extremely improbable that I would meet my partner that night, but I had to be somewhere and she had to be somewhere and happily for us our somewheres coincided." The economist and Nobel laureate Robert Shiller tells the story of how

Henry Ford decided to hire workers at the then-astonishingly high rate of $5 a day, which convinced both his grandfathers to move to Detroit to work for Ford. If someone had made one of his grandfathers a better job offer, if one of his grandfathers had been kicked in the head by a horse, if someone had convinced Ford he was crazy to pay $5 a day . . . if an almost infinite number of events had turned out differently, Robert Shiller would not have been born. But rather than see fate in his improbable existence, Shiller repeats the story as an illustration of how radically indeterminate the future is. "You tend to believe that history played out in a logical sort of sense, that people ought to have foreseen, but it's not like that," he told me. "It's an illusion of hindsight."[30]

Even in the face of tragedy, the probabilistic thinker will say, "Yes, there was an almost infinite number of paths that events could have taken, and it was incredibly unlikely that events would take the path that ended in my child's death. But they had to take a path and that's the one they took. That's all there is to it." In Kahneman's terms, probabilistic thinkers take the outside view toward even profoundly identity-defining events, seeing them as quasi-random draws from distributions of once-possible worlds.

Or, in Kurt Vonnegut's terms, "Why me? Why *not* me?"

If it's true that probabilistic thinking is essential to accurate forecasting, and it-was-meant-to-happen thinking undermines probabilistic thinking, we should expect superforecasters to be much less inclined to see things as fated. To test this, we probed their reactions to pro-fate statements like these:

Events unfold according to God's plan.

Everything happens for a reason.

There are no accidents or coincidences.

We also asked them about pro-probability statements like these:

Nothing is inevitable.

Even major events like World War II or 9/11 could have turned out very differently.

Randomness is often a factor in our personal lives.

We put the same questions to regular volunteer forecasters, undergraduates at the University of Pennsylvania, and a broad cross section of adult Americans. On a 9-point "fate score," where 1 is total rejection of it-was-meant-to-happen thinking and 9 is a complete embrace of it, the mean score of adult Americans fell in the middle of the scale. The Penn undergrads were a little lower. The regular forecasters were a little lower still. And the superforecasters got the lowest score of all, firmly on the rejection-of-fate side.

For both the superforecasters and the regulars, we also compared individual fate scores with Brier scores and found a significant correlation—meaning the more a forecaster inclined toward it-was-meant-to-happen thinking, the less accurate her forecasts were. Or, put more positively, the more a forecaster embraced probabilistic thinking, the more accurate she was.

So finding meaning in events is positively correlated with well-being but negatively correlated with foresight. That sets up a depressing possibility: Is misery the price of accuracy?

I don't know. But this book is not about how to be happy. It's about how to be accurate, and the superforecasters show that probabilistic thinking is essential for that. I'll leave the existential issues to others.

7

Supernewsjunkies?

Superforecasting isn't a paint-by-numbers method but superforecasters often tackle questions in a roughly similar way—one that any of us can follow: Unpack the question into components. Distinguish as sharply as you can between the known and unknown and leave no assumptions unscrutinized. Adopt the outside view and put the problem into a comparative perspective that downplays its uniqueness and treats it as a special case of a wider class of phenomena. Then adopt the inside view that plays up the uniqueness of the problem. Also explore the similarities and differences between your views and those of others—and pay special attention to prediction markets and other methods of extracting wisdom from crowds. Synthesize all these different views into a single vision as acute as that of a dragonfly. Finally, express your judgment as precisely as you can, using a finely grained scale of probability.

Done well, this process is as demanding as it sounds, taking a lot of time and mental energy. And yet it is literally just the beginning.

Forecasts aren't like lottery tickets that you buy and file away until the big draw. They are judgments that are based on available information and that should be updated in light of changing information. If new polls show a candidate has surged into a comfortable lead, you should boost the probability that the candidate will win. If a competitor unexpectedly declares bankruptcy, revise expected sales accordingly. The IARPA tournament was no different. After Bill Flack did all his difficult initial work and concluded there was a 60% chance that polonium would be detected in Yasser Arafat's remains, he could raise or lower his forecast as often as he liked, for any reason. So he followed the news closely and updated his forecast whenever he saw good reason to do so. This is obviously important. A forecast that is updated to reflect the latest available information is likely to be closer to the truth than a forecast that isn't so informed.

Devyn Duffy is a fantastic updater. He is also a superforecaster with the unusual distinction of having volunteered for the Good Judgment Project because he was unemployed, at the age of thirty-six, after losing his job when the factory he worked in closed. The Pittsburgh native is now an income maintenance caseworker with the state government. "My most useful talent is the ability to do well on tests, especially multiple-choice," Devyn told me in an e-mail. "This has made me appear more intelligent than I actually am, often even to myself." Needless to say, Devyn has a cutting sense of humor.

Like many superforecasters, Devyn follows developments closely by using Google alerts. If he makes a forecast about Syrian refugees, for example, the first thing he will do is set an alert for "Syrian refugees" and "UNHCR," which will net any news that mentions both Syrian refugees and the UN agency that monitors their numbers. Devyn will set the alert to report daily if he thinks that events may change rapidly—say, the risk of a military coup in Thailand—otherwise, weekly. Devyn reads the alerts as soon as they come in, thinks through what they imply about the future, and updates his forecasts to reflect the new information. In the third season alone, Devyn made 2,271 forecasts on 140 questions. That's more than 16 forecasts, on average, for each question. "I would attribute my GJP success so far, such as it has been," Devyn wrote, "to good luck and frequent updating."

Devyn is not unusual. Superforecasters update much more frequently, on average, than regular forecasters. That obviously matters.

An updated forecast is likely to be a better-informed forecast and therefore a more accurate forecast. "When the facts change, I change my mind," the legendary British economist John Maynard Keynes declared. "What do you do, sir?" The superforecasters do likewise, and that is another big reason why they are super.

But that raises a suspicion. Maybe all the careful cognitive labor and granular judgment that goes into the initial forecast doesn't explain superforecasters' success. Maybe their forecasts are better simply because they spend a lot more time watching the news and updating. I once asked a famous political scientist who runs a lucrative consultancy providing political forecasts to major corporations if he would like to try his hand in the IARPA tournament. He was interested until he learned that the tournament required updating. He had no interest in "competing with unemployed newsjunkies," he said.

I didn't like his attitude but I got the point. Superforecasters do monitor the news carefully and factor it into their forecasts, which is bound to give them a big advantage over the less attentive. If that's the decisive factor, then superforecasters' success would tell us nothing more than "it helps to pay attention and keep your forecast up to date"—which is about as enlightening as being told that when polls show a candidate surging into a comfortable lead he is more likely to win.

But that's not the whole story. For one thing, superforecasters' *initial* forecasts were at least 50% more accurate than those of regular forecasters. Even if the tournament had asked for only one forecast, and did not permit updating, superforecasters would have won decisively.

More important, it is a huge mistake to belittle belief updating. It is not about mindlessly adjusting forecasts in response to whatever is on CNN. Good updating requires the same skills used in making the initial forecast and is often just as demanding. It can even be *more* challenging.

THE OVER-UNDER

"My fellow Americans—tonight, I want to speak to you about what the United States will do with our friends and allies to degrade and ultimately destroy the terrorist group known as ISIL," President Obama said at the beginning of an address televised live on the evening of September 10, 2014. "I have made it clear that we will hunt down terrorists who threaten our country, wherever they are. That means I will not hesitate to take action against ISIL in Syria, as well as Iraq."

Superforecasters took note. Whether a foreign military would carry out operations within Syria before December 1, 2014, was a live question in the tournament. This announcement made a yes all but certain. A flurry of updating followed.

Like new polls showing a surge in support for a candidate, President Obama's announcement obviously called for an update. And what the update should be—a bump up to near certainty—was also obvious. But a development like this, and the response it calls for, are clear to everyone, and no one can produce superior forecasts only by staying on top of what everyone knows. What makes the difference is correctly identifying and responding to subtler information so you zero in on the eventual outcome faster than others.[1]

Long after Bill Flack made his initial forecast on the Arafat-polonium question, the Swiss research team announced that it would be late releasing its results because it needed to do more—unspecified—testing. What did that mean? It could be irrelevant. Maybe a technician had celebrated his birthday a little too heartily and missed work the next day. There was no way to find out. But by then Bill knew a lot about polonium, including the fact that it can be found in a body as a result of it being introduced in that form, or it can be produced in the body when naturally occurring lead decays. To identify the true source, analysts remove all the polonium, wait long enough for more of the lead—if present—to decay into polonium, then test again. The Swiss team's delay suggested it had detected polonium and was now testing to rule out lead as its source. But that was only one possible explanation, so Bill cautiously raised his forecast to 65% yes. That's smart updating. Bill spotted subtly diagnostic information and moved the forecast in the right direction before everyone else—as the Swiss team did, in fact, find polonium in Arafat's remains. Bill's final Brier score on this question was 0.36. That may not sound terribly impressive but remember that Brier scores only have meaning in relation to the difficulty of the problem at hand, and most experts were shocked by the results. At the close of trading, a prediction market operating inside the IARPA tournament put the probability of yes at a mere 4.27%, which translates into a Brier score five times worse than Bill's. Given the difficulty of the problem, the fact that Bill mostly saw a positive test result as being more likely than not is truly impressive accuracy.

But as Bill also demonstrated, even the best updaters make mistakes. In 2013, when IARPA asked whether the Japanese prime minister, Shinzo Abe, would visit the Yasukuni Shrine, Bill strongly believed the answer was no. Yasukuni was founded in 1869 to honor Japan's war dead and now lists almost 2.5 million soldiers. Conservatives like Abe revere it. But included among the names of the honored dead are those of about one thousand war criminals, including fourteen "class A" criminals. Visits to Yasukuni by Japanese leaders outrage the Chinese and Korean governments, and the government of the United States, Japan's chief ally, constantly urges Japanese prime ministers not to damage relations this way. Looking at these facts, Bill thought Abe wouldn't go. That was a reasonable forecast. But then someone close to Abe said, unofficially, that he would. Time for an update? Bill thought it made so little sense for Abe to make the visit that he discounted the statement and didn't update. On December 26, Abe visited Yasukuni—and Bill's Brier score took a hit.

These stories suggest that if you spot potentially insightful new evidence, you should not hesitate to turn the ship's wheel hard. But consider what happened when Doug Lorch sailed into the Arctic Ocean.

"On 15 September 2014, will the Arctic sea ice extent be less than that of 15 September 2013?" IARPA asked that question on August 20, 2014. Even though it was only a twenty-six-day forecast, it was a tough call. Scientists track Arctic sea ice with amazing precision, reporting results daily, and in mid-August 2014 the ice extent was almost exactly the same as it had been a year earlier. So would there be more or less ice on September 15 than a year earlier? Everyone from scientists to superforecasters agreed it would be close. Doug hedged his opening forecast. He took a prudent 55% position that, yes, there would be less ice than a year earlier.

Two days later, a member of Doug's team discovered a report from the Sea Ice Prediction Network. It was a gem. Scientists had made twenty-eight separate projections using four different methods and all but three predicted less ice in September 2014 than a year earlier. The only catch? The report was a month old. When you're dealing with a reality that changes daily, and the forecast only looks twenty-eight days out, a month is a long time. Still, Doug told me, "It was pretty darned convincing." Doug spun the ship's wheel hard to 95% yes.

Over the next few weeks, ice loss slowed. On September 15, there was more ice than a year earlier. Doug's score suffered for it.[2]

So there are two dangers a forecaster faces after making the initial call. One is not giving enough weight to new information. That's underreaction. The other danger is overreacting to new information, seeing it as more meaningful than it is, and adjusting a forecast too radically.

Both under- and overreaction can diminish accuracy. Both can also, in extreme cases, destroy a perfectly good forecast.

UNDER

Underreaction can happen for any number of reasons, some of them prosaic. "Shoot, I have done a poor job of updating my forecast here," Joshua Frankel wrote after the US Air Force attacked targets in Syria on September 22, 2014—closing the question about whether foreign militaries would intervene in Syria before December 1, 2014. Frankel's mistake? Like everyone else, he saw Obama announce his intention to go after ISIL in Syria. But he didn't raise his forecast from 82% to 99%, as he later said he should have, because events unfolded quickly and he was "too swamped with work to stay on top of it." Some updating does reduce to good housekeeping—sweeping out old forecasts.

But there is a subtler explanation for Bill Flack's underreaction to a Japanese official saying Shinzo Abe would visit the Yasukuni Shrine. The political costs of visiting Yasukuni were steep. And Abe had no pressing need to placate his conservative constituents by going, so the benefit was negligible. Conclusion? Not going looked like the rational decision. But Bill ignored Abe's own feelings. Abe is a conservative nationalist. He had visited Yasukuni before, although not as prime minister. He wanted to go again. Reflecting on his mistake, Bill told me, "I think that the question I was really answering wasn't 'Will Abe visit Yasukuni?' but 'If I were PM of Japan, would I visit Yasukuni?' "[3] That's astute. And it should sound familiar: Bill recognized that he had unconsciously pulled a bait and switch on himself, substituting an easy question in place of a hard one. Having strayed from the real question, Bill dismissed the new information because it was irrelevant to his replacement question.

That's an example of an updating error rooted in psychological bias. They are always a challenge to spot. But one psychological source of error is particularly tenacious—and likely to produce forecast-wrecking underreaction.

On December 7, 1941, when the Japanese Imperial Navy attacked the United States at Pearl Harbor, Americans were shocked not only because they had suddenly been thrust into World War II but because the attack revealed a danger few had imagined: if Hawaii was vulnerable, so was California. Defenses were hurriedly bolstered, but many top officials worried that all their preparations could be undone by spies and saboteurs. Japanese Americans "may well be the Achilles' heel of the entire civilian defense effort," warned Earl Warren. At the time, Warren was attorney general of California. Later, he became governor, then chief justice of the US Supreme Court—and is remembered today as the liberal champion of school desegregation and civil rights.[4]

But civil rights were not at the tip of Warren's nose in World War II. Security was. His solution to the perceived threat was to round up and imprison every man, woman, and child of Japanese descent, a plan carried out between mid-February and August 1942, when 112,000 people—two-thirds of whom had been born in the United States—were shipped to isolated camps ringed with barbed wire and armed guards.

There was no sabotage in the ten weeks before the internment, or in the rest of 1942. Or in 1943. Some advocates of internment felt that this evidence, and the major setbacks suffered by the Japanese military, meant the policy could be eased. Not Warren and other hard-liners. The danger was real and it had not lessened, they insisted.[5]

This is an extreme case of what psychologists call "belief perseverance." People can be astonishingly intransigent—and capable of rationalizing like crazy to avoid acknowledging new information that upsets their settled beliefs. Consider the 1942 argument of General John DeWitt, a strong supporter of the internment of Japanese Americans: "The very fact that no sabotage has taken place to date is a disturbing and confirming indication that such action will be taken."[6]—or to put that more bluntly, "The fact that what I expected to happen didn't happen proves that it will." Fortunately, such extreme obstinacy is rare. More commonly, when we are confronted by facts impossible to ignore, we budge, grudgingly, but the *degree* of change is likely to be less than it should be. As we saw in chapter 2, the brain likes things neat and orderly and once it has things that way it tries to keep disturbances to a minimum.

But not all disturbances are equal. Remember that Keynes quotation about changing your mind in light of changed facts? It's cited in countless books, including one written by me and another by my coauthor. Google it and you will find it's all over the Internet. Of the many famous things Keynes said it's probably the most famous. But while researching this book, I tried to track it to its source and failed. Instead, I found a post by a *Wall Street Journal* blogger, which said that no one has ever discovered its provenance and the two leading experts on Keynes think it is apocryphal.[7] In light of these facts, and in the spirit of what Keynes apparently never said, I concluded that I was wrong. And I have now confessed to the world. Was that hard? Not really. Many smart people made the same mistake, so it's not embarrassing to own up to it. The quotation wasn't central to my work and being right about it wasn't part of my identity.

But if I had staked my career on that quotation, my reaction might have been less casual. Social psychologists have long known that getting people to publicly commit to a belief is a great way to freeze it in place, making it resistant to change. The stronger the commitment, the greater the resistance.[8]

Jean-Pierre Beugoms is a superforecaster who prides himself on his willingness "to change my opinions a lot faster than my other teammates," but he also noted "it is a challenge, I'll admit that, especially if it's a question that I have a certain investment in." For Beugoms, that means military questions. He is a graduate of West Point who is writing his PhD dissertation on American military history. "I feel like I should be doing better than most [on military questions]. So if I realize that I'm wrong, I might spend a few days in denial about it before I critique myself." [9]

Commitment can come in many forms, but a useful way to think of it is to visualize the children's game Jenga, which starts with building blocks stacked one on top of another to form a little tower. Players take turns removing building blocks until someone removes the block that topples the tower. Our beliefs about ourselves and the world are built on each other in a Jenga-like fashion. My belief that Keynes said "When the facts change, I change my mind" was a block sitting at the apex. It supported nothing else, so I could easily pick it up and toss it without disturbing other blocks. But when Jean-Pierre makes a forecast in his specialty, that block is lower in the structure, sitting next to a block of self-perception, near the tower's core. So it's a lot harder to pull that block out without upsetting other blocks—which makes Jean-Pierre reluctant to tamper with it.

The Yale professor Dan Kahan has done much research showing that our judgments about risks—Does gun control make us safer or put us in danger?—are driven less by a careful weighing of evidence than by our identities, which is why people's views on gun control often correlate with their views on climate change, even though the two issues have no logical connection to each other. Psycho-logic trumps logic. And when Kahan asks people who feel strongly that gun control increases risk, or diminishes it, to imagine conclusive evidence that shows they are wrong, and then asks if they would change their position if that evidence were handed to them, they typically say no. That belief block is holding up a lot of others. Take it out and you risk chaos, so many people refuse to even imagine it.

When a block is at the very base of the tower, there's no way to remove it without bringing everything crashing down. This extreme commitment leads to extreme reluctance to admit error, which explains why the men responsible for imprisoning 112,000 innocent people could be so dogged in their belief that the threat of sabotage was severe. Their commitment was massive. Warren was, deep down, a civil libertarian. Admitting to himself that he had unjustly imprisoned 112,000 people would have taken a sledgehammer to his mental tower.

This suggests that superforecasters may have a surprising advantage: they're not experts or professionals, so they have little ego invested in each forecast. Except in rare circumstances—when Jean-Pierre Beugoms answers military questions, for example—they aren't deeply committed to their judgments, which makes it easier to admit when a forecast is offtrack and adjust. This isn't to say that superforecasters have zero ego investment. They care about their reputations among their teammates. And if "superforecaster" becomes part of their self-concept, their commitment will grow fast. But still, the self-esteem stakes are far less than those for career CIA analysts or acclaimed pundits with their reputations on the line. And that helps them avoid underreaction when new evidence calls for updating beliefs.

OVER

Imagine you are a subject in an odd undergraduate psychology experiment. The researcher asks you to read a bit of information about someone. "Robert is a student," it says. "He studies about thirty-one hours each week." You are then asked to predict Robert's grade point average. It's not much to go on, but it matches your stereotype of a good student. So you guess his GPA is pretty high.

Now try this one: David is a psychotherapy patient who is sexually aroused by violent sadomasochistic fantasies. Question: How likely is David to be a child abuser? Again, you have little information, but what you have fits your stereotype of child abusers. So you say there is a good chance he's one.

Now suppose I gave you more facts about Robert. What if I told you he plays tennis three or four times a month? And the longest relationship he has had lasted two months? Would you change your estimate of Robert's GPA?

And here's more information about David: He likes to tell jokes. He once injured his back while skiing. Now, is he more or less likely to be a child abuser?

You may be thinking, "All that additional information is irrelevant. I'd ignore it." And good for you. It was carefully preselected for its total irrelevance.

And yet, irrelevant information of this sort does sway us. In 1989, building on work by the psychologist Richard Nisbett, I ran a study in which randomly selected participants got either the bare minimum facts or that information plus the irrelevant facts and then estimated Robert's GPA or David's proclivity for child abuse. As expected, those who got the irrelevant information lost confidence. Why? With nothing to go on but evidence that fits their stereotype of a good student or a child abuser, the signal feels strong and clear—and our judgment reflects that. But add irrelevant information and we can't help but see Robert or David more as a person than a stereotype, which weakens the fit.[10]

Psychologists call this the dilution effect, and given that stereotypes are themselves a source of bias we might say that diluting them is all to the good. Yes and no. Yes, it is possible to fight fire with fire, and bias with bias, but the dilution effect remains a bias. Remember what's going on here. People base their estimate on what they think is a useful tidbit of information. Then they encounter clearly irrelevant information—meaningless noise—which they indisputably should ignore. But they don't. They sway in the wind, at the mercy of the next random gust of irrelevant information.

Such swaying is overreaction, a common and costly mistake. Look at a typical day in the stock market. The volume and volatility of trading are staggering. The reasons for that are complex and the subject of much research and debate, but it seems clear that at least some of it is due to traders overreacting to new information.[11] Even John Maynard Keynes—he may not have said those famous words but he really did urge people to change their minds in light of changing facts—felt that "day-to-day fluctuations in the profits of existing investments, which are obviously of an ephemeral and nonsignificant character, tend to have an altogether excessive, and even an absurd, influence on the market."[12]

"Many investors move from stock to stock or from mutual fund to mutual fund as if they were selecting and discarding cards in a game of gin rummy," observed the Princeton economist Burton Malkiel.[13] And they pay a price. Many studies have found that those who trade more frequently get worse returns than those who lean toward old-fashioned buy-and-hold strategies. Malkiel cited one study of sixty-six thousand American households over a five-year period in the 1990s when the market had a 17.9% annual return: households that traded the most had an annual return of only 11.4%.[14] Massive time and effort went into those trades and yet the people who made them would have been better off if they had gone golfing.

As with underreaction, the key is commitment—in this case, the absence of commitment. Traders who constantly buy and sell are not cognitively or emotionally connected to their stocks. They expect some to fall and they sell off these losers with a shrug. Malkiel's metaphor is apt. They are no more committed to these stocks than a gin rummy player is to cards in his hand, leaving them free to overreact to information "obviously of an ephemeral and nonsignificant character."

Given superforecasters' modest commitment to their forecasts, we would expect overreactions—like that of Doug Lorch and his team swinging from 55% to 95% on a single, month-old report—to be a greater risk than underreactions. And yet, superforecasters often manage to avoid both errors. They wouldn't be superforecasters if they didn't.

So how do they do it? In the nineteenth century, when prose was never complete without a sage aside to Greek mythology, any discussion of two opposing dangers called for Scylla and Charybdis. Scylla was a rock shoal off the coast of Italy. Charybdis was a whirlpool on the coast of Sicily, not far away. Sailors knew they would be doomed if they strayed too far in either direction. Forecasters should feel the same about under- and overreaction to new information, the Scylla and Charybdis of forecasting. Good updating is all about finding the middle passage.

CAPTAIN MINTO

In the third season of the IARPA tournament, Tim Minto won top spot with a final Brier score of 0.15, an amazing accomplishment, almost in the league of Ken Jennings's winning *Jeopardy!* seventy-four games in a row. A big reason why the forty-five-year-old Vancouver software engineer did so well is his skill at updating.

For his initial forecasts, Tim takes less time than some other top forecasters. "I typically spend five to fifteen minutes, which means maybe an hour or so total when a new batch of six or seven questions come out," he said. But the next day, he'll come back, take another look, and form a second opinion. He also trawls for contrary evidence on the Internet. And he does this five days a week.

All that exploration makes him change his mind a lot. "I update constantly," he said. "That's just the way my mind works, although more typically it applies to real work as opposed to [tournament] questions."[15] By the time a question closes, Tim has usually made a dozen forecasts. Sometimes, the total is closer to forty or fifty. On one question—whether the United States and Afghanistan would reach an agreement on the continued presence of American troops—he made seventy-seven forecasts.

It may look as though Captain Minto is sailing straight for the Charybdis of overreaction. But I haven't yet mentioned the *magnitude* of his constant course corrections. In almost every case they are small. And that makes a big difference.

As the Syrian civil war raged, displacing civilians in vast numbers, the IARPA tournament asked forecasters whether "the number of registered Syrian refugees reported by the United Nations Refugee Agency as of 1 April 2014" would be under 2.6 million. That question was asked in the first week of January 2014, so forecasters had to look three months into the future. The answer turned out to be yes. Here is a chart of how Tim Minto updated his beliefs over those three months.

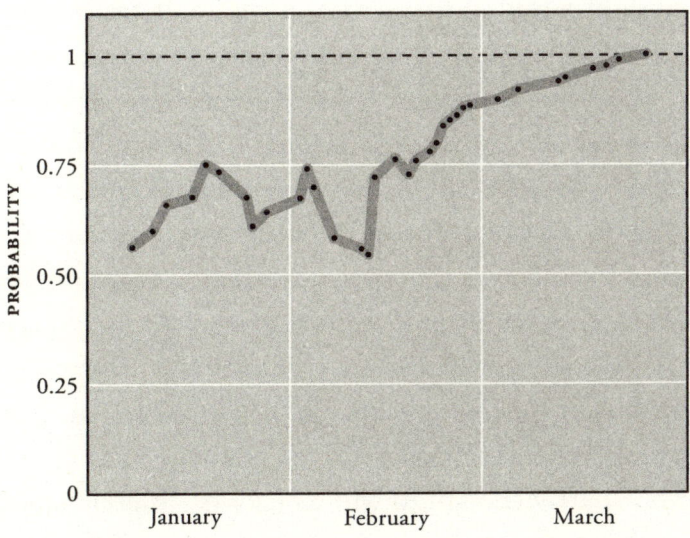

The belief-updating style of a top superforecaster

Tim started off very slightly on the side of yes when the question opened, which made sense at the time. The target number was high, but the situation in Syria was bad and the refugee numbers were rising daily. The chart tells the tale of what followed: Tim changed his forecast thirty-four times. While some of his new forecasts led him away from the correct answer, the trend was mostly in the right direction. Tim's final Brier score was an impressive 0.07.

And notice how small Tim's changes are. There are no dramatic swings of thirty or forty percentage points. The average update was tiny, only 3.5%. That was critical. A few small updates would have put Tim on a heading for underreaction. Many large updates could have tipped him toward overreaction. But with many small updates, Tim slipped safely between Scylla and Charybdis.

It may seem strange to think in terms of such tiny changes—"units of doubt"—but if you think as granularly as Tim does, it comes naturally. Suppose that, in early September 2014, you read that Nate Silver, a prominent poll aggregator, gave Republicans a 60% chance of winning the Senate in the midterm elections. You find that convincing so you set your initial forecast at 60%. The next day you learn a new poll has found Republican support in Colorado's Senate race rising from 45% to 55%. How much should that news increase your estimate? It has to be more than zero. But then you think about how many other races have to tip in favor of the Republicans and you realize that even a win in Colorado doesn't make a big difference. So you think the maximum you should raise your forecast is 10%. It's now between 1% and 10%. How many races look winnable for the Republicans? If the answer is "lots more than needed to take a Senate majority" it suggests the higher end of that range. If it's "barely enough to win a majority," it points toward the lower end. What are the polling trends in those races? Are the factors at work in Colorado relevant there? How far away is the election? How predictive have polls been this far in advance of the election? Each answer helps you to zero in a little more. It's between 2% and

9%, then 3% and 7%. Finally you settle on 4%, and you raise your forecast from 60% to 64%.

It's not dramatic. It's even, to be candid, a tad boring. Tim will never become a guru who shares his visionary insights in TV appearances, bestselling books, and corporate gigs. But Tim's way works. The tournament data prove it: superforecasters not only update more often than other forecasters, they update in smaller increments.

Why this works is no mystery. A forecaster who doesn't adjust her views in light of new information won't capture the value of that information, while a forecaster who is so impressed by the new information that he bases his forecast entirely on it will lose the value of the old information that underpinned his prior forecast. But the forecaster who carefully balances old and new captures the value in both—and puts it into her new forecast. The best way to do that is by updating often but bit by bit.

An old thought experiment illustrates the idea. Imagine you are sitting with your back to a billiards table. A friend rolls a ball onto the table and it stops at a random spot. You want to locate the ball without looking. How? Your friend rolls a second ball, which stops at another random spot. You ask, "Is the second ball to the left or the right of the first?" Your friend says, "To the left." That's an almost trivial scrap of information. But it's not nothing. It tells you that the first ball is not on the extreme left edge of the table. And it makes it just a tad more likely that the first ball is on the right side of the table. If your friend rolls another ball on the table and the procedure is repeated, you get another scrap of information. If he says, "It's to the left," the likelihood of the first ball being on the right side of the table increases a little more. Keep repeating the process and you slowly narrow the range of the possible locations, zeroing in on the truth—although you will never eliminate uncertainty entirely.[16]

If you've taken Statistics 101, you may recall a version of this thought experiment was dreamt up by Thomas Bayes. A Presbyterian minister, educated in logic, Bayes was born in 1701, so he lived at the dawn of modern probability theory, a subject to which he contributed with "An Essay Towards Solving a Problem in the Doctrine of Chances." That essay, in combination with the work of Bayes' friend Richard Price, who published Bayes' essay posthumously in 1761, and the insights of the great French mathematician Pierre-Simon Laplace, ultimately produced Bayes' theorem. It looks like this:

$$P(H|D)/P(-H|D) = P(D|H) \cdot P(D|-H) \cdot P(H)/P(-H)$$

Posterior Odds = Likelihood Ratio • Prior Odds

The Bayesian belief-updating equation

In simple terms, the theorem says that your new belief should depend on two things—your prior belief (and all the knowledge that informed it) multiplied by the "diagnostic value" of the new information. That's head-scratchingly abstract, so let's watch Jay Ulfelder—political scientist, superforecaster, and colleague of mine—put it to concrete use.

In 2013 the Obama administration nominated Chuck Hagel to be defense secretary, but controversial reports surfaced, and a hearing went badly, and some speculated that Hagel might not be confirmed by the Senate. "Will Hagel withdraw?" wrote Tom Ricks, a defense analyst. "I'd say 50-50 . . . But declining by the day. Bottom line: Every business day that the Senate Armed Services Committee doesn't vote to send the nomination to the full Senate, I think the likelihood of Hagel becoming defense secretary declines by about 2%." Was that a solid judgment? "Experienced forecasters often start with the base rate," Ulfelder wrote. "Since the establishment of the [secretary of defense] position soon after World War II, it looks like only one of 24 official nominees has been rejected by the Senate, and none has withdrawn." So the base rate is 96%. If Ulfelder had been asked immediately after Chuck Hagel was nominated whether he would be confirmed, he would say—assuming he didn't factor in any other information—"there is a 96% chance he will." Because this estimate is made prior to the arrival of more information, it is called the "prior."[17]

But then Hagel botched the hearing. Clearly, that reduced his chances. But by how much? To answer that, Ulfelder wrote, "Bayes' theorem requires us to estimate two things: 1) how likely are we to see a poor Senate performance when the nominee is destined to fail and 2) how likely are we to see a poor performance when the nominee is bound for approval?" Ulfelder didn't have those numbers so he started by giving Ricks the benefit of the doubt and tilting his estimates heavily in Ricks's favor, with the implication that if Ricks couldn't be vindicated with those numbers he couldn't be vindicated. "For the sake of argument, I'll assume that only one of every five nominees bound for success does poorly in confirmation hearings, but 19 of 20 bound for failure do." Ulfelder plugged the numbers into Bayes' formula, did the math, and his forecast "tumbles from 96 percent to a lowly . . . 83 percent." Thus, Ulfelder concluded Ricks's estimate was way off and Hagel was still very likely to be confirmed. And he was, two weeks later.[18]

This may cause the math-averse to despair. Do forecasters really have to understand, memorize, and use a—shudder—algebraic formula? For you, I have good news: no, you don't.

The superforecasters are a numerate bunch: many know about Bayes' theorem and could deploy it if they felt it was worth the trouble. But they rarely crunch the numbers so explicitly. What matters far more to the superforecasters than Bayes' theorem is Bayes' core insight of gradually getting closer to the truth by constantly updating in proportion to the weight of the evidence.[19] That's true of Tim Minto. He knows Bayes' theorem but he didn't use it even once to make his hundreds of updated forecasts. And yet Minto appreciates the Bayesian spirit. "I think it is likely that I have a better intuitive grasp of Bayes' theorem than most people," he said, "even though if you asked me to write it down from memory I'd probably fail." Minto is a Bayesian who does not use Bayes' theorem. That paradoxical description applies to most superforecasters.

So we have the winning formula: lots of small updates. Do that and you will be on your way to forecasting glory, right?

I wish it were that simple. True, Tim Minto's approach often works remarkably well, which is why it's common in superforecasters' updating. But it is not a skeleton key that opens all locks. Sometimes it is exactly the wrong thing to do.

Remember Doug Lorch's overreaction to the report about Arctic sea ice? Several days after he raised his forecast to 95% yes, he looked at the most recent data as well as data for the previous twelve years. When he compared the data with the scientists' projections, he saw a big and widening gap between the projections and reality. What should he do? Doug could follow the "many small updates" guideline and gradually lower his forecast as time passed. Or he could take a fresh look. "The only reason I'm at 95% is a report that is clearly failing, so I should ditch the report and make a new forecast." He took the second option. First, he throttled back to 55%, which was his opening forecast. Then he dropped it to 15%. After that, Doug resumed "many small updates," his usual style.

It was the right call. If Doug had stuck with "many small updates" when he was at 95%, his disappointing final score would have been much worse.

In his famous essay "Politics and the English Language," George Orwell concluded with six emphatic rules, including "never use a long word where a short one will do" and "never use the passive where you can use the active." But the sixth rule was the key: "Break any of these rules sooner than saying anything outright barbarous."

I understand the desire for fail-safe rules that guarantee good results. It is the source of our fatal attraction to hedgehog pundits and their false certainty. But there is no magical formula, just broad principles with lots of caveats. Superforecasters understand the principles but also know that their application requires nuanced judgments. And they would rather break the rules than make a barbarous forecast.

8

Perpetual Beta

Failure inspired Mary Simpson to become a superforecaster.

"I really totally missed the 2007 lead-up to the financial crisis and that was frustrating to me because I have the background to understand what went wrong," Simpson said. With a PhD in economics from Claremont Graduate University, Simpson had managed regulatory and financial affairs for the utility Southern California Edison before semiretiring and working as an independent financial consultant in 2007, when the first rumblings of the crisis were felt. At the end of the year, the economy tipped into recession. Worse shocks were felt in the first half of 2008. But like most experts in her field, it wasn't until Lehman Brothers declared bankruptcy on September 15, 2008, that Mary realized the magnitude of the crisis. It was too late. Her retirement savings cratered.

"I really wanted to think more about forecasting," she recalled. It wasn't only financial self-interest that made her want to improve her foresight. It was the sense that she should because, well, she could. "It's one of those things where you feel like, 'I should be better at this.'"[1]

Simpson heard about the Good Judgment Project and volunteered. And she became a very good forecaster, as her superforecaster status attests.

The psychologist Carol Dweck would say Simpson has a "growth mindset," which Dweck defines as believing that your abilities are largely the product of effort—that you can "grow" to the extent that you are willing to work hard and learn.[2] Some people might think that's so obviously true it scarcely needs to be said. But as Dweck's research has shown, the growth mindset is far from universal. Many people have what she calls a "fixed mindset"—the belief that we are who we are, and abilities can only be revealed, not created and developed. People with the fixed mindset say things like "I'm bad at math" and see that as an immutable feature of who they are, like being left-handed or female or tall. This has serious consequences. The person who believes he is bad at math, and always will be, won't try hard to improve, because that would be pointless, and if he is compelled to study math—as we all are in school—he will take any setback as further proof that his limits have been revealed and he should stop wasting his time as soon as possible. Whatever potential he had for improvement will never be realized. Thus, the belief "I am bad at math" becomes self-fulfilling.[3]

In one of many experiments Dweck devised to reveal the crippling power of the fixed mindset, she gave relatively easy puzzles to fifth graders. They enjoyed them. She then gave the children harder puzzles. Some of the children suddenly lost interest and declined an offer to take the puzzles home. Others loved the harder puzzles even more than the easy ones. "Could you write down the name of these puzzles," one child asked, "so my mom can buy me some more when these ones run out?" The difference between the two groups of children was not "puzzle-solving talent." Even among equally adept children, some were turned off by the tougher challenge while others were intrigued. The key factor was mindset. Fixed-mindset kids gave up. Growth-mindset kids knuckled down.

Even when the fixed-minded try, they don't get as much from the experience as those who believe they can grow. In one experiment, Dweck scanned the brains of volunteers as they answered hard questions, then were told whether their answers were right or wrong and given information that could help them improve. The scans revealed that volunteers with a fixed mindset were fully engaged when they were told whether their answers were right or wrong but that's all they apparently cared about. Information that could help improve their answers didn't engage them. "Even when they'd gotten an answer wrong, they were not interested in learning what the right answer was," Dweck wrote. "Only people with a growth mindset paid close attention to information that could stretch their knowledge. Only for them was learning a priority."

To be a top-flight forecaster, a growth mindset is essential. The best illustration is the man who is reputed to have said—but didn't— "When the facts change, I change my mind."

CONSISTENTLY INCONSISTENT

Famous today only for his work on macroeconomic theory, one of John Maynard Keynes's many remarkable accomplishments was his success as an investor.

From the end of World War I to the end of World War II, Keynes handled his own money as well as that of family and friends, two British insurance companies, various investment funds, and Cambridge University's King's College. When he died in 1946, Keynes was an extremely wealthy man, and those whose money he had managed had flourished beyond all reasonable expectation. It would be an impressive record in any era, but this wasn't just any era.[4] Britain's economy stagnated in the 1920s. In the 1930s, the whole world staggered through the Great Depression. "Considering that Keynes was investing during some of the worst years in history, his returns are astounding," noted John F. Wasik, the author of a book on Keynes's investments.[5]

Keynes was breathtakingly intelligent and energetic, which certainly contributed to his success, but more than that he was an insatiably curious man who loved to collect new ideas—a habit that sometimes required him to change his mind. He did so ungrudgingly. Indeed, he took pride in his willingness to squarely admit mistakes and adopt new beliefs, and he urged others to follow his lead. "There is no harm in being sometimes wrong, especially if one is promptly found out," he wrote in 1933.[6]

"Keynes is always ready to contradict not only his colleagues but also himself whenever circumstances make this seem appropriate," reported a 1945 profile of the "consistently inconsistent" economist. "So far from feeling guilty about such reversals of position, he utilizes them as pretexts for rebukes to those he saw as less nimble-minded. Legend says that while conferring with Roosevelt at Quebec, Churchill sent Keynes a cable reading, 'Am coming around to your point of view.' His Lordship replied, 'Sorry to hear it. Have started to change my mind.'"[7]

Keynes's record as an investor was far from unblemished. In 1920 he was nearly wiped out when his foreign currency forecasts turned out to be horribly wrong. He found his footing again and made a fortune for himself and others in the 1920s. But just like Mary Simpson in 2008, Keynes didn't see the disaster of 1929 coming and he again lost big. But he bounced back and did even better than before.

For Keynes, failure was an opportunity to learn—to identify mistakes, spot new alternatives, and try again. After his bad currency calls, Keynes didn't retreat to the safe and easy. He embraced new ideas in the early 1920s, like getting stodgy King's College into stocks at a time when institutions usually stuck to investments like real estate. When he was blindsided by the crash of 1929, he subjected his thinking to withering scrutiny. Keynes concluded that there was something wrong with one of his key theoretical assumptions. Stock prices do not always reflect the true value of companies, so an investor should study a company thoroughly and really understand its business, capital, and management when deciding whether it had sufficient underlying value to make an investment for the long term worthwhile. In the United States, about the same time, this approach was developed by Benjamin Graham, who called it "value investing." It became the cornerstone of Warren Buffett's fortune.

The one consistent belief of the "consistently inconsistent" John Maynard Keynes was that he could do better. Failure did not mean he had reached the limits of his ability. It meant he had to think hard and give it another go. Try, fail, analyze, adjust, try again: Keynes cycled through those steps ceaselessly.

Keynes operated on a higher plane than most of us, but that process—try, fail, analyze, adjust, try again—is fundamental to how all of us learn, almost from the moment we are born. Look at a baby learning to sit up. She's wobbly at first, and when she tilts her head back to have a good long look at the ceiling fan . . . boom! back she goes onto the pillow her mother placed there because babies learning to sit up always flop backward. The mother could skip the drama by putting her baby on her back, or in a chair, but she knows that when her baby flops she learns that she shouldn't tilt her head that far and the next time she sits up she will be a little steadier. The baby will still have to practice this new skill to make it reliable, then habitual, but the initial flop delivers the conceptual breakthrough. The same process plays out thousands of times during childhood, from standing, to walking, to getting on a school bus, to figuring out how to manipulate the two joysticks and all those buttons so the character in the video game leaps at precisely the right moment with exactly the speed necessary to snatch the jewel and score a thousand points.

Adults do it too. The middle-aged accountant who picks up a golf club for the first time is like a baby learning to sit up, and even with professional instruction he will fail often before he can pass as a competent golfer at the club.

We learn new skills by doing. We improve those skills by doing more. These fundamental facts are true of even the most demanding skills. Modern fighter jets are enormously complex flying computers but classroom instruction isn't enough to produce a qualified pilot. Not even time in advanced flight simulators will do. Pilots need hours in the air, the more the better. The same is true of surgeons, bankers, and business executives.

TRY

To demonstrate the limits of learning from lectures, the great philosopher and teacher Michael Polanyi wrote a detailed explanation of the physics of riding a bicycle: "The rule observed by the cyclist is this. When he starts falling to the right he turns the handlebars to the right, so that the course of the bicycle is deflected along a curve towards the right. This results in a centrifugal force pushing the cyclist to the left and offsets the gravitational force dragging him down to the right." It continues in that vein and closes: "A simple analysis shows that for a given angle of unbalance the curvature of each winding is inversely proportional to the square of the speed at which the cyclist is proceeding." It is hard to imagine a more precise description. "But does this tell us exactly how to ride a bicycle?" Polanyi asked. "No. You obviously cannot adjust the curvature of your bicycle's path in proportion to the ratio of your unbalance over the square of your speed; and if you could you would fall off the machine, for there are a number of other factors to be taken into account in practice which are left out in the formulation of this rule."[8]

The knowledge required to ride a bicycle can't be fully captured in words and conveyed to others. We need "tacit knowledge," the sort we only get from bruising experience. To learn to ride a bicycle, we must try to ride one. It goes badly at first. You fall to one side, you fall to the other. But keep at it and with practice it becomes effortless—although if you had to explain how to stay upright, so they can skip the ordeal you just went through, you would succeed no better than Polanyi.

That is blindingly obvious. It should be equally obvious that learning to forecast requires trying to forecast. Reading books on forecasting is no substitute for the experience of the real thing.[9]

FAIL

But not all practice improves skill. It needs to be informed practice. You need to know which mistakes to look out for—and which best practices really are best. So don't burn your books. As noted earlier, randomized controlled experiments have shown that mastering the contents of just one tiny booklet, our training guidelines (see the appendix), can improve your accuracy by roughly 10%. These experiments have also shown how the effects of book knowledge interact with those of practice. People who read the booklet benefited more from practice and people who practiced benefited more from reading the booklet. Fortune favors the prepared mind. The training guidelines help us draw the right lessons from our personal experiences and to strike the right balances between the outside and inside views. And our personal experiences help us infuse pallid public-knowledge abstractions with real-world content.

Effective practice also needs to be accompanied by clear and timely feedback. My research collaborator Don Moore points out that police officers spend a lot of time figuring out who is telling the truth and who is lying, but research has found they aren't nearly as good at it as they think they are and they tend not to get better with experience. That's because experience isn't enough. It must be accompanied by clear feedback.

When an officer decides that a suspect is or isn't lying, the officer doesn't get immediate feedback about the accuracy of her guess (like the suspect saying, "You're right! I *was* lying!"). Instead, events proceed. Charges may be laid, a trial held, and a verdict delivered, or there may be a plea bargain down the road. But this can take months or years, and even when there is a resolution, a huge range of factors could have gone into it. So an officer seldom gets clear feedback that tells her, yes, her judgment was right, or no, it was wrong. Predictably, psychologists who test police officers' ability to spot lies in a controlled setting find a big gap between their confidence and their skill. And that gap grows as officers become more experienced and they assume, not unreasonably, that their experience has made them better lie detectors. As a result, officers grow confident faster than they grow accurate, meaning they grow increasingly over-confident.

Gaps like that are far from unusual. Research on calibration—how closely your confidence matches your accuracy—routinely finds people are too confident.[10] But overconfidence is not an immutable law of human nature. Meteorologists generally do not suffer from it. Neither do seasoned bridge players. That's because both get clear, prompt feedback. The meteorologist who calls for torrential rain tomorrow will know he was off if he wakes to sunshine. Bridge players, who estimate how many "tricks" they will win, get results at the end of each hand. If their forecasts fail, they know it.

That is essential. To learn from failure, we must *know* when we fail. The baby who flops backward does. So does the boy who skins his knee when he falls off the bike. And the accountant who puts an easy putt into a sand trap. And because they know, they can think about what went wrong, adjust, and try again.

Unfortunately, most forecasters do not get the high-quality feedback that helps meteorologists and bridge players improve. There are two main reasons why.

Ambiguous language is a big one. As we saw in chapter 3, vague terms like "probably" and "likely" make it impossible to judge forecasts. When a forecaster says something could or might or may happen, she could or might or may be saying almost anything. The same is true of countless other terms—like Steve Ballmer's reference to "significant market share"—that may sound precise but on close inspection prove as fuzzy as fog. Even an impartial observer would struggle to extract meaningful feedback from vague forecasts, but often the judge is the forecaster herself. That makes the problem even worse.

Consider the Forer effect, named for the psychologist Bertram Forer, who asked some students to complete a personality test, then gave them individual personality profiles based on the results and asked how well the test captured their individual personalities. People were impressed by the test, giving it an average rating of 4.2 out of 5—which was remarkable because Forer had actually taken vague statements like "you have a great need for people to like and admire you" from a book on astrology, assembled them into a profile, and given the same profile to everyone.[11] Vague language is elastic language. The students stretched it to fit their self-images, even though they thought they were judging the test objectively. The lesson for forecasters who would judge their own vague forecasts is: don't kid yourself.

The second big barrier to feedback is time lag. When forecasts span months or years, the wait for a result allows the flaws of memory to creep in. You know how you feel now about the future. But as events unfold, will you be able to recall your forecast accurately? There is a good chance you won't. Not only will you have to contend with ordinary forgetfulness, you are likely to be afflicted by what psychologists call hindsight bias.

If you are old enough now to have been a sentient being in 1991, answer this question: Back then, how likely did you think it was that the incumbent president, George H. W. Bush (now known as Bush 41) would win reelection in 1992? We all know Bush 41 lost to Bill Clinton, but you may recall that he was popular after the victory in the Gulf War. So perhaps you thought his chances were pretty good, but, obviously, he also stood a pretty good chance of losing. Maybe it was fifty-fifty? Or maybe you thought the war gave him the edge, with, say, a 60% or 70% chance of winning? In fact, your memory of your judgment is very likely wrong. And in a predictable direction. I can demonstrate by dredging from the archives a 1991 *Saturday Night Live* skit that captured the received political wisdom in 1991. The scene: a debate among the leading candidates for the Democratic nomination in 1992.

> *Moderator:* Good evening. I'm Fay Sullivan of the League of Women Voters. Welcome to this, the first in a series of debates among the five leading Democrats who are trying to avoid being forced by their party into a hopeless race against President George Bush. Most of them have already announced that they're not interested in the nomination. But each, of course, is under enormous pressure to be the chump who will take on the futile task of running against this very, very popular incumbent. They are . . . Senator Bill Bradley of New Jersey . . .
>
> *Senator Bill Bradley:* I am not a candidate for president in 1992.
>
> *Moderator:* House Majority Leader Dick Gephardt of Missouri . . .
>
> *Congressman Dick Gephardt:* I do not seek my party's nomination.

It gets progressively more absurd. In this debate, each candidate heaps praise on his opponents while savaging himself—because Bush 41 was certain to crush whomever he faced. Everyone knew that. It's why leading Democrats didn't contest the nomination that year, clearing the way for the obscure governor of Arkansas, Bill Clinton.

Once we know the outcome of something, that knowledge skews our perception of what we thought before we knew the outcome:

that's hindsight bias. Baruch Fischhoff was the first to document the phenomenon in a set of elegant experiments. One had people estimate the likelihood of major world events at the time of Fischhoff's research—Will Nixon personally meet with Mao?—then recall their estimate after the event did or did not happen. Knowing the outcome consistently slanted the estimate, even when people tried not to let it sway their judgment. The effect can be subtle, but it can also be quite big. In 1988, when the Soviet Union was implementing major reforms that had people wondering about its future, I asked experts to estimate how likely it was that the Communist Party would lose its monopoly on power in the Soviet Union in the next five years. In 1991 the world watched in shock as the Soviet Union disintegrated. So in 1992–93 I returned to the experts, reminded them of the question in 1988, and asked them to recall their estimates. On average, the experts recalled a number 31 percentage points higher than the correct figure. So an expert who thought there was only a 10% chance might remember herself thinking there was a 40% or 50% chance. There was even a case in which an expert who pegged the probability at 20% recalled it as 70%—which illustrates why hindsight bias is sometimes known as the "I knew it all along" effect.

Forecasters who use ambiguous language and rely on flawed memories to retrieve old forecasts don't get clear feedback, which makes it impossible to learn from experience. They are like basketball players doing free throws in the dark. The only feedback they get are sounds—the clang of the ball hitting metal, the thunk of the ball hitting the backboard, the swish of the ball brushing against the net. A veteran who has taken thousands of free throws with the lights on can learn to connect sounds to baskets or misses. But not the novice. A "swish!" may mean a nothing-but-net basket or a badly underthrown ball. A loud "clunk!" means the throw hit the rim but did the ball roll in or out? They can't be sure. Of course they may convince themselves they know how they are doing, but they don't really, and if they throw balls for weeks they may become more confident—I've practiced so much I must be excellent!—but they won't get better at taking free throws. Only if the lights are turned on can they get clear feedback. Only then can they learn and get better.

When Tim Minto forecast Syrian refugee flows in 2014, he got a Brier score of 0.07. That is clear, precise, and meaningful, an excellent result, the forecasting equivalent of a nothing-but-net free throw. Less happily, Tim's forecast on whether Shinzo Abe would visit the Yakusuni Shrine scored a 1.46, which was like throwing the ball into the trash can at the back of the gymnasium. And Tim knew it. There was no ambiguity in the language to hide behind, no way hindsight bias could subtly fool him into believing his forecast wasn't so bad. Tim blew it and he knew it, which gave him the chance to learn.

By the way, there are no shortcuts. Bridge players may develop well-calibrated judgment when it comes to bidding on tricks, but research shows that judgment calibrated in one context transfers poorly, if at all, to another. So if you were thinking of becoming a better political or business forecaster by playing bridge, forget it. To get better at a certain type of forecasting, that is the type of forecasting you must do—over and over again, with good feedback telling you how your training is going, and a cheerful willingness to say, "Wow, I got that one wrong. I'd better think about why."

ANALYZE AND ADJUST

"We agreed as a team that the half-life of polonium would make detection virtually impossible. We didn't do nearly enough to question that assumption—for example, by considering whether the decay products would be a way to detect polonium, or by asking someone with expertise in the area." That's a message Devyn Duffy posted for his teammates after he and his team took a drubbing on the question about whether Yasser Arafat's remains would test positive for polonium. The lesson he drew: "Be careful about making assumptions of expertise, ask experts if you can find them, reexamine your assumptions from time to time."

Whenever a question closes, it's obvious that superforecasters—in sharp contrast to Carol Dweck's fixed-mindset study subjects—are as keen to know how they can do better as they are to know how they did.

Sometimes they share lengthy postmortems with teammates. These online discussions can go on for pages. And there's a lot more introspection when superforecasters have quiet moments to themselves. "I do that while I'm in the shower or during my morning commute to school or work," Jean-Pierre Beugoms says, "or at random moments during the day when I'm bored or distracted." In the first two seasons of the tournament, Jean-Pierre would often look at his old forecasts and be frustrated that his comments were so sparse that "I often could not figure out why I made a certain forecast" and thus couldn't reconstruct his thought process.[12] So he started leaving more and longer comments knowing it would help him critically examine his thinking. In effect, Beugoms prepares for the postmortem from the moment the tournament question is announced.

Often, postmortems are as careful and self-critical as the thinking that goes into making the initial forecast. Commenting on a question about elections in Guinea—a question his team aced—Devyn emphasized that they couldn't take all the credit. "I think that with Guinea, we were more inclined to believe that the protests wouldn't prevent the elections from taking place. But then they nearly did! So we lucked out, too." That was deeply perceptive. People often assume that when a decision is followed by a good outcome, the decision was good, which isn't always true, and can be dangerous if it blinds us to the flaws in our thinking.[13]

The successful are not usually so open to the idea that they didn't entirely earn their success. In my EPJ research in the late 1980s, I had the experts forecast whether the Communist Party would remain in power in the Soviet Union, whether there would be a violent overthrow of apartheid in South Africa, and whether Quebec would separate from Canada. After the deadlines for three forecasts passed, and the correct answers were clear—no, no, and no—I asked the experts to consider the plausibility of counterfactual scenarios, in which small butterfly-effect tweaks caused history to unfold differently. When the what-iffery implied that their failed forecast would have turned out right—for example, if the coup against Gorbachev in 1991 had been better planned and the plotters had been less drunk and better organized, the Communist Party would still be in power—the experts tended to welcome the what-if tale like an old friend. But when the scenarios implied that their correct forecast could easily have turned out wrong, they dismissed it as speculative. So experts were open to "I was almost right" scenarios but rejected "I was almost wrong" alternatives.

Not Devyn. In triumph, he had no problem saying, "We lucked out."[14]

GRIT

The analogy between forecasting and bicycling is pretty good but, as with all analogies, the fit isn't perfect. With bike riding, the "try, fail, analyze, adjust, and try again" cycle typically takes seconds. With forecasting, it can take months or years. Plus there is the bigger role of chance in forecasting. Cyclists who follow best cycling practices can usually expect excellent outcomes but forecasters should be more tentative. Following best practices improves their odds of winning but less reliably so than in games where chance plays smaller roles.[15] Even with a growth mindset, the forecaster who wants to improve has to have a lot of what my colleague Angela Duckworth dubbed "grit."

Elizabeth Sloane has plenty of grit. Diagnosed with brain cancer, Elizabeth endured chemotherapy, a failed stem-cell transplant, recurrence, and two more years of chemo. But she never relented. She volunteered for the Good Judgment Project to "re-grow her synapses." She also found an article by a top oncologist that described her situation perfectly, leading to a promising new stem-cell transplant. "And here I am about to be cured," she e-mailed GJP project manager Terry Murray. "It is amazing that I have a second chance."

Grit is passionate perseverance of long-term goals, even in the face of frustration and failure. Married with a growth mindset, it is a potent force for personal progress.

When Anne Kilkenny first heard about the GJP, she realized she would be an unusual volunteer. "You want a housewife that hasn't been actively involved in anything geopolitical ever? Four decades removed from having had a real intellectual challenge?" she recalled thinking. "I'll give it a go."

Anne lives in a small town in Alaska. When she graduated from the University of California, Berkeley, in the hippie era, she wanted to be a high school teacher, so she applied to a teaching program but wasn't accepted. She worked as an administrative assistant, a bookkeeper, and a substitute teacher, became a ballroom dancer, sang in choirs, married a carpenter from Alaska, raised a son, and went to church. She ends all her e-mails with her personal motto: "Live simply. Love generously. Care deeply. Speak kindly. Leave the rest to God."

Anne had a brief brush with fame in 2008, when the Republican presidential candidate John McCain announced that his running mate would be the governor of Alaska, Sarah Palin. It was a startling choice. Few outside the state had ever heard of the former mayor of the small town of Wasilla. But Anne Kilkenny had. Wasilla is her hometown and Anne is one of those rare public-spirited citizens who attend town council meetings. So she wrote an e-mail summarizing what Palin had done as mayor and sent it to family and friends outside the state. They wanted to know more, so she added more detail and sent it out again. It went viral. Soon Anne had a reporter from the *New York Times* calling her, then *Newsweek*, the Associated Press, the *Boston Globe*, the *St. Petersburg Times*, and so many more. It was a frenzy.

Anne is a Democrat and her e-mail was largely critical of Palin, so much of the torrent of e-mail sent to her was highly partisan. "I knew it!" someone would write. "I knew Palin was totally ignorant of geopolitics as soon as I saw her face!" And there were bucket loads of praise for Anne; she was courageous, brilliant, fantastic in every way.

But Anne kept her head. Rather than revel in the adulation, she arched a skeptical eyebrow. "How could anybody know these things from a glimpse of the person?" she wrote me. "They couldn't and they didn't. They had their mind made up about [Palin] from the outset because of her partisan affiliation, because she was a woman, etc., and learning facts about her just gave them excuses for their prejudices. Feelings were masquerading as knowledge, as thoughts." That sort of critical, psychologically astute observation helps make a forecaster a superforecaster. So does careful, accurate research. And Anne's famous e-mail held up well when it was scrutinized by national fact-checking organizations—which is particularly impressive considering that Anne thought she was merely drafting a short note for friends and family.[16]

Anne's tenacity is daunting. When the tournament asked a question about refugee numbers in the Central Africa Republic, she went to the UN's website and saw the data were a week old. Rather than assume those were the most recent numbers available,

she e-mailed the agency and asked how often the data were updated
and when the next update could be expected. She also noticed their
data showed large fluctuations. Again, she queried the agency. She
got a response, but it was in French. "Merci," she wrote back, "mais
je ne parle pas français plus bien. S'il vous plait, en anglais?" Back
came a lengthy response, in English, explaining the agency's analytical methods, which was very revealing and a great help in making a forecast.

Anne isn't a superforecaster, at least not yet, but her results are
still impressive. She forecast all 150 questions in year 3, and she had
a pretty inert team, which meant she had to do almost all of the
work herself. Why did she do it? For the same reason a college student might take all the toughest courses with the hardest-grading
professors: she cared more about learning than getting top grades.
"I am always trying to grow, to learn, to change," she wrote me.[17]
We could see that attitude in her behavior as results started coming
in. She thought carefully about them and what they suggested about
how she makes decisions, and often shared thoughtful, introspective
e-mails with our project manager. She kept this up while her Brier
score improved and it looked like she might crack the top ranks.
And she kept at it when some of her high-confidence forecasts ended
badly and her accuracy plunged. Question after question, month
after month, she kept at it. That's grit. It's also why I wouldn't be at
all surprised to see her ultimately become a superforecaster.

Of course that would not be the end of Anne's growth, as the
superforecasters have shown, only the end of the beginning. There
is always more trying, more failing, more analyzing, more adjusting,
and trying again. Computer programmers have a wonderful term
for a program that is not intended to be released in a final version
but will instead be used, analyzed, and improved without end. It is
"perpetual beta."

Superforecasters are perpetual beta.

PULLING IT ALL TOGETHER

We have learned a lot about superforecasters, from their lives to their test scores to their work habits. Taking stock, we can now sketch a rough composite portrait of the modal superforecaster.

In philosophic outlook, they tend to be:

CAUTIOUS: Nothing is certain

HUMBLE: Reality is infinitely complex

NONDETERMINISTIC: What happens is not meant to be and does not have to happen

In their abilities and thinking styles, they tend to be:

ACTIVELY OPEN-MINDED: Beliefs are hypotheses to be tested, not treasures to be protected

INTELLIGENT AND KNOWLEDGEABLE, WITH A "NEED FOR COGNITION": Intellectually curious, enjoy puzzles and mental challenges

REFLECTIVE: Introspective and self-critical

NUMERATE: Comfortable with numbers

In their methods of forecasting they tend to be:

PRAGMATIC: Not wedded to any idea or agenda

ANALYTICAL: Capable of stepping back from the tip-of-your-nose perspective and considering other views

DRAGONFLY-EYED: Value diverse views and synthesize them into their own

PROBABILISTIC: Judge using many grades of maybe

THOUGHTFUL UPDATERS: When facts change, they change their minds

GOOD INTUITIVE PSYCHOLOGISTS: Aware of the value of
checking thinking for cognitive and emotional biases

In their work ethic, they tend to have:

A GROWTH MINDSET: Believe it's possible to get better
GRIT: Determined to keep at it however long it takes

I paint with a broad brush here. Not every attribute is equally
important. The strongest predictor of rising into the ranks of superforecasters is perpetual beta, the degree to which one is committed
to belief updating and self-improvement. It is roughly three times as
powerful a predictor as its closest rival, intelligence. To paraphrase
Thomas Edison, superforecasting appears to be roughly 75% perspi-
ration, 25% inspiration.

And not every superforecaster has every attribute. There are
many paths to success and many ways to compensate for a deficit in
one area with strength in another. The predictive power of perpetual
beta does suggest, though, that no matter how high one's IQ it is difficult to compensate for lack of dedication to the personal project of
"growing one's synapses."

All that said, there is another element that is missing entirely
from the sketch: other people. In our private lives and our work-
places, we seldom make judgments about the future entirely in iso-
lation. We are a social species. We decide together. This raises an
important question.

What happens when superforecasters work in groups?

9

Superteams

On the morning of January 10, 1961, as breakfast was being prepared across America, readers of the *New York Times* opened the newspaper on the kitchen table and read the front-page headline: U.S. Helps Train an Anti-Castro Force at Secret Guatemalan Air-Ground Base. A little inland from Guatemala's Pacific coast "commando-like forces are being drilled in guerrilla warfare tactics by foreign personnel, mostly from the United States." The trainees were identified as Cubans. American aircraft using the base were identified. The American company that built the base was named. "Guatemalan authorities from President Miguel Ydigoras Fuentes down insist that the military effort is designed to meet an assault, expected almost any day, from Cuba," the *Times* reported, but "opponents of the Ydigoras Administration have insisted that the preparations are for an offensive against the regime of Premier Fidel Castro and that they are being planned and directed, and to a great extent paid for, by the United States. The United States embassy is maintaining complete silence on the subject."

In truth, the CIA was training Cuban exiles to land in Cuba and launch a guerrilla war against the new government of Fidel Castro. Secrecy was critical. Once the guerrillas landed, they had to look like an independent force of patriots coming to liberate the nation. To ensure this, no American soldiers would land with the guerrillas, and air support would be provided by old bombers without American markings. No one would know that the United States engineered the whole thing. At least that was the plan.

One might suppose that in Washington, DC, among the planners of this secret mission, the exposure of the scheme on the front page of the *New York Times* would cause concern and reconsideration. There was indeed concern—but no reconsideration. "Somehow the idea took hold around the cabinet table that this would not much matter so long as United States soldiers did not take part in the actual fighting," Arthur M. Schlesinger Jr. recalled. As an adviser to the new president, John F. Kennedy, Schlesinger was part of the inner circle that authorized the mission, and his recollections were filled with amazement at the blunders they made in planning what became known as the Bay of Pigs invasion.[1]

When the CIA-trained guerrillas landed, the Cuban army was waiting and the fourteen hundred men onshore were quickly surrounded by twenty thousand soldiers. Within three days they were all dead or taken prisoner.

The problem was not one of execution. It was the plan. It was harebrained. And that's not hindsight bias. The whole sorry saga has been dissected, and there is rare consensus among historians, left and right, that the plan was riddled with problems that the White House should have spotted but did not. A particularly blatant example was the contingency plan. The CIA assured the president's advisers that if the landing failed the guerrillas could escape to the Escambray Mountains, where they would join other anti-Castro forces. But that idea came from the first version of the plan, which would have landed the guerrillas on the shore at the base of the mountains. The planners had switched the landing site—but didn't consider what that switch meant for the contingency plan. "I don't think we fully realized that the Escambray Mountains lay 80 miles from the Bay of Pigs, across a hopeless tangle of swamps and jungle," Schlesinger recalled.[2]

After the debacle, no one believed that the United States was not involved, and the consequences were immediate and severe. Traditional allies were embarrassed. Latin American nations were outraged. Anti-American protests erupted around the world. Liberals who had high hopes for the new Kennedy administration felt betrayed, while conservatives mocked the novice president's incompetence. Worst of all for the strategic interests of the United States, the Cuban government put itself more firmly inside the Soviet camp. Within eighteen months, an island off the coast of Florida was a base for five thousand Soviet soldiers and an array of Soviet intermediate-range nuclear missiles that could destroy Washington, DC, and New York City, and the two global superpowers were locked in a crisis that Kennedy estimated, in retrospect, had between a one-third and one-half chance of escalating into nuclear war.

The story of the Cuban missile crisis that followed from the Bay of Pigs fiasco is equally familiar, but the similarities end there. Over thirteen terrifying days in October 1962, the Kennedy administration considered a range of dangerous options to counter the Soviet threat—including outright invasion—before settling on a naval blockade. As Soviet ships approached the American red line, each side tried to figure out the other's intentions from its actions and back-channel communications. Finally an agreement was reached, war was averted, and the world exhaled.

If the Bay of Pigs was the Kennedy administration's nadir, the Cuban missile crisis was its zenith, a moment when Kennedy and his team creatively engineered a positive result under extreme pressure. Knowing this, we might assume Kennedy cleaned house after the Bay of Pigs and surrounded himself with far superior advisers in time for the missile crisis. But he didn't. The cast of characters in both dramas is mostly the same: the team that bungled the Bay of Pigs was the team that performed brilliantly during the Cuban missile crisis.

In his 1972 classic, *Victims of Groupthink*, the psychologist Irving Janis—one of my PhD advisers at Yale long ago—explored the decision making that went into both the Bay of Pigs invasion and the Cuban missile crisis. Today, everyone has heard of groupthink, although few have read the book that coined the term or know that Janis meant something more precise than the vague catchphrase groupthink has become today. In Janis's hypothesis, "members of any small cohesive group tend to maintain *esprit de corps* by unconsciously developing a number of shared illusions and related norms that interfere with critical thinking and reality testing."[3] Groups that get along too well don't question assumptions or confront uncomfortable facts. So everyone agrees, which is pleasant, and the fact that everyone agrees is tacitly taken to be proof the group is on the right track. We can't all be wrong, can we? So if a secret American plan to invade Cuba without apparent American involvement happens to be published on the front page of the *New York Times*, the plan can still go ahead—just make sure there are no American soldiers on the beach and deny American involvement. The world will believe it. And if that sounds implausible . . . well, not to worry, no one in the group has objected, which means everyone thinks it's perfectly reasonable, so it must be.

After the fiasco, Kennedy ordered an inquiry to figure out how his people could have botched it so badly. It identified cozy unanimity as the key problem and recommended changes to the decision-making process to ensure it could never develop again. Skepticism was the new watchword. Participants were to speak not only as specialists in their area of expertise but as generalists, with a license to question anything. Special counsel Theodore Sorensen and the president's brother Bobby were designated "intellectual watchdogs," whose job was to "pursue relentlessly every bone of contention in order to prevent errors arising from too superficial an analysis of the issues," Janis noted. "Accepting this role avidly, Robert Kennedy, at the expense of becoming unpopular with some of his associates, barked out sharp and sometimes rude questions. Often, he deliberately became the devil's advocate." Protocol and hierarchy would impede these freewheeling discussions, so they were set aside. New advisers were occasionally brought in to provide fresh perspectives. And John F. Kennedy would sometimes leave the room to let the group talk things through, knowing that there was less true give-and-take when the president was present. That last consideration was crucial. Kennedy started the crisis thinking that, at a minimum, he had to authorize preemptive air attacks on the Soviet missile launchers, but he kept that to himself so it wouldn't be the focus of the discussion. As a result, "by the end of the first day of meetings the committee had seriously discussed ten alternatives," and the president's thinking started to change. It was never easy. There were constant disagreements. The stress was brutal. But it was a process that led to a negotiated peace, not nuclear war.[4]

How the Kennedy White House changed its decision-making culture for the better is a must-read for students of management and public policy because it captures the dual-edged nature of working in groups. Teams can cause terrible mistakes. They can also sharpen judgment and accomplish together what cannot be done alone. Managers tend to focus on the negative or the positive but they need to see both. As mentioned earlier, the term "wisdom of crowds" comes from James Surowiecki's 2004 bestseller of the same name, but Surowiecki's title was itself a play on the title of a classic 1841 book, *Extraordinary Popular Delusions and the Madness of Crowds*, which chronicled a litany of collective folly. Groups can be wise, or mad, or both. What makes the difference isn't just who is in the group, Kennedy's circle of advisers demonstrated. The group is its own animal.

TO TEAM OR NOT TO TEAM?

In the IARPA tournament, our goal was accuracy. Would putting forecasters on teams help? We saw strong arguments for both yes and no. On the negative side, the research literature—as well as my

decades of experience on university committees—suggested that
teams might foster cognitive loafing. Why labor to master a complex
problem when others will do the heavy lifting? When this attitude
is widespread it can sink a team. Worse, forecasters can become too
friendly, letting groupthink set in. These two tendencies can re-
inforce each other. We all agree, so our work is done, right? And
unanimity within a group is a powerful force. If that agreement is
ill-founded, the group slips into self-righteous complacency.

But groups also let people share information and perspectives.
That's good. It helps make dragonfly eye work, and aggregation is
critical to accuracy. Of course aggregation can only do its magic
when people form judgments independently, like the fairgoers guessing the weight of the ox. The independence of judgments ensures that
errors are more or less random, so they cancel each other out. When
people gather and discuss in a group, independence of thought and
expression can be lost. Maybe one person is a loudmouth who domi-
nates the discussion, or a bully, or a superficially impressive talker, or
someone with credentials that cow others into line. In so many ways,
a group can get people to abandon independent judgment and buy
into errors. When that happens, the mistakes will pile up, not cancel
out. This is the root of collective folly, whether it's Dutch investors
in the seventeenth century, who became collectively convinced that a
tulip bulb was worth more than a laborer's annual salary, or American home buyers in 2005, talking themselves into believing that real
estate prices could only go up.

But loss of independence isn't inevitable in a group, as JFK's team
showed during the Cuban missile crisis. If forecasters can keep questioning themselves and their teammates, and welcome vigorous debate, the group can become more than the sum of its parts.

So would groups lift superforecasters up or drag them down?
Some of us suspected one outcome, others the opposite, but deep
down, we knew we were all guessing. Ultimately, we chose to build

teams into our research for two reasons. First, in the real world, people seldom make important forecasts without discussing them with others, so getting a better understanding of forecasting in the real world required a better understanding of forecasting in groups. The other reason? Curiosity. We didn't know the answer and we wanted to, so we took Archie Cochrane's advice and ran an experiment.

In year 1 (2011–12), before a single superforecaster had been tagged and classified, we randomly assigned several hundred forecasters to work alone and several hundred others to work together in teams. The team forecasters wouldn't meet face-to-face, of course, but we created online forums for discussion and team members could communicate by e-mail, Skype, or however else they wanted. They would still be scored as individuals, but individual scores would be pooled to create a team score. Forecasters would see how both they and their team were doing. Beyond that, forecasters could organize however they wished. The goal was accuracy. How they achieved it was up to them.

We also gave teams a primer on teamwork based on insights gleaned from research in group dynamics. On the one hand, we warned, groupthink is a danger. Be cooperative but not deferential. Consensus is not always good; disagreement not always bad. If you do happen to agree, don't take that agreement—in itself—as proof that you are right. Never stop doubting. Pointed questions are as essential to a team as vitamins are to a human body.

On the other hand, the opposite of groupthink—rancor and dysfunction—is also a danger. Team members must disagree without being disagreeable, we advised. Practice "constructive confrontation," to use the phrase of Andy Grove, the former CEO of Intel. Precision questioning is one way to do that. Drawing on the work of Dennis Matthies and Monica Worline, we showed them how to tactfully dissect the vague claims people often make. Suppose someone says, "Unfortunately, the popularity of soccer, the world's favorite pastime, is starting to decline." You suspect he is wrong. How do you question the claim? Don't even think of taking a personal shot like "You're silly." That only adds heat, not light. "I don't think so" only expresses disagreement without delving into why you disagree. "What do you mean?" lowers the emotional temperature with a question but it's much too vague. Zero in. You might say, "What do you mean by 'pastime'?" or "What evidence is there that soccer's popularity is declining? Over what time frame?" The answers to these precise questions won't settle the matter, but they will reveal the thinking behind the conclusion so it can be probed and tested.

Since Socrates, good teachers have practiced precision questioning, but still it's often not used when it's needed most. Imagine how events might have gone if the Kennedy team had engaged in precision questioning when planning the Bay of Pigs invasion:

"So what happens if they're attacked and the plan falls apart?"

"They retreat into the Escambray Mountains, where they can meet up with other anti-Castro forces and plan guerrilla operations."

"How far is it from the proposed landing site in the Bay of Pigs to the Escambray Mountains?"

"Eighty miles."

"And what's the terrain?"

"Mostly swamp and jungle."

"So the guerrillas have been attacked. The plan has fallen apart. They don't have helicopters or tanks. But they have to cross eighty miles of swamp and jungle before they can begin to look for shelter in the mountains? Is that correct?"

I suspect that this conversation would not have concluded "sounds good!"

Questioning like that didn't happen, so Kennedy's first major decision as president was a fiasco. The lesson was learned, resulting in the robust but respectful debates of the Cuban missile crisis—which exemplified the spirit we encouraged among our forecasters.

SUPERTEAMS

At the end of the year, the results were unequivocal: on average, teams were 23% more accurate than individuals.

When year 2 arrived, we all agreed teams should be an essential part of the research design. But we faced another choice. Having identified the top forecasters across experimental conditions, what should we do with these freshly anointed superforecasters? Should they be told of their status? Should they be put together in teams—and hope that superforecasters working with each other would produce superteams?

The risks were obvious. Tell someone they're exceptionally good at something and they may start taking their superiority for granted. Surround them with others who are similarly accomplished, tell them how special they are, and egos may swell even more. Rather than spur a superforecaster to take his game to the next level, it might make him so sure of himself that he is tempted to think his judgment must be right because it is his judgment. This is a familiar paradox: success can lead to acclaim that can undermine the habits of mind that produced the success. Such hubris often afflicts highly accomplished individuals. In business circles, it is called CEO disease.

Again we rolled the theoretical dice. We created teams of superforecasters, with a dozen people on each. We gave them more guidance about how high-performance teams function and created special forums to help them communicate online. The teams did not meet face-to-face, which had its own pluses and minuses. On the minus side, it's easier to disregard people we have never met. It could even foster conflict. Look at how quickly discussion on the Internet can degenerate into poisonous harangues. On the plus side, distance could make it easier to manage disputes and maintain a critical perspective.

Joining a team for the first time, superforecasters like Elaine

Rich had more immediate concerns. "I was pretty intimidated by my team," she told me. Elaine lives in Washington, DC, and works as a pharmacist at the Walter Reed Medical Center. Some of the people on her team "announced huge, impressive credentials," she recalled. "And I had no credentials." At first she stayed quiet, making forecasts but rarely venturing opinions. It wasn't only that her team-mates had credentials and confidence. She found it difficult to ques-tion the views of teammates who were, after all, strangers. People take things differently. What one person would consider a helpful inquiry another might take as an aggressive criticism. And some of the questions touched on issues many people feel passionately about, so talking about them felt like walking through a minefield. The Arafat-polonium discussion was the worst. "There was a lot of ten-sion around that," Elaine said. "It was almost a taboo question."

"There was a lot of what I'll call dancing around," recalled Marty Rosenthal of his first year on a team. People would disagree with someone's assessment, and want to test it, but they were too afraid of giving offense to just come out and say what they were thinking. So they would "couch it in all these careful words," circling around, hoping the point would be made without their having to make it.

Experience helped. Seeing this "dancing around," people realized that excessive politeness was hindering the critical examination of views, so they made special efforts to assure others that criticism was welcome. "Everybody has said, 'I want push-back from you if you see something I don't,'" said Rosenthal. That made a difference. So did offering thanks for constructive criticism. Gradually, the danc-ing around diminished.

Research on teams often assumes they have leaders and norms and focuses on ensuring these don't hinder performance. The usual solutions are those the Kennedy administration implemented after the Bay of Pigs invasion—bring in outsiders, suspend hierarchy, and keep the leader's views under wraps. There's also the "premortem," in which the team is told to assume a course of action has failed and to explain why—which makes team members feel safe to express doubts they may have about the leader's plan. But the superteams did not start with leaders and norms, which created other challenges.

Marty Rosenthal is semiretired now, but for decades he was a management consultant who specialized in building teams. Doing that with no organizational structure is a challenge, he knew, and doing that without meeting face-to-face is tougher still. Someone could step forward and start giving directions, but among strangers that can backfire. "I saw the gaps in how we were forming up as a team, wanted to address some of that, but also didn't want to be seen as, you know, taking over," he said. "And so a lot of what I did was what I think of as leading from behind. I just tried to lead by example." When Marty felt people weren't explaining their forecasts enough to get good discussions going, he explained his in greater detail and invited comments. He also organized a conference call to hash out workloads, with details handled by him—and most of the team signed up. "The feedback afterward was people loved it," Marty said. "I think people felt a little stronger commitment to the team coming out of that."

There were also two opportunities for superforecasters to meet teammates face-to-face, at the end of the second and third years, when GJP project manager Terry Murray hosted conferences at the Wharton School and the University of California, Berkeley. The official goal of the gatherings was to share knowledge: the researchers presented data and the superforecasters offered their views. The unofficial goal was to add a human dimension to the teams. Many superforecasters made the most of it. Marty lives less than a mile from the Berkeley campus so he invited his teammates—most came to the conference—to his house for a barbecue and beer. Modest as this and his other efforts were, Marty thinks they made a difference. "Definitely it's helped our ability to push back on each other and feel a commitment that we really need to step up and share information when we have it."[5]

That sense of belonging developed in Elaine Rich. She did well, boosting her confidence, and her sense of responsibility grew with it. "I felt that I had to be really careful that I was sharing, shouldering my part of the burden, rather than being a freeloader by reading what other people wrote," and not offering thoughts and research, "which is always a temptation."

Most teams have a nucleus of five or six members who do most of the work. Within that core, we might expect to see a division of labor that reduces the amount of effort any one person needs to invest in the task, at least if he or she approached forecasting as work, not play. But we saw the opposite on the best teams: workloads were divided, but as commitment grew, so did the amount of effort forecasters put into it. Being on the team was "tons more work," Elaine said. But she didn't mind. She found it far more stimulating than working by herself. "You could be supporting each other, or helping each other, or building on ideas," she said. "It was a rush."[6]

Committed superteams did some impressive digging. On a question about who would win the 2013 presidential election in Honduras, Paul Theron, a South African superforecaster—and an investment manager who hosts *Hot Stoxx* on CNBC Africa—located a political scientist who specializes in Honduran politics and was told, among other tidbits, that although polls showed a candidate named Castro with a slight lead, the polls were dodgy. Theron also found an analysis of Honduran politics on an obscure website and was so impressed by its thoroughness and the author's credentials that he e-mailed him and had an informative discussion. Paul changed his forecast, giving Castro's opponent Hernández the edge. Hernández won—and Paul's considerable effort paid off. And since Paul shared everything he learned with his teammates, they benefited too. "The team is so much more effective at gathering information than one person could ever be," Paul told me. "There is simply no way that any individual could cover as much ground as a good team does. Even if you had unlimited hours, it would be less fruitful, given different research styles. Each team member brings something different."[7]

The results speak for themselves. On average, when a forecaster did well enough in year 1 to become a superforecaster, and was put on a superforecaster team in year 2, that person became 50% more accurate. An analysis in year 3 got the same result. Given that these were collections of strangers tenuously connected in cyberspace, we found that result startling.

Even more surprising was how well superteams did against prediction markets.

Most economists would say markets are the most effective mechanism for collecting widely dispersed information and distilling it down to a single judgment. Markets do that with trading. If I think a stock is a good value at a certain price, I may offer to buy yours. If you agree with my judgment, you won't sell. If you think I'm wrong, you will. Of course, in reality, trades happen for other reasons—you and I may have different financial needs steering us in different directions—but in general markets create incentives for people to relentlessly second-guess each other. The aggregation of all those judgments—and the information they are based on—is expressed in the price. If many people agree with me that a stock is worth more than it's selling for, they will try to buy it. Increasing demand pushes the price up. In that way, all the individual judgments of the buyers, and all the information guiding those judgments, becomes "priced in."

None of this means markets are perfect, or such efficient aggregators of information that no mortal should ever be so foolish as to aspire to beat them. That's the strong version of what economists call the efficient market hypothesis (EMH), and it's hard to square with what we have learned from psychology and experience. Markets make mistakes. Sometimes they lose their collective minds. But even if markets are far less efficient than ardent proponents of the EMH suppose, it is still very hard to consistently beat markets, which is why so few can plausibly claim to have done it.

Prediction markets are simply markets that trade in predictions, meaning traders buy and sell contracts on specified outcomes—such as "Hillary Clinton will be elected president of the United States in 2016." When the election of 2016 is held, that contract is settled. If Clinton loses, the contract pays out nothing. If she wins, it pays out $1. If the contract is currently selling for 40 cents and I think Clinton has a 60% or 70% chance of winning, I should buy. If lots of traders agree with me, demand for the contract will be strong and the price will rise—until it reaches a level where more traders think it's about right and buying slackens. If a new event suggests Clinton will not win, there will be a rush to sell and the price will decline. By aggregating all these judgments, the contract price should, in theory, closely track the true probability of Hillary Clinton winning.

Prediction markets like the famous Iowa Electronic Markets have an impressive track record. And they have a theory, backed by a battalion of Nobel laureates, going for them. So who would win in a battle between superteams and prediction markets? Most economists would say it's no contest. Prediction markets would mop the floor with the superteams.

We put that proposition to the test by randomly assigning regular forecasters to one of three experimental conditions. Some worked alone. Others worked in teams. And some were traders in prediction markets run by companies such as Inkling and Lumenogic. Of course, after year 1—when the value of teams was resoundingly demonstrated—nobody expected forecasters working alone to compete at the level of teams or prediction markets, so we combined all their forecasts and calculated the unweighted average to get the "wisdom of the crowd." And of course we had one more competitor: superteams.

The results were clear-cut each year. Teams of ordinary forecasters beat the wisdom of the crowd by about 10%. Prediction markets beat ordinary teams by about 20%. And superteams beat prediction markets by 15% to 30%.

I can already hear the protests from my colleagues in finance that the only reason the superteams beat the prediction markets was that our markets lacked liquidity: real money wasn't at stake and we didn't have a critical mass of traders. They may be right. It is a testable idea, and one worth testing. It's also important to recognize that while superteams beat prediction markets, prediction markets did a pretty good job of forecasting complex global events.

How did superteams do so well? By avoiding the extremes of groupthink and Internet flame wars. And by fostering minicultures that encouraged people to challenge each other respectfully, admit ignorance, and request help. In key ways, superteams resembled the best surgical teams identified by Harvard's Amy Edmondson, in which the nurse doesn't hesitate to tell the surgeon he left a sponge behind the pancreas because she knows it is "psychologically safe" to correct higher-ups. Edmondson's best teams had a shared purpose. So did our superteams. One sign of that was linguistic: they said "our" more than "my."

A team like that should promote the sort of actively open-minded thinking that is so critical to accurate forecasting, as we saw in chapter 5. So just as we surveyed individuals to test their active open-mindedness (AOM), we surveyed teams to probe their attitudes toward the group and patterns of interaction within the group—that is, we tested the *team's* AOM. As expected, we found a correlation between a team's AOM and its accuracy. Little surprise there. But what makes a team more or less actively open-minded?

You might think it's the individuals on the team. Put high-AOM people in a team and you'll get a high-AOM team; put lower-AOM people in a team and you'll get a lower-AOM team. Not so, as it turns out. Teams were not merely the sum of their parts. How the group thinks collectively is an emergent property of the group itself, a property of communication patterns among group members, not just the thought processes inside each member.[8] A group of open-minded people who don't care about one another will be less than the sum of its open-minded parts. A group of opinionated people who engage one another in pursuit of the truth will be more than the sum of its opinionated parts.

All this brings us to the final feature of winning teams: the fostering of a culture of sharing. My Wharton colleague Adam Grant categorizes people as "givers," "matchers," and "takers." Givers are those who contribute more to others than they receive in return; matchers give as much as they get; takers give less than they take. Cynics might say that *giver* is a polite word for *chump*. After all, anyone inclined to freeload will happily take what they give and return nothing, leaving the giver worse off than if he weren't so generous. But Grant's research shows that the pro-social example of the giver can improve the behavior of others, which helps everyone, including the giver—which explains why Grant has found that givers tend to come out on top.

Marty Rosenthal is a giver. He wasn't indiscriminately generous with his time and effort. He was generous in a deliberate effort to change the behavior of others for the benefit of all. Although Marty didn't know Grant's work, when I described it to him, he said, "You got it." There are lots more givers on the superteams. Doug Lorch distributed programming tools, which got others thinking about creating and sharing their own. Tim Minto contributed an analysis that showed how to make valuable automatic tweaks to forecasts with the passage of time. All are givers. None is a chump. In fact, Doug Lorch's individual score was the best in year 2, while Tim Minto topped the chart in year 3. And each man's team won the team competition.[9]

But let's not take this too far. A busy executive might think "I want some of those" and imagine the recipe is straightforward: shop for top performers, marinate them in collaborative teams, strain out the groupthink, sprinkle in some givers, and wait for the smart decisions and money to start flowing. Sadly, it isn't that simple. Replicating this in an existing organization with real employees would be a challenge. Singling out people for "super" status may be divisive and transferring people into cross-functional teams can be disruptive. And there's no guarantee of results. There were eccentric exceptions to the tendencies outlined above, such as the few teams who were not mutually supportive but who nonetheless did well. One of the best superforecasters even refused to leave comments for his teammates, saying he didn't want to risk groupthink.

This is the messy world of psychological research. Solid conclusions take time and this work, particularly on superteams, is in its infancy. There are many questions we have only begun to explore.

One involves the provocative phrase "diversity trumps ability," coined by my colleague (and former competitor in the IARPA tournament) Scott Page.[10] As we have seen, the aggregation of different perspectives is a potent way to improve judgment, but the key word is *different*. Combining uniform perspectives only produces more of the same, while slight variation will produce slight improvement. It is the diversity of the perspectives that makes the magic work. Superteams were fairly diverse—because superforecasters are fairly diverse—but we didn't design them with that in mind. We put ability first. If Page is right, we might have gotten even better results if we had made diversity the key determinant of team membership and let ability take care of itself. Again, though, flag the false dichotomy. The choice is not ability or diversity; it is fine-tuning the mixes of ability and diversity and gauging which work best in which situations.

To appreciate this balancing act—and how promising it is— think back to President Obama asking each member of his team of advisers how likely it was that the unusually tall man in the mystery house in Pakistan was Osama bin Laden. The answers ranged from 30% to 95%, most well over 50%. Add them up and divide by the number of advisers and, from the sketchy reports available, it averages out to roughly 70%. That's the wisdom of the crowd. It's a hard-to-beat number that should have been given more respect than it got in that meeting. But could President Obama have done even better than that?

Our research suggests yes—depending on the diversity of his team. The more diverse his team, the greater the chance that some advisers will possess scraps of information that others don't. And since these scraps mostly point toward "it's bin Laden," if all the advisers were given all the scraps they don't have, they would individually raise their estimate. And that would boost the "wisdom of the crowd" figure—maybe to 80% or 85%.

That's the thinking behind the extremizing algorithm I mentioned in chapter 4. It works superbly, but its effectiveness depends on diversity.[11] A team with zero diversity—its members are clones and everyone knows everything that everyone else knows—should not be extremized at all. Of course no team matches that description. But some teams are good at sharing information and that reduces diversity somewhat. Superforecaster teams were like that, which is why extremizing didn't help them much. But regular forecasting teams weren't as good at sharing information. As a result, we got major gains when we extremized them. Indeed, extremizing gave regular forecaster teams a big enough boost to pass some superteams, and extremizing a large pool of regular forecasters produced, as we saw earlier, tournament-winning results.

These tools won't replace intelligence analysts or the officials who synthesize their conclusions. And they shouldn't. As far as I can see, there will always be a need for a chief executive to be surrounded by a smart team of advisers, as John F. Kennedy was during the Cuban missile crisis. But the tools are good enough that the remarkably inexpensive forecasts they generate should be on the desks of decision makers, including the president of the United States.

10

The Leader's Dilemma

Leaders must decide, and to do that they must make and use forecasts. The more accurate those forecasts are, the better, so the lessons of superforecasting should be of intense interest to them. But leaders must also act and achieve their goals. In a word, they must lead. And anyone who has led people may have doubts about how useful the lessons of superforecasting really are for leaders.

Ask people to list the qualities an effective leader must have, or consult the cottage industry devoted to leadership coaching, or examine rigorous research on the subject, and you will find near-universal agreement on three basic points. Confidence will be on everyone's list. Leaders must be reasonably confident, and instill confidence in those they lead, because nothing can be accomplished without the belief that it can be. Decisiveness is another essential attribute. Leaders can't ruminate endlessly. They need to size up the situation, make a decision, and move on. And leaders must deliver a vision—the goal that everyone strives together to achieve.

But look at the style of thinking that produces superforecasting and consider how it squares with what leaders must deliver. How can leaders be confident, and inspire confidence, if they see nothing as certain? How can they be decisive and avoid "analysis paralysis" if their thinking is so slow, complex, and self-critical? How can they act with relentless determination if they readily adjust their thinking in light of new information or even conclude they were wrong? And underlying superforecasting is a spirit of humility—a sense that the complexity of reality is staggering, our ability to comprehend limited, and mistakes inevitable. No one ever described Winston Churchill, Steve Jobs, or any other great leader as "humble." Well, maybe Gandhi. But try to name a second and a third.

And consider how the superteams operated. They were given guidance on how to form an effective team, but nothing was imposed. No hierarchy, no direction, no formal leadership. These little anarchist cells may work as forums for the endless consideration and reconsideration superforecasters like to engage in but they're hardly organizations that can pull together and get things done. That takes structure—and a leader in charge.

This looks like a serious dilemma. Leaders must be forecasters *and* leaders but it seems that what is required to succeed at one role may undermine the other.

Fortunately, the contradiction between being a superforecaster and a superleader is more apparent than real. In fact, the superforecaster model can help make good leaders superb and the organizations they lead smart, adaptable, and effective. The key is an approach to leadership and organization first articulated by a nineteenth-century Prussian general, perfected by the German army of World War II, made foundational doctrine by the modern American military, and deployed by many successful corporations today. You might even find it at your neighborhood Walmart.

MOLTKE'S LEGACY

"In war, everything is uncertain," wrote Helmuth von Moltke.[1] In the late nineteenth century, Moltke was famous the world over after he led Prussian forces to victory against Denmark in 1864, Austria in 1866, and France in 1871—victories that culminated in the unification of Germany. His writings on war—which were themselves influenced by the great theorist Carl von Clausewitz—profoundly shaped the German military that fought the two world wars. But Moltke was no Napoleon. He never saw himself as a visionary leader directing his army like chess pieces. His approach to leadership and organization was entirely different.

The Prussian military had long appreciated uncertainty—they had invented board games with dice to introduce the element of chance missing from games like chess—but "everything is uncertain" was for Moltke an axiom whose implications needed to be teased out. The most urgent is to never entirely trust your plan. "No plan of operations extends with certainty beyond the first encounter with the enemy's main strength," he wrote. That statement was refined and repeated over the decades and today soldiers know it as "no plan survives contact with the enemy." That's much snappier. But notice that Moltke's original was more nuanced, which is typical of his thinking. "It is impossible to lay down binding rules" that apply in all circumstances, he wrote. In war, "two cases never will be exactly the same." Improvisation is essential.[2]

Moltke trusted that his officers were up to the task. In addition to their military training, they received what we today would consider a liberal arts education with an emphasis on critical thinking. Even when the curriculum focused on purely military matters, students were expected to think hard. In other nations of that era—including the United States—instructors laid out problems, told students the right answer, and expected them to nod and memorize. In Germany's war academies, scenarios were laid out and students were invited to suggest solutions and discuss them collectively. Disagreement was not only permitted, it was expected, and even the instructor's views could be challenged because he "understood himself to be a comrade among others," noted the historian Jörg Muth. Even the views of generals were subject to scrutiny. "German junior officers were regularly asked for their opinions and they would criticize the outcome of a large maneuver with several divisions before the attending general had the floor."[3]

The acceptance of criticism went beyond the classroom, and under extraordinary circumstances more than criticism was tolerated. In 1758, when Prussia's King Frederick the Great battled Russian forces at Zorndorf, he sent a messenger to the youngest Prussian general, Friedrich Wilhelm von Seydlitz, who commanded a cavalry unit. "Attack," the messenger said. Seydlitz refused. He felt the time wasn't right and his forces would be wasted. The messenger left but later returned. Again he told Seydlitz the king wanted him to attack. Again Seydlitz refused. A third time the messenger returned and he warned Seydlitz that if he didn't attack immediately, the king would have his head. "Tell the King that after the battle my head is at his disposal," Seydlitz responded, "but meanwhile I will make use of it." Finally, when Seydlitz judged the time right, he attacked and turned the battle in Prussia's favor. Frederick the Great congratulated his general and let him keep his head. This story, and others like it, notes Muth, "were collective cultural knowledge within the Prussian officer corps, recounted and retold countless times in an abundance of variations during official lectures, in the officer's mess, or in the correspondence between comrades." The fundamental message: think. If necessary, discuss your orders. Even criticize them. And if you absolutely must—and you better have a good reason—disobey them.[4]

All this may sound like a recipe for a fractious organization that can't get anything done, but that danger was avoided by balancing those elements that promoted independent thinking against those that demanded action.

The time devoted to a decision was constrained by circumstances, so decision making could be leisurely and complex or—when bullets were flying—abrupt and simple. If this meant a decision wasn't as informed as it could be, that was fine. An imperfect decision made in time was better than a perfect one made too late. "Clarification of the enemy situation is an obvious necessity, but waiting for information in a tense situation is seldom the sign of strong leadership—more often of weakness," declared the command manual of the Wehrmacht (the German military) published in 1935 and in force throughout World War II. "The first criterion in war remains decisive action."[5]

The Wehrmacht also drew a sharp line between deliberation and implementation: once a decision has been made, the mindset changes. Forget uncertainty and complexity. Act! "If one wishes to attack, then one must do so with resoluteness. Half measures are out of place," Moltke wrote. Officers must conduct themselves with "calm and assurance" to "earn the trust of the soldier." There is no place for doubt. "Only strength and confidence carry the units with them and produce success." The wise officer knows the battlefield is shrouded in a "fog of uncertainty" but "at least one thing must be certain: one's own decision. One must adhere to it and not allow oneself to be dissuaded by the enemy's actions until this has become unavoidably necessary."[6]

So a leader must possess unwavering determination to overcome obstacles and accomplish his goals—while remaining open to the possibility that he may have to throw out the plan and try something else. That's a lot to ask of anyone, but the German military saw it as the essence of the leader's role. "Once a course of action has been initiated it must not be abandoned without overriding reason," the Wehrmacht manual stated. "In the changing situations of combat, however, inflexibly clinging to a course of action can lead to failure. The art of leadership consists of the timely recognition of circumstances and of the moment when a new decision is required."[7]

What ties all of this together—from "nothing is certain" to "unwavering determination"—is the command principle of *Auftragstaktik*. Usually translated today as "mission command," the basic idea is simple. "War cannot be conducted from the green table,"

Moltke wrote, using an expression that referred to top commanders at headquarters. "Frequent and rapid decisions can be shaped only on the spot according to estimates of local conditions."[8] Decision-making power must be pushed down the hierarchy so that those on the ground—the first to encounter surprises on the evolving battlefield—can respond quickly. Of course those on the ground don't see the bigger picture. If they made strategic decisions the army would lose coherence and become a collection of tiny units, each seeking its own ends. *Auftragstaktik* blended strategic coherence and decentralized decision making with a simple principle: commanders were to tell subordinates what their goal is but not how to achieve it.

Imagine a top-down, command-and-control military unit approaching a town. A captain is ordered to take the town. How? Approach from the southwest, skirt the factory on the outskirts, seize the canal bridge, then occupy the town hall. Why? Not his business. The captain's job is to salute and do as he is told. What if the situation in the town turns out to be different from what headquarters expects? That won't happen. But what if it does? There is no answer. The captain will be unsure of what to do other than asking headquarters for new orders. Worse, he and his men will be rattled. As Moltke observed, "It shakes the trust of subordinates and gives the units a feeling of uncertainty if things happen entirely differently from what orders from higher headquarters had presumed."[9]

In the Wehrmacht, by contrast, a captain would be told to take the town. How? That's up to him. Why? Because his superior has been ordered to prevent enemy reinforcements from reaching the region on the other side of the town and taking the town will sever a key road. Thanks to *Auftragstaktik*, the captain can devise a plan for capturing the town that takes into account the circumstances he encounters, not those headquarters expects him to encounter. And he can improvise. If he comes across a bridge on another road that HQ thought had been destroyed but wasn't, he will realize it could be used to move enemy reinforcements. So he should destroy it. No need to ask HQ. Act now.

Orders in the Wehrmacht were often short and simple—even when history hung in the balance. "Gentlemen, I demand that your divisions completely cross the German borders, completely cross the Belgian borders and completely cross the River Meuse," a senior officer told the commanders who would launch the great assault into Belgium and France on May 10, 1940. "I don't care how you do it, that's completely up to you."[10] And *Auftragstaktik* wasn't limited to senior officers, or even officers. Right down to junior officers, NCOs, and the lowliest private, soldiers were told what the commander wanted accomplished but were expected to use their judgment about how best to do that given what they were seeing. The battlefield "requires soldiers who can think and act independently, who can make calculated, decisive, and daring use of every situation, and who understand that victory depends on each individual," the command manual stated.[11]

This is the opposite of the image most people have of Germany's World War II military. The Wehrmacht served a Nazi regime that preached total obedience to the dictates of the führer, and everyone remembers the old newsreels of German soldiers marching in goose-stepping unison: They don't even look like individual men. They look like they have been assembled, like engine parts and a tank's armor plates, into a mindless, obedient, brutally efficient war machine. But what is often forgotten is that the Nazis did not create the Wehrmacht. They inherited it. And it could not have been more different from the unthinking machine we imagine—as the spectacular attack on the Belgian fortress of Eben Emael demonstrated.

In the early morning darkness of May 10, 1940, dozens of gliders flew silently toward Eben Emael, a massive, largely underground fortress that was the centerpiece in Belgium's extensive effort to ensure it would never again be used by Germany as the front gate to France.

Most of the gliders landed in fields. Soldiers scrambled out and attacked Belgian troops guarding bridges. Nine gliders landed on the roof of the fort. Soldiers rushed out and destroyed the heavy guns. Case Yellow—the invasion of Belgium and France—had begun. Eben Emael's defenders surrendered.

That's how the story is usually told. What's left out is that the Germans gave command of this critical operation to a young lieutenant, Rudolf Witzig, whose own glider had to make an emergency landing in Germany, 100 kilometers off target. Flying in radio silence to avoid alerting the Belgians, the other troops only discovered on landing that they had lost their commander and much of their force. Meanwhile, another glider that was to be part of the assault on the bridges had landed 60 kilometers from its target. At this point, the operation could easily have failed. But on top of Eben Emael, a sergeant took charge of the remaining troops and knocked out the Belgian guns. Then another glider swooped down and landed on the fort. Out hopped Rudolf Witzig, who had secured another plane and glider and gotten to Eben Emael only a little behind schedule. As for the other errant glider, the sergeant in charge commandeered two vehicles, drove into Belgium, and improvised a ground attack that netted 121 prisoners.[12]

"Great success requires boldness and daring, but good judgment must take precedence," the Wehrmacht manual stated. "The command of an army and its subordinate units requires leaders capable of judgment, with clear vision and foresight, and the ability to make independent and decisive decisions and carry them out unwaveringly and positively."[13] In our terms, it takes individuals who are both superforecasters and superleaders. Not all the Wehrmacht's officers were, of course, but enough were, particularly at the operational and tactical levels, that the German military was able to conquer most of Europe and hold on to it for years even though, throughout most of the war, it was heavily outnumbered and outgunned. "Despite the evil nature of the regime that it served," noted the historian James Corum, "it must be admitted that the Germany Army of World War II was, man for man, one of the most effective fighting forces ever seen."[14]

Ultimately, the Wehrmacht failed. In part, it was overwhelmed by its enemies' superior resources. But it also made blunders—often because its commander in chief, Adolf Hitler, took direct control of operations in violation of Helmuth von Moltke's principles, nowhere with more disastrous effect than during the invasion of Normandy. The Allies feared that after their troops landed, German tanks would drive them back to the beaches and into the sea, but Hitler had directed that the reserves could only move on his personal command. Hitler slept late. For hours after the Allies landed on the beaches, the dictator's aides refused to wake him to ask if he wanted to order the tanks into battle.

Ironically, a nineteenth-century German general was vindicated by the German defeat in Normandy—at the hands of Dwight Eisenhower, an American general of German descent who had a keener understanding of Moltke's philosophy than Germany's Supreme Commander.

I LIKE IKE

In contrast to authoritarian Germany's Wehrmacht, free and democratic America's army of the same era had little use for independent thinking.

Shortly after World War I, Eisenhower, then a junior officer who had some experience with the new weapons called tanks, published an article in the US Army's *Infantry Journal* making the modest argument that "the clumsy, awkward and snail-like progress of the old tanks must be forgotten, and in their place we must picture this speedy, reliable and efficient engine of destruction." Eisenhower was dressed down. "I was told my ideas were not only wrong but dangerous, and that henceforth I was to keep them to myself," he recalled. "Particularly, I was not to publish anything incompatible with solid infantry doctrine. If I did, I would be hauled before a court-martial."[15]

In the army, subordinates were to salute and obey superiors without question. Orders were long and detailed—"the orders for the American forces to land in North Africa were the size of a Sears Roebuck catalogue," Jörg Muth wrote—and left little room for individual initiative.[16] There were smart and creative American officers, but they valued individual initiative *despite* their training, not because of it. George Patton was one. "Never tell people how to do things," he wrote, succinctly capturing the spirit of *Auftragstaktik:* "Tell them what to do, and they will surprise you with their ingenuity."[17]

Patton's lifelong friend Dwight Eisenhower was another. Like Moltke, Eisenhower knew that nothing was certain. His first act after giving the irrevocable order to go ahead with the D-Day invasion was to write a note taking personal responsibility, which was to be released in the event of failure. Like Moltke, who was famously quiet, almost serene, Eisenhower understood that a cool and assured appearance could do more to spread confidence and boost morale than false claims of certainty. In private, Eisenhower could be a moody, brooding chain-smoker. With the troops, he always had a smile and a steady word.

Eisenhower also expected his officers to engage in open debate. He respected well-founded criticisms and readily acknowledged mistakes. In 1954, when Eisenhower was president, the army chief of staff, Matthew Ridgway, advised against intervening in Vietnam, saying it would take a massive effort of more than half a million soldiers. Eisenhower respected Ridgway's judgment because in 1943 Ridgeway had resisted Eisenhower's order to drop an airborne division on Rome and Eisenhower later decided Ridgeway had been right.[18]

After World War II, the US military was slow to learn the lessons of the Wehrmacht. It was the new Israeli military that appreciated the value of individual initiative. "Plans are merely a platform for change" was a popular Israeli Defense Forces slogan of the era. An Israeli officer commenting on the performance of a division in the 1956 war with Egypt proudly noted that "almost all the plans were foiled during the fighting but all objectives were attained in full— and faster than expected." The Israeli system wasn't explicitly patterned on any foreign model, however, "if only because the German *Auftragstaktik* could never be acknowledged."[19]

The time for *Auftragstaktik* finally came in the early 1980s. Tensions were mounting and the Soviets had a huge numerical lead in men and tanks, forcing NATO to do more with less. Generals in the United States combed through the writings of historians and theorists and scrutinized Israeli experience. Some even consulted old Wehrmacht generals. In 1982 "mission command" became part of official American doctrine.

Whether the army is as decentralized as it should be is debatable, but the initiative of on-site commanders has indisputably produced some big successes in the modern era. During the 2003 invasion of Iraq, as Iraqi forces crumbled in the open desert and American forces approached Baghdad, and there were fears that grinding urban warfare would follow, a raid later dubbed "thunder run" sent a heavily armored column racing along main roads to the newly captured airport. Iraqi forces were caught completely off guard and the column got through with the loss of only one vehicle. Two days later, an entire brigade conducted a thunder run along the same route, but with a turn into the main government district—which it seized and held, ensuring the rapid collapse of Iraqi defenses. Key to the victory was the empowerment of ground commanders, who made the critical decisions—including the gutsy call to stay in the government district despite running low on ammunition.

The insurgency that blossomed after the fall of Baghdad was not forecast by the military leadership, and for months, even years, they had little idea how to respond. Local commanders struggled to deal with it as best they could. In the northern Iraqi city of Mosul, General David Petraeus, commander of the 101st Airborne, drew on his extensive knowledge of military history to improvise strategies he hoped would "secure and serve" the people of the city and thereby deny the insurgents popular support. It was all on his own initiative. "Petraeus informed his superiors in Baghdad what he was up to," wrote the journalist Fred Kaplan, "but he never asked permission and certainly didn't await instructions, knowing there wouldn't be any."[20] Petraeus's efforts paid off. The insurgency that became a firestorm elsewhere was starved of oxygen in Mosul as long as he was in command.

In 2007, when the insurgency was consuming the country and seemed unbeatable to many, Petraeus was given overall command in Iraq. He brought in like-minded officers, "flexible commanders able to think independently," and the counterinsurgency strategies he tested in Mosul were implemented vigorously throughout the country.[21] Violence plummeted. It's never clear how much credit any one person deserves, but most observers agree that Petraeus deserves some, and perhaps a lot.

I talked to David Petraeus about his philosophy of leadership and it was easy to hear echoes of Moltke. He even invoked the mantras "no plan survives contact with the enemy" and "nothing is certain." But it's easy to spout platitudes, Petraeus noted. What matters, he said, is "beyond the bumper sticker, what do you do to prepare for that?"

To develop flexible thinking, Petraeus pushes people out of their "intellectual comfort zone." When he was a brigade commander in the 82nd Airborne Division, Petraeus was unhappy with live-fire training exercises that were so choreographed nothing surprising ever happened. "You basically handed the company commander almost a script," he said, and "the company commander walks a hundred meters and crosses a particular road and he knows this is where he's supposed to call for this particular type of indirect fire or employ attack helicopters or what have you." In reality, commanders run into surprises and have to improvise. So why the script? Safety. This training uses real weapons and explosives. According to Petraeus, it was a huge challenge to develop exercises that were reasonably safe but also forced officers to deal with surprises. But they figured it out because "that's how you develop flexible leaders who can deal with uncertainty."

Petraeus also supports sending officers to top universities for graduate education, not to acquire a body of knowledge, although that is a secondary benefit, but to encounter surprises of another kind. "It teaches you that there are seriously bright people out in the world who have very different basic assumptions about a variety of different topics and therefore arrive at conclusions on issues that are very, very different from one's own and very different from mainstream kind of thinking, particularly in uniform," Petraeus said. Like encountering shocks on a battlefield, grappling with other ways of thinking trains officers to be mentally flexible. Petraeus speaks from experience. Thirteen years after graduating from West Point, he earned a PhD in international relations from Princeton University, an experience he calls "invaluable."

Petraeus's insistence on intellectual flexibility—"the most powerful tool any soldier carries is not his weapon but his mind," he says—is still controversial in the army. "Hamlet thinks too much," wrote Ralph Peters, a retired colonel, in a 2007 magazine article that ran alongside a piece by Petraeus in support of sending officers to universities. "Chewing every side of the argument to mush, he lacks the courage to swallow hard and kill an assassin at prayer—a philosophical 'war crime.' The archetypal academic, theory-poisoned and indecisive, Hamlet should have stayed at the university in Witten-berg, where his ability to prattle without resolution surely would have gained him tenure." What the military needs are doers, not thinkers, wrote Peters—Henry V, not Hamlet. "King Harry could make a decision."[22]

But Petraeus sees the divide between doers and thinkers as a false dichotomy. Leaders must be both. "The bold move is the right move except when it's the wrong move," he says. A leader "needs to figure out what's the right move and then execute it boldly."[23] That's the tension between deliberation and implementation that Moltke em-phasized and Petraeus balanced in Iraq.

How skillfully leaders perform this balancing act determines how successfully their organizations can cultivate superteams that can replicate the balancing act down the chain of command. And this is not something that one isolated leader can do on his own. It requires a wider willingness to hear unwelcome words from others—and the creation of a culture in which people feel comfortable speak-ing such words. What was done to the young Dwight Eisenhower was a serious mistake, Petraeus says. "You have to preserve and pro-mote the out-of-the-box thinkers, the iconoclasts."[24]

AUFTRAGSTAKTIK IN BUSINESS

Armies are unusual organizations, but bosses everywhere feel the tension between control and innovation, which is why Moltke's spirit can be found in organizations that have nothing to do with bullets and bombs.

"We let our people know what we want them to accomplish. But—and it is a very big 'but'—we do not tell them how to achieve those goals."[25] That is a near-perfect summary of "mission com-mand." The speaker is William Coyne, who was senior vice president of research and development at 3M, the famously innovative manufacturing conglomerate.

"Have backbone; disagree and commit" is one of Jeff Bezos's fourteen leadership principles drilled into every new employee at Amazon. It continues: "Leaders are obligated to respectfully challenge decisions when they disagree, even when doing so is uncomfortable or exhausting. Leaders have conviction and are tenacious. They do not compromise for the sake of social cohesion. Once a decision is determined, they commit wholly."[26] The language is a little blunt for Moltke, but it wouldn't look out of place in the Wehrmacht command manual or in my conversation with David Petraeus.

When Walmart found it was building stores faster than it could develop store managers, it created a "leadership academy" to get prospects ready for promotion sooner. The academy was designed by the British consulting firm McKinney Rogers, which is headed by Damian McKinney, a former British Royal Marine. It is modeled after military academies, with the "mission command" philosophy at its foundation.[27]

And McKinney is far from alone in bringing his military experience to the corporate world. Many former officers, including David Petraeus, have followed the same path. They often encounter the perception that militaries are strictly hierarchical organizations in which subordinates snap salutes to superiors and mechanically obey. That image is laughably out of date. In fact, ex–military officers advising corporations often find themselves telling executives to worry less about status and more about empowering their people and teams to choose the best ways to achieve shared goals. "Ironically," Damian McKinney told the *Financial Times*, "companies are much more focused on what I call 'command and control' than their military counterparts."[28]

A PECULIAR TYPE OF HUMILITY

But there's still the vexing question of humility.

No one ever called Winston Churchill or Steve Jobs humble. Same with David Petraeus. From West Point cadet onward, Petraeus believed he had the right stuff to become a top general.

The same self-assurance can be seen in many of the leaders and thinkers whose judgment I have singled out in this book: Helmuth von Moltke, Sherman Kent, even Archie Cochrane, who had the chutzpah to call out the most eminent authorities. John Maynard Keynes always thought he was the smartest man in the room. And George Soros was a Wall Street hedge fund manager who worked under extreme pressure at a pace that would drive many to nervous exhaustion with stakes that would make many executives go weak in the knees. Soros's most famous bet, shorting the British pound in 1992, which earned him an estimated $1.1 billion, required him to sell sterling worth almost $10 billion. "There is nothing like danger to focus the mind," Soros once said. That does not sound like someone who worries that he's not up to the job.

Even Dwight Eisenhower, the plainspoken man from Abilene, Kansas, had a substantial ego. After World War II, Eisenhower was immensely popular and both parties all but begged him to accept their nominations for the presidency. President Truman even offered to step aside for him. Eisenhower always refused. He sincerely did not want the job. But as the race for the 1952 election shaped up, it became clear that the Republican nomination, and likely the presidency, would be won by an isolationist who promised to bring all American troops home to "the Gibraltar of freedom." Eisenhower thought this would be a catastrophe that he—and he alone—could stop. "He wanted what was best for his country," one biographer wrote, "and in the end he decided that he was the best and would have to serve."[29] Clearly, he had no shortage of self-regard.

So how do we square all that with the apparently critical need for a forecaster to be humble? The answer lies in something Annie Duke told me.

We met Duke earlier. She believes she is one of the world's best poker players, which is no small claim, but she has a long record of accomplishments—including a World Series of Poker championship—that suggest her confidence is reasonable. But Duke also knows there is danger in confidence. When making a decision, a smart person like Duke is always tempted by a simple cognitive shortcut: "I know the answer. I don't need to think long and hard about it. I am a very successful person with good judgment. The fact that *I* believe my judgment is correct proves it is." Make decisions like that and you are only looking at reality from the tip of your nose. That's a dangerous way to make decisions, no matter who you are. To avoid this trap, Duke carefully distinguishes what she is confident about—and what she's not.

"You have to have tremendous humility in the face of the game because the game is extremely complex, you won't solve it, it's not like tic-tac-toe or checkers," she says. "It's very hard to master and if you're not learning all the time, you will fail. That being said, humility in the face of the game is extremely different than humility in the face of your opponents." Duke feels confident that she can compete with most people she sits down with at a poker table. "But that doesn't mean I think I've mastered this game."[30]

The humility required for good judgment is not self-doubt—the sense that you are untalented, unintelligent, or unworthy. It is *intellectual* humility. It is a recognition that reality is profoundly complex, that seeing things clearly is a constant struggle, when it can be done at all, and that human judgment must therefore be riddled with mistakes. This is true for fools and geniuses alike. So it's quite possible to think highly of yourself and be intellectually humble. In fact, this combination can be wonderfully fruitful. Intellectual humility compels the careful reflection necessary for good judgment; confidence in one's abilities inspires determined action.

"With firmness in the right, as God gives us to see the right, let us strive on to finish the work we are in," Abraham Lincoln declared in his second inaugural address. It's a statement of fierce conviction and determination. But it is also a humble acknowledgment—"as God gives us to see the right"—that our vision is limited, our judgment flawed, and even firmest belief may be wrong.

POSTSCRIPT

There is a dangling question: Did I have to choose the Wehrmacht? Other organizations illustrate how thinking like a superforecaster can improve leader performance. So why make the point with an army that served the evilest cause in modern history?

Understanding what worked in the Wehrmacht requires engaging in the toughest of all forms of perspective taking: acknowledging that something we despise possesses impressive qualities. Forecasters who can't cope with the dissonance risk making the most serious possible forecasting error in a conflict: underestimating your opponent.

There is no divinely mandated link between morality and competence. If the Puritan poet John Milton could portray Satan as both evil and resourceful in *Paradise Lost,* is it too much to acknowledge the same could be true of the Wehrmacht? Forecasters who see illusory correlations and assume that moral and cognitive weakness run together will fail when we need them most. We don't want intelligence analysts to assume jihadist groups must be inept or that vicious regimes can't be creatively vicious.

Coping with dissonance is hard. "The test of a first-rate intelligence is the ability to hold two opposed ideas in mind at the same time and still retain the ability to function," F. Scott Fitzgerald observed in "The Crack-Up." It requires teasing apart our feelings about the Nazi regime from our factual judgments about the Wehrmacht's organizational resilience—and to see the Wehrmacht as both a horrific organization that deserved to be destroyed *and* an effective organization with lessons to teach us. There is no logical contradiction, just a psycho-logical tension. If you want to become a superforecaster, you must overcome it.

It's a challenge. Even superforecasters who excel at aggressive self-criticism sometimes conflate facts and values. Early in the Syrian civil war, Doug Lorch flubbed a question on whether the rebels would take the city of Aleppo. When he considered why, he realized he had let his loathing of the Assad regime lead him to the wishful conclusion that the rebels would win, despite evidence they were outgunned. Joshua Frankel floundered forecasting whether North Korea would detonate a nuclear weapon because he "was influenced by optimism and hope for progress," he recalled. He didn't sense it at the time. But "a couple of weeks before the closing date a conversation with a good friend, who happens to have family members who escaped from North Korea at the time of the Korean War, made me realize this" and he flipped his forecast.[31]

So why use the Wehrmacht as an illustration even though it makes us squirm? Precisely because it makes us squirm.

11

Are They Really So Super?

For as long as I have been running forecasting tournaments—from Ronald Reagan and Red Army parades to today—I have been talking with Daniel Kahneman about my work. For that, I have been supremely fortunate. Kahneman is the accidental Nobelist, the cognitive psychologist who had no training in economics but whose work shook the foundations of the field. He is also a superb conversationalist who moves fluidly between casual banter and incisive dissection of casual banter. Talking to Kahneman can be a Socratic experience: energizing as long as you don't hunker down into a defensive crouch. So in the summer of 2014, when it was clear that superforecasters were not merely superlucky, Kahneman cut to the chase: "Do you see them as different kinds of people, or as people who do different kinds of things?"

My answer was, "A bit of both." They score higher than average on measures of intelligence and open-mindedness, although they are not off the charts. What makes them so good is less what they are than what they do—the hard work of research, the careful thought and self-criticism, the gathering and synthesizing of other perspectives, the granular judgments and relentless updating.

But how long can they sustain it? As we saw, people can, in principle, use conscious System 2 reflection to catch mistakes arising from a rapid, unconscious System 1 operations. Superforecasters put enormous effort into doing just that. But the continuous self-scrutiny is exhausting, and the *feeling* of knowing is seductive. Surely even the best of us will inevitably slip back into easier, intuitive modes of thinking.

Consider a 2014 interview with General Michael Flynn, who summed up his view of the world shortly before retiring as head of the Defense Intelligence Agency (DIA), the Pentagon's equivalent of the CIA with seventeen thousand employees. "I come into this office every morning, and other than a short jog to clear my head, I spend two to three hours reading intelligence reports," he said. "I will frankly tell you that what I see each day is the most uncertain, chaotic, and confused international environment that I've witnessed in my entire career. There were probably more dangerous times such as when the Nazis and [Japanese] imperialists were trying to dominate the world, but we're in another very dangerous era. . . . I think we're in a period of prolonged societal conflict that is pretty unprecedented."[1]

Much of what Flynn said is too vague to be judged, but his final line isn't. In the context of the interview—the reporter had mentioned conflicts in Ukraine, Korea, and the Middle East—that statement makes it clear that Flynn believes "societal conflict" is at a "pretty unprecedented" level. That is an empirical claim that can be checked by reviewing the many reports that have quantified global violence since World War II. And what they all show, broadly, is that interstate wars have been declining since the 1950s and civil wars have been declining since the end of the Cold War in the early 1990s. This is reflected in the number of battle deaths per year, which, with a few blips, declined throughout the period.[2]

You don't have to be the head of the DIA to find those reports. Googling "global conflict trends" will suffice. But Flynn saw no need to do so before drawing his sweeping conclusion and sharing it. Why not? The same reason Peggy Noonan saw no need to consult the data on other former presidents' approval ratings when she judged the meaning of President Bush's rising appeal. At work in each case was Kahneman's WYSIATI—What You See Is All There Is—the mother of all cognitive illusions, the egocentric worldview that prevents us from seeing any world beyond the one visible from the tips of our noses. Flynn saw mountains of bad news on his desk every day, and his conclusion felt right—so That Was All There Was. As a lifelong intelligence officer, Flynn knew the importance of checking assumptions, no matter how true they feel, but he didn't because it didn't feel like an assumption. It felt true. It's the oldest trick in the psychological book and Flynn fell for it.

I am not belittling Michael Flynn. Quite the opposite: the fact that a man so accomplished made so obvious an error is precisely what makes the error notable. We are *all* vulnerable. And there's no way to make ourselves bulletproof, as the famous Müller-Lyer optical illusion illustrates:

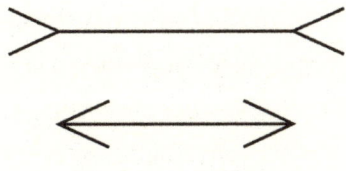

Müller-Lyer illusion

The top horizontal line looks longer than the line below it, but it's not. If you are unsure, take out a ruler and measure. Once you are fully satisfied that the lines are identical, look again, but now try to see the lengths of the two lines accurately. No luck? You know the lines are the same. You want to see them that way. But you can't. Not even *knowing* it's an illusion can switch off the illusion. The cognitive illusions that the tip-of-your-nose perspective sometimes generates are similarly impossible to stop. We can't switch off the tip-of-our-nose perspective. We can only monitor the answers that bubble up into consciousness—and, when we have the time and cognitive capacity, use a ruler to check.

Viewed in this light, superforecasters are always just a System 2 slipup away from a blown forecast and a nasty tumble down the rankings. Kahneman and I agree about that. But I am more optimistic that smart, dedicated people can inoculate themselves to some degree against certain cognitive illusions. That may sound like a tempest in an academic teapot, but it has real-world implications. If I am right, organizations will have more to gain from recruiting and training talented people to resist biases.

Although Kahneman officially retired long ago, he still practices adversarial collaboration, his commitment as a scientist to finding common ground with those who hold different views. So just as Kahneman worked with Gary Klein to resolve their disputes about expert intuition, he worked with Barbara Mellers, to explore the capacity of superforecasters to resist a bias of particularly deep relevance to forecasting: scope insensitivity.

Kahneman first documented scope insensitivity thirty years ago when he asked a randomly selected group in Toronto, the capital city of Ontario, how much they would be willing to pay to clean up the lakes in a small region of the province. On average, people said about $10.[3] Kahneman asked another randomly selected group how much they would be willing to pay to clean up every one of the 250,000 lakes in Ontario. They too said about $10. Later research got similar results. One study informed people that each year 2,000 migratory birds drown in oil ponds. How much would you be willing to pay to stop that? Other subjects were told 20,000 birds died each year. A third group was told it was 200,000 birds. And yet in each case, the average amount people said they would be willing to pay was around $80. What people were responding to, Kahneman later wrote, was the prototypical image that came to them—a polluted lake or a drowning, oil-soaked duck. "The prototype automatically evokes an affective response, and the intensity of that emotion is then mapped onto the dollar scale." It's classic bait and switch. Instead of answering the question asked—a difficult one that requires putting a money value on things we never monetize—people answered "How bad does this make me feel?" Whether the question is about 2,000 or 200,000 dying ducks, the answer is roughly the same: bad. Scope recedes into the background—and out of sight, out of mind.

What do polluted lakes have to do with the Syrian civil war or any of the other geopolitical problems posed in the IARPA tournament? If you are as creative as Daniel Kahneman, the answer is "a lot."

Flash back to early 2012. How likely is the Assad regime to fall? Arguments against a fall include (1) the regime has well-armed core supporters; (2) it has powerful regional allies. Arguments in favor of a fall include (1) the Syrian army is suffering massive defections; (2) the rebels have some momentum, with fighting reaching the capital. Suppose you weight the strength of these arguments, they feel roughly equal, and you settle on a probability of roughly 50%.

But notice what's missing? The time frame. It obviously matters. To use an extreme illustration, the probability of the regime falling in the next twenty-four hours must be less—likely a lot less—than the probability that it will fall in the next twenty-four months. To put this in Kahneman's terms, the time frame is the "scope" of the forecast.

So we asked one randomly selected group of superforecasters, "How likely is it that the Assad regime will fall in the next three months?" Another group was asked how likely it was in the next six months. We did the same experiment with regular forecasters.

Kahneman predicted widespread "scope insensitivity." Unconsciously, they would do a bait and switch, ducking the hard question that requires calibrating the probability to the time frame and tackling the easier question about the relative weight of the arguments for and against the regime's downfall. The time frame would make no difference to the final answers, just as it made no difference whether 2,000, 20,000, or 200,000 migratory birds died. Mellers ran several studies and found that, exactly as Kahneman expected, the vast majority of forecasters were scope insensitive. Regular forecasters said there was a 40% chance Assad's regime would fall over three months and a 41% chance it would fall over six months.

But the superforecasters did much better: They put the probability of Assad's fall at 15% over three months and 24% over six months. That's not perfect scope sensitivity (a tricky thing to define), but it was good enough to surprise Kahneman. If we bear in mind that no one was asked both the three- and six-month version of the question, that's quite an accomplishment. It suggests that the superforecasters not only paid attention to the time frame in the question but also thought about other possible time frames—and thereby shook off a hard-to-shake bias.

I wish I could take credit for that. Our advanced training guidelines urge forecasters to mentally tinker with "the question asked" and explore how their answers to a timing question might change if the cutoff date were six months out instead of twelve, or if the target price for oil were 10% lower, or some other relevant variation. Running such "thought experiments" inside your head is a good way to stress-test the adequacy of your mental model of the problem and ensure you are scope sensitive. But the truth is superforecasters were talking about problems of scope insensitivity—although they didn't use that term—before we started to study it, and their thinking helped inform our training guidelines as much as our training guidelines informed their thinking.

My sense is that some superforecasters are so well practiced in System 2 corrections—such as stepping back to take the outside view—that these techniques have become habitual. In effect, they are now part of their System 1. That may sound bizarre but it's not an unusual process. Any golfer can recall the first time she stood at a tee and was told to bend at the knees, tilt her head just so, raise one shoulder, drop the other, lift the elbow . . . It was awkward and required self-conscious monitoring. The second time she set up at the tee, she had to laboriously work through this mental checklist ("bend at knees, tilt head, raise shoulder . . .") and even with great mental effort she still forgot something and had to be corrected. The third time was the same. But slowly, it got easier. A golfer who keeps at it will eventually bury those instructions in System 1 and do it all gracefully. No matter how physically or cognitively demanding a task may be—cooking, sailing, surgery, operatic singing, flying fighter jets—deliberative practice can make it second nature. Ever watch a child struggling to sound out words and grasp the meaning of a sentence? That was you once. Fortunately, reading this sentence isn't nearly so demanding for you now.

So how long can superforecasters defy the laws of psychological gravity? The answer to that depends on how heavy their cognitive loads are. Turning a self-conscious System 2 correction into an unconscious System 1 operation may lighten the load considerably. So may the software tools some superforecasters have developed—like Doug Lorch's new-source selection program designed to correct the System 1 bias in favor of the like-minded.

But still, superforecasting remains hard work. Those who do it well appreciate the fragility of their success. They expect to stumble. And when they do, they will get up, try to draw the right lessons, and keep forecasting.

But another friend and colleague is not as impressed by the superforecasters as I am. Indeed, he suspects this whole research program is misguided.

ENTER THE BLACK SWAN

Nassim Taleb is a former Wall Street trader whose thinking about uncertainty and probability has produced three enormously influential books and turned "black swan" into a common English phrase.

For those unfamiliar with the concept, imagine you are a European living four centuries ago. You have seen many swans in your life to date. All were white. If you were asked to envision all the possible swans you might ever encounter, you would probably imagine lots and lots of swans that vary in size and shape, but all would be white, because your experience has taught you all swans are white. But then a ship returns from Australia. On board is a swan—a *black* swan. You are stunned. The "black swan" is therefore a brilliant metaphor for an event so far outside experience we can't even imagine it until it happens.

But Taleb isn't interested only in surprise. A black swan must be impactful. Indeed, Taleb insists that black swans, and black swans alone, determine the course of history. "History and societies do not crawl," he wrote. "They make jumps."[4] The implication for my efforts to improve foresight are devastating: IARPA has commissioned a fool's errand. What matters can't be forecast and what can be forecast doesn't matter. Believing otherwise lulls us into a false sense of security. In this view, I have taken a scientific step backward. In my EPJ research, I got it roughly right with the punch line about experts and the dart-throwing chimp. But my Good Judgment Project is premised on misconceptions, panders to desperation, and fosters foolish complacency.

I respect Taleb. He and I have even cowritten a paper on a key area where we agree. I think his critique makes deep points that future tournaments will have to struggle to address. But I see another false dichotomy rearing its head: "forecasting is feasible if you follow my formula" versus "forecasting is bunk."

Dispelling the dichotomy requires putting the beguiling black swan metaphor under the analytic microscope. What exactly *is* a black swan? The stringent definition is something literally inconceivable before it happens. Taleb has implied as much on occasion. If so, many events dubbed black swans are actually gray.

Consider the 9/11 terrorist attacks, the prototypic black swan in which one dazzling sunny morning in September, a bolt from the blue changed history. But 9/11 was not unimaginable. In 1994 a plot to hijack a jet and crash it into the Eiffel Tower was broken up. In 1998 the US Federal Aviation Administration examined a scenario in which terrorists hijacked FedEx cargo planes and crashed them into the World Trade Center. The danger was so well known in security circles that in August 2001, a government official asked Louise Richardson, a Harvard terrorism expert, why no terrorist group had ever used an airplane as a flying bomb. "My answer was far from helpful," she later wrote. "I said that the tactic was very much under consideration and I suspected that some terrorist groups would use it sooner rather than later."[5]

Other events that have been called black swans—such as the outbreak of World War I, which was preceded by more than a decade of fretting about the danger of war among the great powers—also fail the unimaginability test. If black swans must be inconceivable before they happen, a rare species of event suddenly becomes a lot rarer.

But Taleb also offers a more modest definition of a black swan as a "highly improbable consequential event."[6] These are not hard to find in history. And as Taleb and I explored in our joint paper, this is where the truth in his critique can be found.

If forecasters make hundreds of forecasts that look out only a few months, we will soon have enough data to judge how well calibrated they are. But by definition, "highly improbable" events almost never happen. If we take "highly improbable" to mean a 1% or 0.1% or 0.0001% chance of an event, it may take decades or centuries or millennia to pile up enough data. And if these events have to be not only highly improbable but also impactful, the difficulty multiplies. So the first-generation IARPA tournament tells us nothing about how good superforecasters are at spotting gray or black swans. They may be as clueless as anyone else—or astonishingly adept. We don't know, and shouldn't fool ourselves that we do.

Now if you believe that only black swans matter in the long run, the Good Judgment Project should only interest short-term thinkers. But history is not just about black swans. Look at the inch-worm advance in life expectancy. Or consider that an average of 1% annual global economic growth in the nineteenth century and 2% in the twentieth turned the squalor of the eighteenth century and all the centuries that preceded it into the unprecedented wealth of the twenty-first.[7] History does sometimes jump. But it also crawls, and slow, incremental change can be profoundly important.

A useful analogy lies in the world of investing. Vinod Khosla is the cofounder of Sun Microsystems and a Silicon Valley venture capitalist. He is also a big fan of Nassim Taleb. Investing in the notoriously volatile world of technology, Khosla has watched countless forecasts fail and he knows he can't specify the next big thing with exactitude. So he spreads his investments around, expecting most to fail, but hoping that he will, occasionally, find one or two of the rare start-ups that beat the odds and yield a Google-size fortune. Most people lack the stomach for this because they look at it the wrong way, he told me in 2013: "It's funny that a 90% chance of failing people don't like, but a 10% chance of changing the world people love." This is black swan investing, and it's similar to how Taleb himself traded—very successfully—before becoming an author. But it's not the only way to invest. A very different way is to beat competitors by forecasting more accurately—for example, correctly deciding that there is a 68% chance of something happening when others foresee only a 60% chance. This is the approach of the best poker players. It pays off more often, but the returns are more modest, and fortunes are amassed slowly. It is neither superior nor inferior to black swan investing. It is different.

There is another, big reason not to dismiss forecasting tournaments. What elevates a mere surprise to black swan status are the event's consequences. But consequences take time to develop. On July 14, 1789, a mob took control of a prison in Paris known as the Bastille, but we mean something much bigger than what happened that day when we refer today to "the storming of the Bastille." We mean the actual event plus the events it triggered that spiraled into the French Revolution. That's why, centuries later, July 14 is the national holiday of France. "The more you want to explain about a black swan event like the storming of the Bastille," wrote the sociologist Duncan Watts, "the broader you have to draw the boundaries around what you consider to be the event itself."[8]

In this light, black swans are not as wildly unpredictable as supposed.

Three days after terrorists flew jets into the World Trade Center and the Pentagon, the US government demanded that the Taliban rulers of Afghanistan hand over Osama bin Laden and other al-Qaeda terrorists. The Taliban said they would comply if the US government produced satisfactory evidence of al-Qaeda's guilt. The United States prepared for invasion. Still the Taliban refused to hand over bin Laden. Finally, almost a month after 9/11, the United States attacked. Today, when we refer to the black swan of 9/11, we mean the attacks plus the consequences, which include the invasion of Afghanistan. But that sequence of events could arguably have gone differently. Bin Laden and al-Qaeda were Arabic-speaking foreigners in Afghanistan and the Taliban could have decided that sheltering them just wasn't worth incurring the wrath of the world's sole superpower right when they were on the cusp of finally destroying the Northern Alliance, their hated rivals. Or, sensing imminent extradition, bin Laden and his followers could have fled to Pakistan, Somalia, or Yemen. You could imagine a scenario in which there was no invasion of Afghanistan, or no ten-year hunt for Osama bin Laden. And we would then see 9/11 differently—a tragedy, certainly, but not the opening shot in a series of wars that dominated a decade.

We may have no evidence that superforecasters can foresee events like those of September 11, 2001, but we do have a warehouse of evidence that they can forecast questions like: Will the United States threaten military action if the Taliban don't hand over Osama bin Laden? Will the Taliban comply? Will bin Laden flee Afghanistan prior to the invasion? To the extent that such forecasts can anticipate the consequences of events like 9/11, and these consequences make a black swan what it is, we *can* forecast black swans.

ALL THAT SAID . . .

I see Kahneman's and Taleb's critiques as the strongest challenges to the notion of superforecasting. We are far enough apart empirically and close enough philosophically to make communication, even collaboration, possible.

To see how close we are, consider a bureaucratic memo that would never have made it into history's footnotes but for the accident of its timing. On April 11, 2001, Defense Secretary Donald Rumsfeld sent a memo to President George W. Bush and Vice President Dick Cheney. "I ran across this piece on the difficulty of predicting the future," Rumsfeld wrote. "I thought you might find it interesting."[9] The "piece" looks at the strategic situation at the start of each decade between 1900 and 2000 and shows that, in every case, the reality was a stunning change from ten years earlier. "All of which is to say that I'm not sure what 2010 will look like," concluded its author, Linton Wells, "but I'm sure that it will be very little like what we expect, so we should plan accordingly."

Thoughts for the 2001 Quadrennial Defense Review

Lin Wells
CF: Andy

- If you had been a security policy-maker in the world's greatest power in 1900, you would have been a Brit, looking warily at your age-old enemy, France.

- By 1910, you would be allied with France and your enemy would be Germany.

- By 1920, World War I would have been fought and won, and you'd be engaged in a naval arms race with your erstwhile allies, the U.S. and Japan.

- By 1930, naval arms limitation treaties were in effect, the Great Depression was underway, and the defense planning standard said "no war for ten years."

- Nine years later World War II had begun.

- By 1950, Britain no longer was the world's greatest power, the Atomic Age had dawned, and a "police action" was underway in Korea.

- Ten years later the political focus was on the "missile gap," the strategic paradigm was shifting from massive retaliation to flexible response, and few people had heard of Vietnam.

- By 1970, the peak of our involvement in Vietnam had come and gone, we were beginning détente with the Soviets, and we were anointing the Shah as our protégé in the Gulf region.

- By 1980, the Soviets were in Afghanistan, Iran was in the throes of revolution, there was talk of our "hollow forces" and a "window of vulnerability," and the U.S. was the greatest creditor nation the world had ever seen.

- By 1990, the Soviet Union was within a year of dissolution, American forces in the Desert were on the verge of showing they were anything but hollow, the U.S. had become the greatest debtor nation the world had ever known, and almost no one had heard of the internet.

- Ten years later, Warsaw was the capital of a NATO nation, asymmetric threats transcended geography, and the parallel revolutions of information, biotechnology, robotics, nanotechnology, and high density energy sources foreshadowed changes almost beyond forecasting.

- All of which is to say that I'm not sure what 2010 will look like, but I'm sure that it will be very little like we expect, so we should plan accordingly.

Lin Wells

Precisely five months after Rumsfeld wrote his memo, a terrorist cell crashed jets into the Twin Towers and the Pentagon. The decade that followed was yet another that bore little resemblance to what the chattering classes expected at its launch.

Taleb, Kahneman, and I agree there is no evidence that geopolitical or economic forecasters can predict anything ten years out beyond the excruciatingly obvious—"there will be conflicts"—and the odd lucky hits that are inevitable whenever lots of forecasters make lots of forecasts. These limits on predictability are the predictable results of the butterfly dynamics of nonlinear systems. In my EPJ research, the accuracy of expert predictions declined toward chance five years out. And yet, this sort of forecasting is common, even within institutions that should know better. Every four years, Congress requires the Department of Defense to produce a twenty-year forecast of the national security environment. "Enormous effort goes into this Quadrennial Defense Review," noted Richard Danzig, a former secretary of the navy.[10] It was this ritualistic exercise that prompted Lin Wells to commit a modest act of intellectual rebellion and write his article.

Wells hinted at a better way in his closing comment. If you have to plan for a future beyond the forecasting horizon, plan for surprise. That means, as Danzig advises, planning for adaptability and resilience. Imagine a scenario in which reality gives you a smack in the ear and consider how you would respond. Then assume reality will give you a kick in the shin and think about dealing with that. "Plans are useless," Eisenhower said about preparing for battle, "but planning is indispensable."[11]

Taleb has taken this argument further and called for critical systems—like international banking and nuclear weapons—to be made "antifragile," meaning they are not only resilient to shocks but strengthened by them. In principle, I agree. But a point often overlooked is that preparing for surprises—whether we are shooting for resilience or antifragility—is costly. We have to set priorities, which puts us back in the forecasting business. Consider building codes. In Tokyo, big new buildings have to be constructed with advanced engineering to withstand megaquakes. That's expensive. Does it make sense to incur that cost? The timing of earthquakes can't be predicted with precision, but seismologists know where they tend to occur and how big they are likely to be. Tokyo is earthquake central, so expensive engineering standards make sense. But in regions less prone to big quakes, particularly in poorer countries, the same standards make less sense.

These sorts of probability estimates are at the heart of all long-term planning, but they are rarely as explicit as those in earthquake preparation. For decades, the United States had a policy of maintaining the capacity to fight two wars simultaneously. But why not three? Or four? Why not prepare for an alien invasion while we are at it? The answers hinge on probabilities. The two-war doctrine was based on a judgment that the likelihood of the military having to fight two wars simultaneously was high enough to justify the huge expense—but the same was not true of a three-war, four-war, or alien-invasion future. Judgments like these are unavoidable, and if it sometimes looks like we've avoided them in long-term planning that is only because we have swept them under the rug. That's worrisome. Probability judgments should be explicit so we can consider whether they are as accurate as they can be. And if they are nothing but a guess, because that's the best we can do, we should say so. Knowing what we don't know is better than thinking we know what we don't.

This comes into focus if we think about forecasting carefully. But we often don't—leading to absurdities like twenty-year geopolitical forecasts and bestsellers about the coming century. I think both Taleb and Kahneman help explain why we keep making these sorts of mistakes.

Kahneman and other pioneers of modern psychology have revealed that our minds crave certainty and when they don't find it, they impose it. In forecasting, hindsight bias is the cardinal sin. Recall how experts stunned by the Gorbachev surprise quickly became convinced it was perfectly explicable, even predictable, although they hadn't predicted it.

Brushing off surprises makes the past look more predictable than it was—and this encourages the belief that the future is much more predictable than it is. Will China become the world's leading economic power in the mid-twenty-first century? Many are sure it will. And it might. But in the 1980s and early 1990s, there was an even more prevalent belief that Japan would soon dominate the global economy, and its subsequent decline should at least give pause to those asserting China's ascendancy.[12] But it often doesn't because when looking back it seems strange that anyone ever thought Japan would take the lead. Of course Japan would falter! It's obvious—in hindsight—just as the prediction that China will not seems obvious today.

Now consider what happens when this psychology encounters the reality Nassim Taleb describes so well.

In much of daily life, we encounter recurring events that fit the classic bell curve when graphed. For instance, most men are between five and six feet tall, far fewer are around four and seven feet, and there are tiny numbers at three feet (the shortest man ever was just under three feet tall) and eight feet (the tallest was just under nine feet). But the bell curve doesn't fit everything, as the inequality of wealth in the United States demonstrates. Suppose that median household wealth is around $100,000 and 95% of households fall between $10,000 and $1,000,000. If wealth were distributed along a classic bell curve, like that on page 247, we would virtually never encounter a household worth more than $10 million. And coming across a household with a net worth of $1 billion would be a one-in-trillions occurrence. But wealth isn't distributed normally. There are nearly five hundred individuals with a net worth over $1 billion and a handful worth over $10 billion. The true distribution of wealth is a fat-tailed one that permits much more extreme outcomes. The true likelihood of someone in the United States being a billionaire rises sharply from one in trillions to roughly one in every seven hundred thousand.

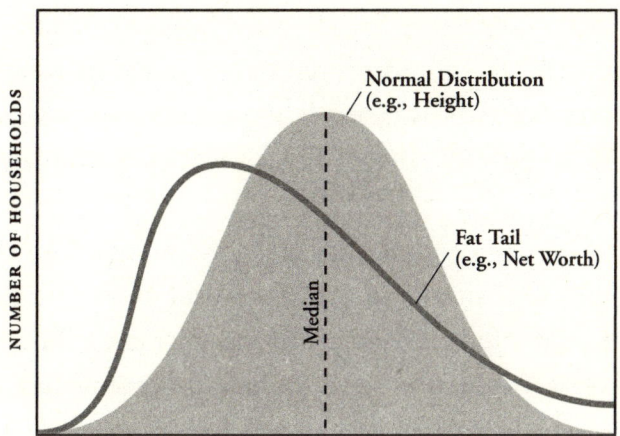

Now comes the hardest-to-grasp part of Taleb's view of the world. He posits that historical probabilities—all the possible ways the future could unfold—are distributed like wealth, not height. That means our world is vastly more volatile than most of us realize and we are at risk of grave miscalculations.

Let's time travel back to the summer of 1914. World War I is about to break out. Imagine a senior official in the British Foreign Office has assumed (incorrectly) that the death tolls from wars up to that point in history are normally distributed around an average of one hundred thousand.[13] His worst-case scenario is thus a war claiming about a million lives. Now he meets a forecaster who claims that Europe is about to plunge into a world war that will kill ten million—followed by another world war that will kill sixty million. The policy maker sees this combination of catastrophes as vanishingly improbable—say, one in several million—so he dismisses the forecaster as a crackpot.

What would have happened if the policy maker had relied on a more realistic fat-tailed distribution of war casualties? He still would have seen the forecast as improbable, but it would now be thousands of times more probable than before.[14] The impact would be analogous to your learning that your personal chances of winning the

Powerball lottery on any ticket purchase have risen from one in five million to one in five hundred. Wouldn't you rush to buy tickets? A policy maker in 1914 who knew the true fat-tail risks of a mega-casualty war might well have tried a lot harder to avert the looming catastrophe.

Or, look at it this way. If height had a fat-tailed distribution, it would still be very unusual to walk down the street and encounter a twelve-foot man—followed by a fifteen-foot man—but such events could conceivably occur in one's lifetime. In the same light, now that we know that war casualties actually do have a fat-tailed distribution, we should not be astonished when military historians tell us that World War II could have claimed far more than sixty million lives if Hitler had launched the invasion of the Soviet Union earlier in 1941 or had intuited the destructive power of the atomic bomb. The possibilities were once real—and numerous.

Some find it hard wrapping their heads around Taleb's idea of statistical distributions of possible worlds. It feels like eggheaded nonsense. There is only one reality: what happened in the past, what we're living in now, and what will happen in the future. But if you are as mathematically inclined as Taleb, you get used to the idea that the world we live in is but one that emerged, quasi-randomly, from a vast population of once-possible worlds. The past did not have to unfold as it did, the present did not have to be what it is, and the future is wide open. History is a virtually infinite array of possibilities. Prudent leaders feel this in their bones, as John F. Kennedy did when he realized the Cuban missile crisis had an array of possible outcomes ranging from peace to nuclear annihilation, which could have pushed the death toll for World War III into the hundreds of millions. Fat tails indeed![15]

Daniel Kahneman makes the point with a characteristically elegant thought experiment. He invites us to consider three leaders whose impact on the twentieth century was massive—Hitler, Stalin, and Mao. Each came to power backed by a political movement that would never have accepted a female leader, but each man's origins can be traced to an unfertilized egg that had a 50% chance of being fertilized by different sperm cells and producing a female zygote that would become a female fetus and finally a female baby. That means there was only a 12.5% chance that all three leaders would be born male, and an 87.5% chance that at least one would be born female. The ripple effects of different results are unknowable but potentially enormous. If Anna Hitler had been born on April 20, 1889, in Braunau am Inn, Austria, World War II might never have happened—or a smarter Nazi dictator might have visited even worse horrors upon us by making shrewder decisions.

All three of us see history this way. Counterfactuals highlight how radically open the possibilities once were and how easily our best-laid plans can be blown away by flapping butterfly wings. Immersion in what-if history can give us a visceral feeling for Taleb's vision of radical indeterminacy. Savoring how history could have generated an infinite array of alternative outcomes and could now generate a similar array of alternative futures, is like contemplating the one hundred billion known stars in our galaxy and the one hundred billion known galaxies. It instills profound humility.[16]

Kahneman, Taleb, and I agree on that much. But I also believe that humility should not obscure the fact that people can, with considerable effort, make accurate forecasts about at least some developments that really do matter. To be sure, in the big scheme of things, human foresight is puny, but it is nothing to sniff at when you live on that puny human scale.

12

What's Next?

For months, the outcome wasn't in doubt. Excluding undecideds, about 43% of Scots said they would vote yes in the September 18, 2014, referendum on Scotland leaving the United Kingdom; 57% favored no. But two weeks before the referendum, the polls shifted rapidly, giving yes the edge. The last few polls before the vote revealed another small shift, putting no in the lead by a nose—with as many as 9% of voters still undecided. Would the 307-year-old United Kingdom survive?

The answer seems obvious now, as it usually does after the fact. It wasn't then. The yes campaign had appealed to nationalist sentiment, the no campaign had countered that Scotland's economy would be crippled by separation. Some pundits argued that nationalist identity politics would trump economic calculations; others expected the reverse. The one highly probable outcome was that whatever happened pundits would immediately explain why.

As it turned out, no won by the surprisingly wide margin of 55.3% to 44.7%. (Superforecasters aced this one, incidentally, even beating British betting markets with real money on the table.)[1]

But one pundit broke ranks. "I was all set to have some fun today writing a post that would have been a 'Choose Your Own Analysis' adventure in the wake of Scotland's referendum," wrote the political scientist and *Washington Post* blogger Daniel Drezner the day after Scotland voted no. It would have had "sentences like, 'Yesterday's referendum is a clear demonstration of [the enduring power of nationalism in the 21st century / the resilience of economics in the minds of voters in the West], and maybe pundits who predicted a [No/Yes] outcome were too quick to discount [the bland appeal of economics / the goods that nationalism cannot deliver.]" I wish Drezner had continued in that vein. It would have been a delightful poke at the insta-analysis of too-sure-of-themselves commentators. But Drezner did something else. He confessed that he had personally been unsure of the outcome and was surprised by the wide margin of no's victory. It was "a teachable moment for punditry," Drezner wrote. "Which is to say—what does one do with data points like this to adjust one's worldview?"[2]

What a fabulous question! On the one hand, the hindsight-tainted analyses that dominate commentary after major events are a dead end. Many factors were at work in the Scottish referendum, so "economics trumped nationalism" leaves too much out. It's even more misguided to blithely conclude that because "economics trumped nationalism" here, it will do so elsewhere. On the other hand, our expectations of the future are derived from our mental models of how the world works, and every event is an opportunity to learn and improve those models.

But as Drezner noted, effective learning from experience can't happen without clear feedback, and you can't have clear feedback unless your forecasts are unambiguous and scorable. Sound familiar? It should. Drezner cited an article about the IARPA tournament. "I'm certainly guilty of the vagary of prediction," he wrote. Prior to the Scottish referendum, he had thought no would win but he wrote a post about why yes might win instead. So what had he forecast? It wasn't clear. How should he change his thinking in light of the outcome? That too wasn't clear. "So, going forward, when I write about a discrete event like the Scottish referendum, I'll try to do two things: make a clear prediction, and offer a confidence interval about that prediction. In other words, I want to keep score."[3]

That was precisely the reaction I hoped for.

With scores and leaderboards, forecasting tournaments may look like games but the stakes are real and substantial. In business, good forecasting can be the difference between prosperity and bankruptcy; in government, the difference between policies that give communities a boost and those that inflict unintended consequences and waste tax dollars; in national security, the difference between peace and war. If the US intelligence community had not told Congress it was certain that Saddam Hussein had weapons of mass destruction, a disastrous invasion might have been averted. IARPA understands the enormous potential in keeping score. That is why it bankrolled this project.

Tournaments help researchers learn what improves forecasting and help forecasters sharpen their skills with practice and feedback. Tournaments could help society, too, by providing tools for structuring our thinking about what is likely to happen if we venture down one policy path or another. Vague expectations about indefinite futures are not helpful. Fuzzy thinking can never be proven wrong. And only when we are proven wrong so clearly that we can no longer deny it to ourselves will we adjust our mental models of the world—producing a clearer picture of reality. Forecast, measure, revise: it is the surest path to seeing better.

Dan Drezner saw that. In my daydreams, so will everyone who reads this book, and serious change will begin. Consumers of forecasting will stop being gulled by pundits with good stories and start asking pundits how their past predictions fared—and reject answers that consist of nothing but anecdotes and credentials. Just as we now expect a pill to have been tested in peer-reviewed experiments before we swallow it, we will expect forecasters to establish the accuracy of their forecasting with rigorous testing before we heed their advice. And forecasters themselves will realize, as Dan Drezner did, that these higher expectations will ultimately benefit them, because it is only with the clear feedback that comes from rigorous testing that they can improve their foresight. It could be huge—an "evidence-based forecasting" revolution similar to the "evidence-based medicine" revolution, with consequences every bit as significant.

Or nothing may change. Revolutionaries aren't supposed to say failure is possible, but let's think like superforecasters here and acknowledge that things may go either way.

In this closing chapter, I size up the strongest force resisting change, and why, despite it, the status quo may be in for a shock. Then I look at something I can control—my future research. Whether it will be conducted amid a tumultuous change, as I hope, or a stagnant status quo, as I fear, will be decided by the people whom political scientists call the "attentive public." I'm modestly optimistic. But readers can make the final forecast.

THE KTO-KOGO STATUS QUO

In the months prior to the 2012 presidential election, Nate Silver's forecasts consistently had Obama leading Mitt Romney. Even when polls showed Romney breathing down Obama's neck, and the phrases "fifty-fifty" and "too close to call" echoed through the media, Silver's forecast never had Obama below a 61% chance of winning. Republicans reviled Silver and accused him of bias. Democrats defended his integrity and praised his forecasting acumen—and showered him with extravagant praise when Obama won. But in March 2014, when Silver issued forecasts that suggested the Republicans would take control of the Senate in that November's midterm elections, many Democrats had a change of heart. Some officials even passed around old forecasts of Silver's that had failed.[4] Same forecaster, same track record—but when his forecasts ceased to align with partisan purposes he was demoted from prophet to stumblebum.

It was an extreme illustration of a problem I swept under the rug in chapter 1, when I said the exclusive goal of forecasting should be accuracy and that would be the sole concern in this book. In reality, accuracy is often only one of many goals. Sometimes it is irrelevant.

This unseemly truth is usually disguised but occasionally the mask falls, as it did when an analyst with the Banco Santander Brasil SA warned wealthy clients that Brazil's stock market and currency would likely decline if a left-wing candidate continued her ascent in the polls. The candidate and her party were livid and demanded the analyst be fired. She was, immediately, because in Brazil it's not good for a bank to be on bad terms with potential future presidents. Whether the analyst's forecast was accurate did not matter in the slightest.[5]

Like many hardball operators before and since, Vladimir Lenin insisted politics, defined broadly, was nothing more than a struggle for power, or as he memorably put it, "*kto, kogo*?" That literally means "who, whom" and it was Lenin's shorthand for "Who does what to whom?" Arguments and evidence are lovely adornments but what matters is the ceaseless contest to be the *kto*, not the *kogo*.[6] It follows that the goal of forecasting is *not* to see what's coming. It is to advance the interests of the forecaster and the forecaster's tribe. Accurate forecasts may help do that sometimes, and when they do accuracy is welcome, but it is pushed aside if that's what the pursuit of power requires. Earlier, I discussed Jonathan Schell's 1982 warning that a holocaust would certainly occur in the near future "unless we rid ourselves of our nuclear arsenals," which was clearly not an accurate forecast. Schell wanted to rouse readers to join the swelling nuclear disarmament movement. He did. So his forecast was not accurate, but did it fail? Lenin would say it did exactly what it was supposed to do.

Dick Morris—a Republican pollster and former adviser to President Bill Clinton—underscored the point days after the presidential election of 2012. Shortly before the vote, Morris had forecast a Romney landslide. Afterward, he was mocked. So he defended himself. "The Romney campaign was falling apart, people were not optimistic, nobody thought there was a chance of victory and I felt that it was my duty at that point to go out and say what I said," Morris said.[7] Of course Morris may have lied about having lied, but the fact that Morris felt this defense was plausible says plenty about the *kto-kogo* world he operates in.

You don't have to be a Marxist-Leninist to concede that Lenin had a point. Self and tribe matter. If forecasting can be co-opted to advance their interests, it will be. From this perspective, there is no need to reform and improve forecasting, and it will not change, because it is already serving its primary purpose well.

But before giving up, let's remember that Lenin was a tad dogmatic. People want power, yes. But they value other things too. And that can make all the difference.

CHANGE

A century ago, as physicians were slowly professionalizing and medicine was on the cusp of becoming scientific, a Boston doctor named Ernest Amory Codman had an idea similar in spirit to forecaster scorekeeping. He called it the End Result System. Hospitals should record what ailments incoming patients had, how they were treated, and—most important—the end result of each case. These records should be compiled and statistics released so consumers could choose hospitals on the basis of good evidence. Hospitals would respond to consumer pressure by hiring and promoting doctors on the same basis. Medicine would improve, to the benefit of all. "Codman's plan disregarded a physician's clinical reputation or social standing as well as bedside manner or technical skills," noted the historian Ira Rutkow. "All that counted were the clinical consequences of a doctor's effort."[8]

Today, hospitals do much of what Codman demanded, and more, and physicians would find it flabbergasting if anyone suggested they stop. But the medical establishment saw it differently when Codman first proposed the idea.

Hospitals hated it. They would have to pay for record keepers. And the physicians in charge saw nothing in it for them. They were already respected. Keeping score could only damage their reputations. Predictably, Codman got nowhere. So he pushed harder—and alienated his colleagues so badly he was booted from Massachusetts General Hospital. Codman opened his own little hospital, where he personally paid for statistics to be compiled and published, and he continued to publicize his ideas, using increasingly intemperate means. At a meeting of a local medical society in 1915, Codman unfurled an enormous cartoon that poked fun at various dignitaries, including the president of Harvard University. Codman was suspended from the medical society and lost his Harvard teaching post. The status quo seemed unassailable.

But "the hue and cry over Codman's cartoon created a nationwide buzz," Rutkow wrote. "Medical efficiency and the end result system were suddenly the hot topic of the day. As the profession and the public learned of Codman's ideas a growing number of hospitals across the country implemented his scheme. Codman became a sought-after speaker and when the fledgling American College of Surgeons formed a commission on hospital standardization, he was appointed its first chairman."[9] Much that Codman advocated was never adopted—he was an inexhaustible idealist—but ultimately his core insight won.

If *kto-kogo* were the decisive force in human affairs that Lenin and others took it to be, evidence-based medicine—which was a threat to everyone who was anyone in the medical hierarchy—would have been stillborn. But Ernest Codman, Archie Cochrane, and many others overcame entrenched interests. They did it not by storming the ramparts. They did it with reason and a relentless focus on the singular goal of making the sick well.

Their success inspired others. Evidence-based policy is a movement modeled on evidence-based medicine, with the goal of subjecting government policies to rigorous analysis so that legislators will
actually know—not merely think they know—whether policies do
what they are supposed to do. As a result, in the United States, the
United Kingdom, and elsewhere, there is probably more top-quality
policy analysis being done than ever before. Of course politics will
always be politics and politicians will always factor in partisan advantage and ideological conviction, but there is plenty of evidence that
rigorous analysis has made a real difference in government policy.[10]

The same thinking is transforming charitable foundations,
which are increasingly making funding contingent on stringent program evaluation. Those that deliver are expanded, those that fail are
shuttered. In line with Bill Gates's insistence on having clear goals
and measures, the Gates Foundation, one of the world's largest, is
renowned for the rigor of its evaluations.

Sports provide striking examples of the growth and power of
evidence-based thinking. As James Surowiecki noted in the *New
Yorker*, both athletes and teams have improved dramatically over the
last thirty or forty years. In part, that's because the stakes are bigger.
But it also happened because what they are doing has increasingly
become evidence based. "When John Madden coached the Oakland
Raiders, he would force players to practice at midday in August in
full pads," Surowiecki noted. "Don Shula, when he was head coach
of the Baltimore Colts, insisted that his players practice without access to water." Thanks to scientific research in human performance,
such gut-informed techniques are going the way of bloodletting in
medicine. Training is "far more rational and data-driven," Surowiecki wrote. So is team development, thanks to rapid advances in
"Moneyball"-style analytics. "A key part of the 'performance revolution' in sports, then, is the story of how organizations, in a systematic
way, set about making employees more effective and productive."[11]

All these changes have been catalyzed by rapid advances in information technology. We can count and test like never before. And we are. Seen in this broader perspective, an evidence-based forecasting movement would not be a startling change springing up out of nothing. It would be another manifestation of a broad and deep shift away from decision making based on experience, intuition, and authority—"Do this because I think it will work and I'm an expert"—toward quantification and analysis. Far from being surprising, one might even think, "What took so long?"

Perhaps the best reason to hope for change is the IARPA tournament itself. If someone had asked me a decade ago to list the organizations that most needed to get serious about forecasting but were least likely to do so, the intelligence community would have been at the top. Why? *Kto-kogo*. Evidence-based forecasting will improve their work in the long run, but it's dangerous in the short run.

Recall the wrong-side-of-maybe fallacy that leads people to conclude a forecast of "There is a 70% chance an event will happen" is wrong if the event doesn't happen. It was a big reason why Sherman Kent's modest proposal to attach numerical ranges to forecasts went nowhere. Use the number and you risk being unfairly blamed. Stick with phrases as fuzzy as a puff of smoke and you are safe.

This thinking is tempting in many organizations but it's irresistible in the intelligence community, which has so often been whipsawed between condemnations. After 9/11, the IC was blamed for failing to connect the dots and underestimating the risk of terrorist attacks. After the 2003 invasion of Iraq, the IC was blamed for connecting unconnected dots and overestimating the risk of weapons of mass destruction. Each time this happens, the IC responds by going to extremes to avoid making the sort of mistake it just made. If it failed to raise an alarm when a threat was real, it raises alarms at the slightest sign of trouble. If it raised a false alarm, it becomes wary of crying wolf. This blame-game ping-pong does nothing to make the intelligence community improve. It even prevents the long-term investments necessary to get better at forecasting.[12]

What *would* help is a sweeping commitment to evaluation: Keep score. Analyze results. Learn what works and what doesn't. But that requires numbers, and numbers would leave the intelligence community vulnerable to the wrong-side-of-maybe fallacy, lacking any cover the next time they blow a big call. Imagine a director of National Intelligence in a congressional hearing to explain why intelligence analysts didn't see some huge event coming—a revolution or a terrorist strike—before it was too late. "Well, we're generally pretty good at these things and getting better," he says, taking out a chart. "See? Our evaluations show the Brier scores of our analysts are solid and there has been significant improvement over time. We have even caught up with those annoying superforecasters. So while it's true we missed this important event, and terrible consequences followed, it's important to keep these statistics in mind."

And yet, despite all this, the intelligence community *did* fund the IARPA tournament. I've also seen strong interest from the director of National Intelligence in making scorekeeping an integral part of intelligence analysis. Of course it could all be undone in a heartbeat. But still, that's an amazing and welcome change. History may be on our side—in the long run.

THE HUMANISTS' OBJECTION

Balancing it all out, count me as cautiously optimistic that my work may contribute to an evidence-based forecasting movement. But this is not a prospect everyone embraces. I need only imagine how my life might have gone differently to know how the objection might be framed.

In 1976 I was a clueless twenty-two-year-old Canadian who, like countless others, was about to make choices that would shape the rest of my life. I had just graduated from the University of British Columbia. I thought I might accept a Commonwealth scholarship to study the humanities at Oxford. My adviser, Peter Suedfeld, thought that was a terrible idea. Go to the United States and commit to the scientific method, he said. I took his advice, but only hesitantly. My decision could have gone the other way. And if I had left for Oxford and a career in the humanities, I can easily guess what I would have said about the research outlined in this book, and the next steps it will take.

Numbers are fine and useful things, I would say in that alternate universe, but we must be careful not to be smitten with them. "Not everything that counts can be counted," goes a famous saying, "and not everything that can be counted counts."[13] In this era of computers and algorithms, some social scientists have forgotten that. As the cultural critic Leon Wieseltier put it in the *New York Times*, "There are 'metrics' for phenomena that cannot be metrically measured. Numerical values are assigned to things that cannot be captured by numbers."[14] This naive positivism is running rampant, taking over domains it has no business being in. As Wieseltier poetically put it, "Where wisdom once was, quantification will now be."

I actually feel that there is a lot of truth in this perspective. Far too many people treat numbers like sacred totems offering divine insight. The truly numerate know that numbers are tools, nothing more, and their quality can range from wretched to superb. A crude version of Codman's End Results System that simply tracked patient survival might result in a hospital boasting that 100% of its patients live—without mentioning that the hospital achieves this bragging right by turning away the sickest patients. Numbers must be constantly scrutinized and improved, which can be an unnerving process because it is unending. Progressive improvement is attainable. Perfection is not.[15]

This is how I see Brier scoring of forecast accuracy. It is a work in progress. One problem is that Brier scores treat false alarms the same as misses. But when it comes to things like terrorist attacks, people are far more concerned about misses than false alarms. Fortunately, adjusting the scoring to capture this concern is easy. Forecasters just have to be told in advance what the ground rules are—"False positives will cost you one-tenth as much as false negatives"—so they can adjust their judgments accordingly.

But don't suppose that because a scoring system needs tweaking it isn't a big improvement. Consider consumer credit ratings, whose flaws are so often criticized. Decades ago, before credit scores, loan officers could make decisions almost whimsically and your fate could hinge on whether you reminded them of someone, or they had slept poorly the night before, or they harbored stereotypes of "shiftless blacks" and "flighty women." Credit scores may be miles from perfect but they're a huge advance from that. Similarly, while I can't claim my scoring system is perfect, it is a big improvement on judging a forecaster by the criteria used nowadays—titles, confidence, skill at spinning a story, number of books sold, CNN appearances, and time spent at Davos.

But even the most skeptical humanities professor would concede these points, I suspect. The challenge runs deeper, and it brings us back to that line about the countable not always being worth counting.

THE QUESTION THAT COUNTS

In the spring of 2013 I met with Paul Saffo, a Silicon Valley futurist and scenario consultant. Another unnerving crisis was brewing on the Korean peninsula, so when I sketched the forecasting tournament for Saffo, I mentioned a question IARPA had asked: Will

North Korea "attempt to launch a multistage rocket between 7 January 2013 and 1 September 2013?" Saffo thought it was trivial. A few colonels in the Pentagon might be interested, he said, but it's not the question most people would ask. "The more fundamental question is 'How does this all turn out?'" he said. "That's a much more challenging question." He then offered a long answer that glided smoothly from country to country and leader to leader, a bravura performance of the sort that anyone who attends think-tank conferences or watches pundit panels on TV would recognize. But was Saffo right? Even today, I don't know. What he said was just too vague to judge. That's typical of the answers to big, important questions like "How does this all turn out?"

So we confront a dilemma. What matters is the big question, but the big question can't be scored. The little question doesn't matter but it *can* be scored, so the IARPA tournament went with it. You could say we were so hell-bent on looking scientific that we counted what doesn't count.

That is unfair. The questions in the tournament had been screened by experts to be both difficult and relevant to active problems on the desks of intelligence analysts. But it *is* fair to say these questions are more narrowly focused than the big questions we would all love to answer, like "How does this all turn out?" Do we really have to choose between posing big and important questions that can't be scored or small and less important questions that can be? That's unsatisfying. But there is a way out of the box.

Implicit within Paul Saffo's "How does this all turn out?" question were the recent events that had worsened the conflict on the Korean peninsula. North Korea launched a rocket, in violation of a UN Security Council resolution. It conducted a new nuclear test. It renounced the 1953 armistice with South Korea. It launched a cyber attack on South Korea, severed the hotline between the two governments, and threatened a nuclear attack on the United States.

Seen that way, it's obvious that the big question is composed of many small questions. One is "Will North Korea test a rocket?" If it does, it will escalate the conflict a little. If it doesn't, it could cool things down a little. That one tiny question doesn't nail down the big question, but it does contribute a little insight. And if we ask *many* tiny-but-pertinent questions, we can close in on an answer for the big question. Will North Korea conduct another nuclear test? Will it rebuff diplomatic talks on its nuclear program? Will it fire artillery at South Korea? Will a North Korean ship fire on a South Korean ship? The answers are cumulative. The more yeses, the likelier the answer to the big question is "This is going to end badly."

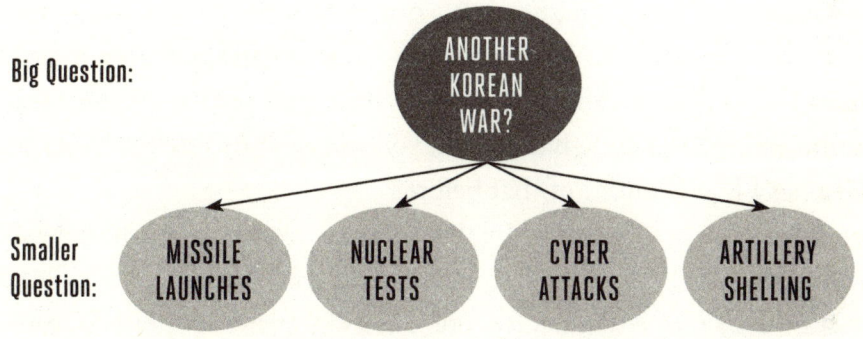

Question clustering to accelerate learning

I call this Bayesian question clustering because of its family resemblance to the Bayesian updating discussed in chapter 7. Another way to think of it is to imagine a painter using the technique called pointillism. It consists of dabbing tiny dots on the canvas, nothing more. Each dot alone adds little. But as the dots collect, patterns emerge. With enough dots, an artist can produce anything from a vivid portrait to a sweeping landscape.

There were question clusters in the IARPA tournament, but they arose more as a consequence of events than a diagnostic strategy. In future research, I want to develop the concept and see how effectively we can answer unscorable "big questions" with clusters of little ones.

But the Leon Wieseltiers are still not likely to be mollified. For one thing, I called my research program the Good Judgment Project, which seems to imply that accurate forecasting and good judgment are one and the same. But that's not what I intended. Foresight is one element of good judgment, but there are others, including some that cannot be counted and run through a scientist's algorithms—moral judgment, for one.

Another critical dimension of good judgment is asking good questions. Indeed, a farsighted forecast flagging disaster or opportunity can't happen until someone thinks to pose the question. What qualifies as a good question? It's one that gets us thinking about something worth thinking about. So one way to identify a good question is what I call the smack-the-forehead test: when you read the question after time has passed, you smack your forehead and say, "If only I had thought of that before!"

Here is one Tom Friedman posed in September 2002: "As I think about President Bush's plans to take out Saddam Hussein and rebuild Iraq into a democracy, one question gnaws at me: Is Iraq the way it is today because Saddam Hussein is the way he is? Or is Saddam Hussein the way he is because Iraq is the way it is? I mean, is Iraq a totalitarian dictatorship under a cruel, iron-fisted man because the country is actually an Arab Yugoslavia—a highly tribalized, artificial state. . . . Or, has Iraq, by now, congealed into a real nation? And once the cruel fist of Saddam is replaced by a more enlightened leadership, Iraq's talented educated people will slowly produce a federal democracy."[16] Friedman's questioning drew attention to what we now know were key drivers of later events, including the savage sectarianism that has devastated Iraq since the US invasion of 2003. So it passes the smack-the-forehead test. That's particularly remarkable because Friedman became a strong supporter of the invasion in part because his expectations of how things would unfold were presumably quite different from what actually happened.

While we may assume that a superforecaster would also be a superquestioner, and vice versa, we don't actually know that. Indeed, my best scientific guess is that they often are not. The psychological recipe for the ideal superforecaster may prove to be quite different from that for the ideal superquestioner, as superb question generation often seems to accompany a hedgehog-like incisiveness and confidence that one has a Big Idea grasp of the deep drivers of an event. That's quite a different mindset from the foxy eclecticism and sensitivity to uncertainty that characterizes superb forecasting.

This suggests a different way to look at an analysis like Friedman's. Consider a column Friedman wrote in December 2014 about the ramifications of the plunging price of oil. "The last time the world witnessed such a steep and sustained drop in oil prices—from 1986 to 1999—it had some profound consequences for oil-dependent states and those who depended on their largesse," Friedman wrote. "The Soviet empire collapsed; Iran elected a reformist president; Iraq invaded Kuwait; and Yasir Arafat, having lost his Soviet backer and Arab bankers, recognized Israel—to name but a few." Friedman's conclusion? "If today's falloff in oil prices is sustained, we'll also be in for a lot of surprises"—particularly in the petro-states of Venezuela, Iran, and Russia.[17]

Here was a vague warning of unspecified surprises in unspecified time frames. As a forecast, that's not terribly helpful. This sort of thing is why some people see Friedman as a particularly successful and slippery pundit who has mastered the art of appearing to go out on a limb without ever venturing out. But the same column can be read less as a forecast than an attempt to draw the attention of forecasters to something they should be thinking about. In other words, it is a question, not an answer.

Whether superforecasters can outpredict Friedman is both unknown and, for present purposes, beside the point. Superforecasters and superquestioners need to acknowledge each other's complementary strengths, not dwell on each other's alleged weaknesses. Friedman poses provocative questions that superforecasters should use to sharpen their foresight; superforecasters generate well-calibrated answers that superquestioners should use to fine-tune and occasionally overhaul their mental models of reality. The "Tom versus Bill" frame with which we started the book is our final false dichotomy. We need a Tom-Bill symbiosis.

That's a tall order. But there's a much bigger collaboration I'd like to see. It would be the Holy Grail of my research program: using forecasting tournaments to depolarize unnecessarily polarized policy debates and make us collectively smarter.

ONE LAST IDEA

In October 2014 Bloomberg reporters did me a big favor by contacting the signatories of the letter I wrote about in chapter 3—the one sent to Fed chairman Ben Bernanke in November 2010, which warned that Bernanke's planned asset purchases "risk currency debasement and inflation." Bernanke ignored that warning and forged ahead. In the following years, the US dollar did not weaken and inflation did not rise. Many critics said that proved the signatories were wrong, but as I discussed in chapter 3 the actual wording of the letter was so vague it was impossible to say that definitively.

Several months after I wrote that chapter, Bloomberg reporters asked the signatories how they felt about the letter in hindsight. Those who responded unanimously said they were right. They wouldn't change a word.

Their reasons fell into two categories. One, the forecast only appeared to have failed because people were looking at the wrong measure. "I think there's plenty of inflation," the financial commentator James Grant told Bloomberg, "not at the checkout counter, necessarily, but on Wall Street." Two, if you look carefully at the language of the letter, it clearly has not been proved wrong. "Note the word 'risk.' And note the absence of a date," Niall Ferguson told Bloomberg. "There is in fact still a risk of currency debasement and inflation."[18]

That captures perfectly what's wrong with so many public debates today.

Recall that the severe economic turmoil of 2008 and 2009 generated a fierce policy debate. Two camps coalesced: the Keynesians and the Austerians. The Keynesians called for heroic improvisation by central banks and aggressive deficit spending by governments. The Austerians called for austerity—government budget cuts—and warned that the Keynesian policies would ignite inflation and sink currencies. Ultimately, governments struck various compromises. In some countries, the Keynesians got more of what they wanted; in others, the Austerians did. Time passed. And then? What should have happened is a comparison of what people predicted and what actually happened, and to the extent that people were wrong, they would say so, and adjust their thinking accordingly. That's only rational. As J. M. Keynes is reputed to have said but did not, "When the facts change, I change my mind. What do you do, sir?"

As it turned out, not much, sir. People so rarely adjusted their thinking that when the president of the Federal Reserve Bank of Minneapolis, an Austerian, announced publicly that events had shown the Keynesians were closer to the truth, it made headlines— that could have read "Man Changes His Mind in Response to Evidence." The 2014 Bloomberg follow-up to the 2010 letter illustrates failure. I am not saying the letter writers were wrong on substance. I am agnostic on issues outside my field. The failure is one of process: In 2010 one group spelled out their beliefs in writing, and warned that if Bernanke pursued his policy certain results would follow.

Another group vehemently disagreed. Four years passed and no one budged. That should be unsatisfactory to everyone, no matter what their views on the merits.

There were attempts to extract lessons from events during those years, but they mostly involved brute force. Hammering opponents both for their forecasting failures and for not acknowledging them was a standard theme in the columns of Paul Krugman, whose Nobel Prize in economics and *New York Times* bully pulpit made him the most prominent Keynesian. Krugman's opponents hammered back. Niall Ferguson wrote a three-part catalog of Krugman's alleged failures. Back and forth it went, with each side poring over the other's forecasts, looking for failures, deflecting attacks, and leveling accusations. For fans of one side or the other, it may have been thrilling. For those who hope that we can become collectively wiser, it was a bewildering fracas that looked less like a debate between great minds and more like a food fight between rival fraternities. These are accomplished people debating pressing issues, but nobody seems to have learned anything beyond how to defend their original position.

We can do better. Remember the "adversarial collaboration" between Daniel Kahneman and Gary Klein? These two psychologists won acclaim by developing apparently contradictory schools of thought, making each man a threat to the legacy of the other. But they were committed to playing by scientific ground rules, so they got together to discuss why they had such different views and how they could be reconciled. Something similar could, in principle, be done in forecasting.

When a debate like "Keynesians versus Austerians" emerges, key figures could work together—with the help of trusted third parties—to identify what they disagree about and which forecasts would meaningfully test those disagreements. The key is precision. It's one thing for Austerians to say a policy will cause inflation and Keynesians to say it won't. But how much inflation? Measured by what benchmark? Over what time period? The result must be a fore-cast question that reduces ambiguity to an absolute minimum.

A single dot on a canvas is not a painting and a single bet cannot resolve a complex theoretical dispute. This will take many questions and question clusters. Of course it's possible that if large numbers of questions are asked, each side may be right on some forecasts but wrong on others and the final outcome won't generate the banner headlines that celebrity bets sometimes do. But as software engineers say, that's a feature, not a bug. A major point of view rarely has zero merit, and if a forecasting contest produces a split decision we will have learned that the reality is more mixed than either side thought. If learning, not gloating, is the goal, that is progress.

The catch is that the Kahneman-Klein collaboration presumed good faith. Each side wanted to be right but they wanted the truth more. Sadly, in noisy public arenas, strident voices dominate debates, and they have zero interest in adversarial collaboration. But let's not make the cynic's mistake of thinking that those who dominate de-bates are the only debaters. We hear them most because they are the loudest and the media reward people who shout into bullhorns. But there are less voluble and more reasonable voices. With their adver-saries and a moderator, let them design clear tests of their beliefs. When the results run against their beliefs, some will try to rational-ize away the facts, but they will pay a reputational price. Others will do the honorable thing and say, "I was wrong." But most important, we can all watch, see the results, and get a little wiser. [19]

All we have to do is get serious about keeping score.

Epilogue

A s I was finishing this manuscript, I shared the first chapter with
Bill Flack, who confessed he is not quite a "native Cornhusker,"
as I identified him. Bill was born in Kansas City, Missouri, and his
family moved to Nebraska when he was seven. Whether he qualifies
as a native depends on which dictionary one consults.

Some might dismiss that as hair-splitting. But I see precision—
one reason why Bill Flack is a superforecaster.

Here's another: Bill doesn't think he should be invited to Davos.
"I'd have to go to Google just to find out who the prime minister of Fanatistan is," he wrote. "The seats at Davos should be saved
for people who can lecture without notes on Fanatistani politics and
economics and demographics, and who know that the Prime Minister and the General-in-Chief have hated each other ever since the
PM's brother-in-law made a noisy drunken spectacle of himself at
the General-in-Chief's daughter's wedding." Recognize that? It's intellectual humility. Bill knows what he doesn't know, and respects
those who do. "The Tom Friedmen of the world possess that kind of
in-depth knowledge, and that makes them valuable."

Still, Bill Flack has an outstanding record of forecasting tough,
real-world questions, and he has the Brier score to prove it. The "Tom
Friedmen of the world" do not. Some people in Bill's position might
get cocky, but not Bill. He doesn't dismiss pundits. He uses them:
"There are good pundits and bad pundits for my purposes, of course.
The bad ones issue their predictions with no supporting arguments,
expecting their readers to treat their pronouncements like the word

from Mt. Sinai; or they back their forecasts with anecdotes rather than useful facts. The good ones argue the case for their forecasts; in fact, I see them as functioning something like lawyers in an adversarial judicial system: they put forth the best argument they can for why X is going to happen, and I consider everybody's arguments, dig further into background as necessary, and come up with my own forecast as a weighted sum of theirs."

I share Bill's dragonfly-eyed view of how he and Tom Friedman complement each other. And I would tack on a baseball metaphor to his courtroom metaphor. Big strategic thinkers like Friedman will probably never step to the plate and let us compare their batting averages with those of superforecasters like Bill. But they might be amenable to pitching forecasting questions at aspiring batters. Friedman pitched some great questions on Iraq in 2002 and some of his 2014 petro-state questions may prove tricky to hit.

Bill knows there is no guarantee he will continue to be a great batter. He also knows that his success hinges on more than the quality of the pitching. Slumps are inevitable because we frequently pass through phases of history riddled with irreducible uncertainty—phases in which luck trumps skill. These are the moments when the laws of statistics tell us to shift bets and put our money on massive regression to the mean.

How would he react when that happens? "That possibility is very much before my eyes," he wrote. "I know well that luck played a part in the success that I've had." That luck may turn. "An overconfident forecast that goes bad can hit one hard in the Brier score, and a few such could make the difference between a terrific season and a terrible one. It probably wouldn't shatter my image of myself as a reasonably competent superforecaster, but it'd probably make me more cautious and less prone to extreme forecasts. . . . This would probably be a salutary thing, of course: the Brier score gives me feedback on whether I'm under- or overconfident, and I modify my forecasting behavior in response to it."[1]

I can't imagine a better description of the "try, fail, analyze, adjust, try again" cycle—and of the grit to keep at it and keep improving. Bill Flack is perpetual beta.

And that, too, is why he is a superforecaster.

An Invitation

If you like what you've read about superforecasters and the Good Judgment Project, please consider joining us. You'll be improving your own forecasting skills and helping science at the same time. You can learn more at www.goodjudgment.com.

APPENDIX

Ten Commandments for Aspiring Superforecasters

The guidelines sketched here distill key themes in this book and in training systems that have been experimentally demonstrated to boost accuracy in real-world forecasting contests. For more details, visit www.goodjudgment.com.

(1) Triage.

Focus on questions where your hard work is likely to pay off. Don't waste time either on easy "clocklike" questions (where simple rules of thumb can get you close to the right answer) or on impenetrable "cloud-like" questions (where even fancy statistical models can't beat the dart-throwing chimp). Concentrate on questions in the Goldilocks zone of difficulty, where effort pays off the most.

For instance, "Who will win the presidential election, twelve years out, in 2028?" is impossible to forecast now. Don't even try. Could you have predicted in 1940 the winner of the election, twelve years out, in 1952? If you think you could have known it would be a then-unknown colonel in the United States Army, Dwight Eisenhower, you may be afflicted by one of the worst cases of hindsight bias ever documented by psychologists.

Of course, triage judgment calls get harder as we come closer to home. How much justifiable confidence can we place in March 2015 on who will win the 2016 election? The short answer is not a lot but still a lot more than we can for the election in 2028. We can at least narrow the 2016 field to a small set of plausible contenders, which is a lot better than the vast set of unknown (Eisenhower-ish) possibilities lurking in 2028.

Certain classes of outcomes have well-deserved reputations for being radically unpredictable (e.g., oil prices, currency markets). But we usually don't discover how unpredictable outcomes are until we have spun our wheels for a while trying to gain analytical traction. Bear in mind the two basic errors it is possible to make here. We could fail to try to predict the potentially predictable or we could waste our time trying to predict the unpredictable. Which error would be worse in the situation you face?

(2) Break seemingly intractable problems into tractable sub-problems.

Channel the playful but disciplined spirit of Enrico Fermi who— when he wasn't designing the world's first atomic reactor—loved ballparking answers to head-scratchers such as "How many extraterrestrial civilizations exist in the universe?" Decompose the problem into its knowable and unknowable parts. Flush ignorance into the open. Expose and examine your assumptions. Dare to be wrong by making your best guesses. Better to discover errors quickly than to hide them behind vague verbiage.

Superforecasters see Fermi-izing as part of the job. How else could they generate quantitative answers to seemingly impossible-to-quantify questions about Arafat's autopsy, bird-flu epidemics, oil prices, Boko Haram, the Battle of Aleppo, and bond-yield spreads.

We find this Fermi-izing spirit at work even in the quest for love, the ultimate unquantifiable. Consider Peter Backus, a lonely guy in London, who guesstimated the number of potential female partners in his vicinity by starting with the population of London (approximately six million) and winnowing that number down by the proportion of women in the population (about 50%), by the proportion of singles (about 50%), by the proportion in the right age range (about 20%), by the proportion of university graduates (about 26%), by the proportion he finds attractive (only 5%), by the proportion likely to find him attractive (only 5%), and by the proportion likely to be compatible with him (about 10%). Conclusion: roughly twenty-six women in the pool, a daunting but not impossible search task. [1]

There are no objectively correct answers to true-love questions, but we can score the accuracy of the Fermi estimates that superforecasters generate in the IARPA tournament. The surprise is how often remarkably good probability estimates arise from a remarkably crude series of assumptions and guesstimates.

(3) Strike the right balance between inside and outside views.

Superforecasters know that there is nothing new under the sun. Nothing is 100% "unique." Language purists be damned: uniqueness is a matter of degree. So superforecasters conduct creative searches for comparison classes even for seemingly unique events, such as the outcome of a hunt for a high-profile terrorist (Joseph Kony) or the standoff between a new socialist government in Athens and Greece's creditors. Superforecasters are in the habit of posing the outside-view question: How often do things of this sort happen in situations of this sort?

So too apparently is Larry Summers, a Harvard professor and former Treasury secretary. He knows about the planning fallacy: when bosses ask employees how long it will take to finish a project, employees tend to underestimate the time they need, often by factors of two or three. Summers suspects his own employees are no different. One former employee, Greg Mankiw, himself now a famous economist, recalls Summers's strategy: he doubled the employee's estimate, then moved to the next higher time unit. "So, if the research assistant says the task will take an hour, it will take two days. If he says two days, it will take four weeks."[2] It's a nerd joke: Summers corrected for employees' failure to take the outside view in making estimates by taking the outside view toward employees' estimates, and then inventing a funny correction factor.

Of course Summers would adjust his correction factor if an employee astonished him and delivered on time. He would balance his outside-view expectation of tardiness against the new inside-view evidence that a particular employee is an exception to the rule. Because each of us is, to some degree, unique.

(4) Strike the right balance between under- and overreacting to evidence.

Belief updating is to good forecasting as brushing and flossing are to good dental hygiene. It can be boring, occasionally uncomfortable, but it pays off in the long term. That said, don't suppose that belief updating is always easy because it sometimes is. Skillful updating requires teasing subtle signals from noisy news flows—all the while resisting the lure of wishful thinking.

Savvy forecasters learn to ferret out telltale clues before the rest of us. They snoop for nonobvious lead indicators, about what would have to happen before X could, where X might be anything from an expansion of Arctic sea ice to a nuclear war in the Korean peninsula. Note the fine line here between picking up subtle clues before everyone else and getting suckered by misleading clues. Does the appearance of an article critical of North Korea in the official Chinese press signal that China is about to squeeze Pyongyang hard—or was it just a quirky error in editorial judgment? The best forecasters tend to be incremental belief updaters, often moving from probabilities of, say, 0.4 to 0.35 or from 0.6 to 0.65, distinctions too subtle to capture with vague verbiage, like "might" or "maybe," but distinctions that, in the long run, define the difference between good and great forecasters.

Yet superforecasters also know how to jump, to move their probability estimates fast in response to diagnostic signals. Superforecasters are not perfect Bayesian updaters but they are better than most of us. And that is largely because they value this skill and work hard at cultivating it.

(5) Look for the clashing causal forces at work in each problem.

For every good policy argument, there is typically a counterargument that is at least worth acknowledging. For instance, if you are a devout dove who believes that threatening military action never brings peace, be open to the possibility that you might be wrong about Iran. And the same advice applies if you are a devout hawk who believes that soft "appeasement" policies never pay off. Each side should list, in advance, the signs that would nudge them toward the other.

Now here comes the really hard part. In classical dialectics, thesis meets antithesis, producing synthesis. In dragonfly eye, one view meets another and another and another—all of which must be synthesized into a single image. There are no paint-by-number rules here. Synthesis is an art that requires reconciling irreducibly subjective judgments. If you do it well, engaging in this process of synthesizing should transform you from a cookie-cutter dove or hawk into an odd hybrid creature, a dove-hawk, with a nuanced view of when tougher or softer policies are likelier to work.

(6) Strive to distinguish as many degrees of doubt as the problem permits but no more.

Few things are either certain or impossible. And "maybe" isn't all that informative. So your uncertainty dial needs more than three settings. Nuance matters. The more degrees of uncertainty you can distinguish, the better a forecaster you are likely to be. As in poker, you have an advantage if you are better than your competitors at separating 60/40 bets from 40/60—or 55/45 from 45/55. Translating vague-verbiage hunches into numeric probabilities feels unnatural at first but it can be done. It just requires patience and practice. The superforecasters have shown what is possible.

Most of us could learn, quite quickly, to think in more granular ways about uncertainty. Recall the episode in which President Obama was trying to figure out whether Osama bin Laden was the mystery occupant of the walled-in compound in Abbottabad. And recall the probability estimates of his intelligence officers and the president's reaction to their estimates: "This is fifty-fifty . . . a flip of the coin." Now suppose that President Obama had been shooting the breeze with basketball buddies and each one offered probability estimates on the outcome of a college game—and those estimates corresponded exactly to those offered by intelligence officers on the whereabouts of Osama bin Laden. Would the president still have shrugged and said, "This is fifty-fifty," or would he have said, "Sounds like the odds fall between three to one and four to one"? I bet on the latter. The president is accustomed to granular thinking in the domain of sports. Every year, he enjoys trying to predict the winners of the March Madness basketball tournament, a probability puzzle that draws the attention of serious statisticians. But, like his Democratic and Republican predecessors, he does not apply the same rigor to national security decisions. Why? Because different norms govern different thought processes. Reducing complex hunches to scorable probabilities is de rigueur in sports but not in national security.[3]

So, don't reserve rigorous reasoning for trivial pursuits. George Tenet would not have dared utter "slam dunk" about weapons of mass destruction in Iraq if the Bush 43 White House had enforced standards of evidence and proof that are second nature to seasoned gamblers on sporting events. Slam dunk implies one is willing to offer infinite odds—and to lose everything if one is wrong.

(7) Strike the right balance between under- and overconfidence, between prudence and decisiveness.

Superforecasters understand the risks both of rushing to judgment and of dawdling too long near "maybe." They routinely manage the trade-off between the need to take decisive stands (who wants to listen to a waffler?) and the need to qualify their stands (who wants to listen to a blowhard?). They realize that long-term accuracy requires getting good scores on both calibration and resolution—which requires moving beyond blame-game ping-pong. It is not enough just to avoid the most recent mistake. They have to find creative ways to tamp down both types of forecasting errors—misses and false alarms—to the degree a fickle world permits such uncontroversial improvements in accuracy.

(8) Look for the errors behind your mistakes but beware of rearview-mirror hindsight biases.

Don't try to justify or excuse your failures. Own them! Conduct unflinching postmortems: Where exactly did I go wrong? And remember that although the more common error is to learn too little from failure and to overlook flaws in your basic assumptions, it is also possible to learn too much (you may have been basically on the right track but made a minor technical mistake that had big ramifications). Also don't forget to do postmortems on your successes too. Not all successes imply that your reasoning was right. You may have just lucked out by making offsetting errors. And if you keep confidently reasoning along the same lines, you are setting yourself up for a nasty surprise.

(9) Bring out the best in others and let others bring out the best in you.

Master the fine arts of team management, especially perspective taking (understanding the arguments of the other side so well that you can reproduce them to the other's satisfaction), precision questioning (helping others to clarify their arguments so they are not misunderstood), and constructive confrontation (learning to disagree without being disagreeable). Wise leaders know how fine the line can be between a helpful suggestion and micromanagerial meddling or between a rigid group and a decisive one or between a scatterbrained group and an open-minded one. Tommy Lasorda, the former coach of the Los Angeles Dodgers, got it roughly right: "Managing is like holding a dove in your hand. If you hold it too tightly you kill it, but if you hold it too loosely, you lose it."[4]

(10) Master the error-balancing bicycle.

Implementing each commandment requires balancing opposing errors. Just as you can't learn to ride a bicycle by reading a physics textbook, you can't become a superforecaster by reading training manuals. Learning requires doing, with good feedback that leaves no ambiguity about whether you are succeeding—"I'm rolling along smoothly!"—or whether you are failing—"crash!" Also remember that practice is not just going through the motions of making forecasts, or casually reading the news and tossing out probabilities. Like all other known forms of expertise, superforecasting is the product of deep, deliberative practice.

(11) Don't treat commandments as commandments.

"It is impossible to lay down binding rules," Helmuth von Moltke warned, "because two cases will never be exactly the same."[5] As in war, so in all things. Guidelines are the best we can do in a world where nothing is certain or exactly repeatable. Superforecasting requires constant mindfulness, even when—perhaps especially when—you are dutifully trying to follow these commandments.

Acknowledgments

PHIL TETLOCK

Although I wrote this book in the first person singular, that should not obscure the profoundly collaborative nature of the Good Judgment Project. My research partner, Barbara Mellers, also happens to be my life partner. We launched this project together in the midst of personal tragedy, the passing of our beloved daughter, Jenny, to whom this book is dedicated. The project filled our empty lives with a measure of meaning. We believe that if the message of this book is taken to heart, it has the potential to make a crazy world a bit saner.

The list of key contributors is long. Without Terry Murray and David Wayrynen, the project would have collapsed countless times. Without Steve Rieber and Jason Matheny, a bureaucratic Goliath, the intelligence community, never would have funded a bunch of wannabe Davids with slingshot money. Without the statistical savvy and programming skills of Lyle Ungar, Angela Minster, David Scott, Jon Baron, Eric Stone, Sam Swift, Phillip Rescober, and Ville Satopää, we could not have won the forecasting tournament. Without the political science expertise of Mike Horowitz and his question-generation team (Katie Cochran, Jay Ulfelder, Allison Balls, Janna Rappoport, and Regina Joseph), the tournament would not have been stocked with so many synapse-stimulating challenges, and we would not see nearly as clearly as we now do how to make the next generation of forecasting tournaments even more exciting and useful. Without Terry Murray, Eva Chen, Tom Hoffman, Michael Bishop, and Catherine Wright, the project would have dissolved into administrative chaos.

Among the postdoctoral fellows and graduate students, Eva Chen deserves special mention for her selfless dedication and willingness to do whatever it took to make things work. Pavel Atanasov and Phillip Rescober played pivotal roles in running prediction market operations. Eva and Pavel—plus Katrina Fincher and Welton Chang—showed it is possible to teach real-world forecasting skills, a great discovery.

And there is my gratitude toward the many friends and colleagues who commented on drafts of this book, including Daniel Kahneman, Paul Schoemaker, Terry Murray, Welton Chang, Jason Matheny, Angela Duckworth, Aaron Brown, Michael Mauboussin, Katrina Fincher, Eva Chen, Michael Horowitz, Don Moore, John Katz, John Brockman, Greg Mitchell, and, of course, Barbara Mellers.

Finally, three closing notes. First, I thank my long-suffering co-author, Dan Gardner, and editor, Amanda Cook, who helped me tell my story far better than I could have—and who had to wrestle for two years against my professorial propensity to "complexify" fundamentally simple points. Fortunately for readers, they usually won. Foxes will need to parse the endnotes. Second, but for the courageous bureaucratic decision of IARPA to sponsor a David-versus-Goliath forecasting tournament, we never would have discovered the superforecasters. I know of no other intelligence agency on the planet that would have allowed such a totally unclassified competition and then placed zero constraints on researchers' ability to publish the results. And then there are, of course, the superforecasters themselves, too numerous to mention by name, without whom there would have been no story to tell. They have shown what is possible when smart people commit to pushing themselves to the limit. They surprised us all. Now I hope they will inspire readers to hone their own forecasting skills.

DAN GARDNER

I'll second Phil's acknowledgments, and add him to the list with an explanation that comes from the inscription at the St. Paul's tomb of the architect Christopher Wren: "look around you."

I'll also add the names of four extraordinary women: Amanda Cook, my wife, my mother, and Queen Elizabeth. Amanda edited this book and without her sometimes astonishing patience and perseverance it would not exist. Ditto for my wife, Sandra, because I'm useless without her, and my mother, June, who made me, which was inarguably a necessary antecedent to my participation in this book's creation. And the Queen is the Queen, dammit. Long may she reign.

NOTES

1. AN OPTIMISTIC SKEPTIC

1. Why single out Tom Friedman when so many other celebrity pundits could have served the purpose? The choice was driven by a simple formula: (status of pundit) X (difficulty of pinning down his/her forecasts) X (relevance of pundit's work to world politics). Highest score wins. Friedman has high status; his claims about possible futures are highly difficult to pin down—and his work is highly relevant to geopolitical forecasting. The choice of Friedman was in no way driven by an aversion to his editorial opinions. Indeed, I reveal in the last chapter a sneaky admiration for some aspects of his work. Exasperatingly evasive though Friedman can be as a forecaster, he proves to be a fabulous source of forecasting questions.

2. Again, this is not to imply that Friedman is unusual in this regard. Virtually every political pundit on the planet operates under the same tacit ground rules. They make countless claims about what lies ahead but couch their claims in such vague verbiage that it is impossible to test them. How should we interpret intriguing claims like "expansion of NATO *could* trigger a ferocious response from the Russian bear and *may* even lead to a new Cold War" or "the Arab Spring *might* signal that the days of unaccountable autocracy in the Arab world are numbered" or . . . ? The key terms in these semantic dances, *may* or *could* or *might*, are not accompanied by guidance on how to interpret them. *Could* could mean anything from a 0.0000001 chance of "a large asteroid striking our planet in the next one hundred years" to a 0.7 chance of "Hillary Clinton winning the presidency in 2016." All this makes it impossible to track accuracy across time and questions. It also gives pundits endless flexibility to claim credit when something happens (I told you it could) and to dodge blame when it does not (I merely said it could happen). We shall encounter many examples of such linguistic mischief.

3. It is as though we have collectively concluded that sizing up the starting lineup for the Yankees deserves greater care than sizing up the risk of genocide in the South Sudan. Of course the analogy between baseball and politics is imperfect. Baseball is played over and over under standard conditions. Politics is a quirky game in which the rules are continually being contorted and contested. So scoring political forecasting is much harder than compiling baseball statistics. But "harder" doesn't mean impossible. It turns out to be quite possible.

There is also another objection to the analogy. Pundits do more than forecasting. They put events in historical perspective, offer explanations, engage in policy advocacy, and pose provocative questions. All true, but pundits also make lots of implicit or explicit forecasts. For instance, the historical analogies pundits invoke contain implicit forecasts: the Munich appeasement analogy is trotted out to support the conditional forecast "if you appease country X, it will ramp up its demands"; and the World War I analogy is trotted out to support "if you use threats, you will escalate the conflict." I submit that it is logically impossible to engage in policy advocacy (which pundits routinely do) without making assumptions about whether we would be better or worse off if we went down one or another policy path. Show me a pundit who does not make at least implicit forecasts and I will show you one who has faded into Zen-like irrelevance.

4. See James Gleick, *Chaos: Making a New Science* (New York: Viking, 1987); Donald N. McCloskey, "History, Differential Equations, and the Problem of Narration," *History and Theory* 30 (1991): 21–36.

5. Pierre-Simon Laplace, *A Philosophical Essay on Probabilities*, trans. Frederick Wilson Truscott and Frederick Lincoln Emory (New York: Dover Publications, 1951), p. 4.

6. Yet even historians who should know better continue to make grand pronouncements like this one, by Oxford professor Margaret MacMillan, quoted in Maureen Dowd's September 7, 2014, *New York Times* column: "the 21st century will be a series of low grade, very nasty wars that will go on and on without clear outcomes, doing dreadful things to any civilians in their paths"—a good summary of the recent past but a dubious guide to the world of 2083. Books like *The Next 100 Years: A Forecast for the 21st Century* continue to become bestsellers. The author of the latter, incidentally, is George Friedman, the CEO of Stratfor, a firm that provides geopolitical forecasting to deep-pocketed clients in the public and private sectors. A mere two years after it was published the Arab Spring turned the Middle East topsy-turvy, but I can't find it in Friedman's book, which casts some doubt on his forecasts for the remaining ninety-eight years. Friedman is also the author of the 1991 book *The Coming War with Japan*—that's the coming *American* war with Japan—which has yet to prove its prescience.

7. For islands of professionalism in a sea of malpractice, see the forecasting concepts and tools reviewed in Nate Silver, *The Signal and the Noise: Why So*

Many Predictions Fail—but Some Don't (New York: Penguin Press, 2012); J. Scott Armstrong, ed., *Principles of Forecasting: A Handbook for Researchers and Practitioners* (Boston: Kluwer, 2001); and Bruce Bueno de Mesquita, *The Predictioneer's Game* (New York: Random House, 2009). Expanding these islands has proven hard. There is often little transfer of classroom statistical concepts, like regression toward the mean, to problems that students later encounter in life. See D. Kahneman and A. Tversky, "On the Study of Statistical Intuitions," *Cognition* 11 (1982): 123–41. This poses a big challenge for the efforts of the Good Judgment Project to train people to think like superforecasters.

8. "Bill Gates: My Plan to Fix the World's Biggest Problems," *Wall Street Journal*, January 25, 2013, http://www.wsj.com/articles/SB10001424127887323539804578261780648285770.

9. B. Fischhoff and C. Chauvin, eds., *Intelligence Analysis: Behavioral and Social Scientific Foundations* (Washington, DC: National Academies Press, 2011); Committee on Behavioral and Social Science Research to Improve Intelligence Analysis for National Security, Board on Behavioral, Cognitive, and Sensory Sciences, Division of Behavioral and Social Sciences and Education, National Research Council, *Intelligence Analysis for Tomorrow: Advances from the Behavioral and Social Sciences* (Washington, DC: National Academies Press, 2011).

10. P. E. Tetlock, B. Mellers, N. Rohrbaugh, and E. Chen, "Forecasting Tournaments: Tools for Increasing Transparency and Improving the Quality of Debate," *Current Directions in Psychological Science* (2014): 290–95.

11. Aaron Brown, in discussion with the author, April 30, 2013.

12. Paul Meehl, *Clinical Versus Statistical Prediction* (Minneapolis: University of Minnesota Press, 1954).

13. Stephen Baker, *Final Jeopardy* (Boston: Houghton Mifflin Harcourt, 2011), p. 35.

14. David Ferrucci, in discussion with the author, July 8, 2014.

2. ILLUSIONS OF KNOWLEDGE

1. Archibald L. Cochrane with Max Blythe, *One Man's Medicine: An Autobiography of Professor Archie Cochrane* (London: British Medical Journal, 1989).

2. Ibid., p. 171.

3. Ibid.

4. Druin Burch, *Taking the Medicine: A Short History of Medicine's Beautiful Idea, and Our Difficulty Swallowing It* (London: Vintage, 2010), p. 4.

5. Ibid., p. 37.

6. Ira Rutkow, *Seeking the Cure: A History of Medicine in America* (New York: Scribner, 2010), p. 98.

7. Ibid., p. 94.

8. Burch, *Taking the Medicine*, p. 158.

9. Richard Feynman, commencement address at the California Institute of Technology, Pasadena, 1974.

10. Richard Feynman, *The Meaning of It All: Thoughts of a Citizen-Scientist* (New York: Basic Books, 2005), p. 28.

11. Ibid., p. 27.

12. Cochrane with Blythe, *One Man's Medicine*, pp. 46, 157, 211, 190.

13. Daniel Kahneman, *Thinking, Fast and Slow* (New York: Farrar, Straus and Giroux, 2011), p. 209.

14. If you know cognitive psychology, you know that the heuristics-and-biases school of thought has not gone unchallenged. Skeptics are impressed by how stunningly accurately System 1 can perform. People automatically and seemingly optimally synthesize meaningless photons and sound waves into language we infuse with meaning (Steven Pinker, *How the Mind Works*, New York: Norton, 1997).

There is dispute over how often System 1 heuristics lead us astray (Gerd Gigerenzer and Peter Todd, *Simple Heuristics that Make Us Smart*, New York: Oxford University Press, 1999) and how hard it is to overcome WYSIATI illusions via training or incentives (Philip Tetlock and Barbara Mellers, "The Great Rationality Debate: The Impact of the Kahneman and Tversky Research Program, *Psychological Science* 13, no. 5 [2002]: 94–99). Psychology has yet to piece together the mosaic. It is, however, my view that the heuristics-and-biases perspective still provides the best first-order approximation of the errors that real-world forecasters make and the most useful guidance on how to help forecasters bring their error rates down.

15. Michael Gazzaniga, *The Mind's Past* (Berkeley: University of California Press, 1998), pp. 24–25.

16. Ziva Kunda, *Social Cognition: Making Sense of People* (Cambridge, MA: MIT Press, 1999).

17. Kahneman, *Thinking, Fast and Slow*, p. 212.

18. You can see it at work during elections. When an incumbent president seeks reelection, the question that many voters want answered is "Did he do a good job in his first term?" On close inspection, that is a tough question. It requires a review of what the president did and didn't do over the previous four years, and, even harder, consideration of how things could have turned out differently under different leadership. It would be a ton of work even for a journalist covering the White House and impossible for someone who doesn't follow politics closely. Not surprisingly, voters do a bait and switch. How voters feel about local economic conditions, as well as those of the country, in the six months prior to the election sways how they judge the job the president has done over the previous four years. So "Do I feel the country has been roughly on the right track over the last six months?" replaces "Did the president do a good job over the last four years?" Few voters explicitly say to themselves, "It's too hard to judge the president's record so I'll use a proxy question instead." But many of us implicitly do exactly that. See, for example, Christopher Achen and Larry Bartels, "Musical Chairs: Pocketbook Voting and the Limits of Democratic Accountability," paper presented at the 2004 annual meeting of the American Political Science Association, Chicago.

19. Daniel Kahneman and Gary Klein, "Conditions for Intuitive Expertise: A Failure to Disagree," *American Psychologist* 64, no. 6 (September 2009): 515–26.

20. W. G. Chase and H. A. Simon, "The Mind's Eye in Chess," in *Visual Information Processing*, ed. W. G. Chase (New York: Academic Press, 1973).

21. Kahneman and Klein, "Conditions for Intuitive Expertise," p. 520.

22. Ibid.

23. Nigel Farndale, "Magnus Carlsen: Grandmaster Flash," *Observer*, October 19, 2013.

24. Peggy Noonan, "Monday Morning," *Wall Street Journal*, November 5, 2012, http://blogs.wsj.com/peggynoonan/2012/11/05/monday-morning/.

3. KEEPING SCORE

1. Mark Spoonauer, "The Ten Worst Tech Predictions of All Time," *Laptop*, August 7, 2013, blog.laptopmag.com/10-worst-tech-predictions-of-all-time.

2. Bryan Glick, "Timing Is Everything in Steve Ballmer's Departure—Why Microsoft Needs a New Vision," *Computer Weekly Editor's Blog*, August 27, 2013, http://www.computerweekly.com/blogs/editors-blog/2013/08/timing-is-everything-in-steve.html.

3. "Starr Report: Narrative." Nature of President Clinton's Relationship with Monica Lewinsky (Washington, DC: US Government Printing Office, 2004), footnote 1128.

4. Sameer Singh, *Tech-Thoughts*, November 18, 2013, http://www.tech-thoughts.net/2013/11/smartphone-market-share-by-country-q3-2013.html#.VQM0QEJYW-Q.

5. Barry Ritholtz, "2010 Reminder: QE = Currency Debasement and Inflation," *The Big Picture*, November 15, 2013, http://www.ritholtz.com/blog/2013/11/qe-debasement-inflation/print/.

6. A similar problem bedevils Steve Ballmer's iPhone prediction. The iPhone

market-share numbers I presented are from six years after its launch and they were higher after seven years. So, in principle, Ballmer could argue his forecast had an implicit time frame of two, three, or five years. That's basically the opposite of the "just wait, it's coming" defense. It may be tendentious and self-serving, but it is an argument that could be made—which would lead to precisely the sort of back-and-forth bickering we want to avoid when we judge forecasting accuracy.

7. Jonathan Schell, *The Fate of the Earth* and *The Abolition* (Stanford, CA: Stanford University Press, 2000), p. 183.

8. Brian Till, "Mikhail Gorbachev: The West Could Have Saved the Russian Economy," *Atlantic*, June 16, 2001, http://www.theatlantic.com/international /archive/2011/06/mikhail-gorbachev-the-west-could-have-saved-the-russian -economy/240466/.

9. Sherman Kent, "Estimates and Influence," *Studies in Intelligence* (Summer 1968): 35.

10. Sherman Kent, "Words of Estimative Probability," in *Sherman Kent and the Board of National Estimates*, ed. Donald P. Steury (Washington, DC: History Staff, Center for the Study of Intelligence, CIA, 1994), pp. 134–35.

11. Ibid., p. 135.

12. Richard E. Neustadt and Ernest R. May, *Thinking in Time* (New York: Free Press, 1988).

13. *Sherman Kent and the Profession of Intelligence Analysis*, Center for the Study of Intelligence, Central Intelligence Agency, November 2002, p. 55.

14. Ibid.

15. David Leonhardt, "When the Crowd Isn't Wise," *New York Times*, July 7, 2012.

16. Henry Blodget, "Niall Ferguson: Okay, I Admit It—Paul Krugman Was Right," *Business Insider*, January 30, 2012, http://www.businessinsider.com/niall -ferguson-paul-krugman-was-right-2012-1.

17. Brier scoring is "proper" because it incentivizes forecasters to report their true beliefs and to resist bending them to political pressures. A forecaster who cares only about her Brier score will report her true belief that there is, say, a 4% chance of an Iranian nuclear test in 2015, but a forecaster worried about blame-game fallout might pump up that probability to preempt later possible recriminations— "you said it only had a 4% chance!" Brier scoring imposes reputational penalties for overconfidence that are tied to the financial penalties that gamblers would incur from the same errors. If you aren't willing to bet on the odds implied by your probability estimate, rethink your estimate. Glenn W. Brier, "Verification of Forecasts Expressed in Terms of Probability," *Monthly Weather Review* 78, no. 1 (1950): 1–3; Robert L. Winkler, "Evaluating Probabilities: Asymmetric Scoring Rules," *Management Science* 40, no. 11 (1994): 1395–405.

18. Larry Kudlow fits the profile of hedgehogs in EPJ, but he was not one of the anonymous forecasters in EPJ. And I certainly did not choose him because he is conservative. EPJ offers many examples of left-wing hedgehogs. Indeed, as I show in EPJ, many hedgehogs, left and right, see "hedgehog" as a compliment, not an insult. They are more incisive and decisive than those equivocating foxes. Remember the battle of the partisan spinmeisters in the 2004 presidential election? Was John Kerry a flexible tactician or an opportunistic flip-flopper? Was George W. Bush a principled leader or a dogmatic dimwit? "Fox" and "hedgehog" are labile labels.

19. Larry Kudlow, "Bush Boom Continues," *National Review*, December 10, 2007, http://nationalreview.com/article/223061/bush-boom-continues/larry-kudlow.

20. Larry Kudlow, "Bush's 'R' is for 'Right'," Creators.com, May 2, 2008, http://www. creators.com/opinion/lawrence-kudlow-bush-s-r-is-for-right.html.

21. Larry Kudlow, "If Things Are So Bad . . . ," *National Review*, July 25, 2008.

22. Annie Duke, in discussion with the author, April 30, 2013. This is no quirk of poker players. Imagine you suffer from insomnia and haven't slept properly in days and you lose your temper and shout at a colleague. Then you apologize. What does this incident say about you? It says you need your sleep. Beyond that, it says nothing. But imagine you see someone who snaps, shouts, then apologizes and explains that he has insomnia and hasn't slept properly in days. What does that incident say about that person? Logically, it should say about him what it said

about you, but decades of research suggest that's not the lesson you will draw. You will think this person is a jerk. Psychologists call this the fundamental attribution error. We are fully aware that situational factors—like insomnia—can influence our own behavior, and we rightly attribute our behavior to those factors, but we routinely don't make the same allowance for others and instead assume that their behavior reflects who they are. Why did that guy act like a jerk? Because he is a jerk. This is a potent bias. If a student is told to speak in support of a Republican candidate, an observer will tend to see the student as pro-Republican even if the student only did what she was told to do—and even if *the observer* is the one who gave the order! Stepping outside ourselves and seeing things as others do is that hard. See Lee Ross, "The Intuitive Psychologist and His Shortcomings: Distortions in the Attribution Process," in *Advances in Experimental Social Psychology*, ed. Leonard Berkowitz, vol. 10 (New York: Academic Press, 1977), 173–220; Daniel T. Gilbert, "Ordinary Personology," in *The Handbook of Social Psychology*, vol. 2, ed. Daniel T. Gilbert, Susan T. Fiske, and Gardner Lindzey (New York: Oxford University Press, 1998): 89–150.

23. It can be a good career move in academia to stake out a provocatively extreme position on issues where the truth falls in the murky middle. Case in point: are our styles of thinking fixed by personality, or can we shift styles of thinking as readily as we take on one social role or another? Murky-middle-but-true answer: it depends on the flexibility of the person—and the power of the situation. Case in point: we observed markedly less overconfidence among forecasters in the IARPA tournaments with open competition and public leaderboards than we did in the earlier EPJ research that guaranteed all forecasters anonymity. One result: the hedgehog-fox distinction mattered far less in the IARPA tournaments.

4. SUPERFORECASTERS

1. National Intelligence Estimate background debriefing at the White House on weapons of mass destruction in Iraq, October 2001, http://fas.org/irp/cia/product/iraq-wmd.html.

2. Condoleezza Rice, interview with Wolf Blitzer, CNN, September 8, 2002.

3. Committee on Behavioral and Social Science Research to Improve Intelli-

gence Analysis for National Security, Board on Behavioral, Cognitive, and Sensory Sciences, Division of Behavioral and Social Sciences and Education, National Research Council, *Intelligence Analysis for Tomorrow: Advances from the Behavioral and Social Sciences* (Washington, DC: National Academies Press, 2011).

4. In cost-benefit analysis terms, the question is how much should the United States be willing to pay for an improved probability estimation system that would lower the risk of a $2 trillion slam-dunk "mistake" by, say, 20% or 30%? Expected-value theory suggests an answer in the hundreds of billions of dollars. By this standard, the Good Judgment Project is the bargain of the century. But note the scare quotes around "mistake." The 2003 Iraq invasion is widely seen as a mistake, but no one knows how bad off we would be today if Saddam Hussein had clung to power—or how much we would have spent on national security in that world. My personal guesstimate is that the tournament would still be a bargain, even if we paint a grim what-if baseline-comparison world.

5. The Commission on the Intelligence Capabilities of the United States Regarding Weapons of Mass Destruction, *Report to the President of the United States* (Washington, DC: March 31, 2005), p. 155.

6. Robert Jervis, in discussion with the author, March 27, 2013.

7. Committee on Behavioral and Social Science Research to Improve Intelligence Analysis for National Security, *Intelligence Analysis for Tomorrow*, National Academies Press, 2011.

8. Generating Goldilocks-zone questions was hard. It required winnowing out questions that were too easy (had less than 10% or greater than 90% chance of occurrence) or intractably difficult (questions to which no one could be reasonably supposed to know the answer). Michael Horowitz's question-generation team deserves credit here.

9. Credit for this insight goes to two colleagues at the University of Pennsylvania, Lyle Ungar and Jonathan Baron. Lyle is responsible for all algorithms deployed by our project, with the exception of "L2E" developed by David Scott at Rice University.

10. David Ignatius, "More Chatter Than Needed," *Washington Post*, Novem-

ber 1, 2013. Ignatius must have talked to someone with access to classified sources inside the US government.

11. Ibid. The IC has never disputed the Ignatius story. And I believe it to be true. Indeed, I am willing to make a big reputational bet that the superforecasters beat the intelligence analysts in each year in which such comparisons were possible.

The true explanation for why superforecasters outperformed intelligence analysts is unknown. But I doubt it is because superforecasters are smarter or more open-minded. I suspect they did better because they treat forecasting as a cultivatable skill whereas analysts work inside an organization that treats prediction as a sideshow, not part of the analyst's real job. Consider the views of Thomas Fingar, a former chairman of the National Intelligence Council: "Prediction is not—and should not be—the goal of strategic analysis. . . . The goal is to identify the most important streams of developments, how they interact, where they seem to be headed, what drives the process, and what signs might indicate a change of trajectory"; see Thomas Fingar, *Reducing Uncertainty: Intelligence Analysis and National Security* (Stanford, CA: Stanford University Press, 2011), pp. 53, 74.

Tom Fingar and I served together on the 2010 National Research Council committee that urged the IC to conduct IARPA-style experiments of what works. He is a sophisticated and dedicated public servant. And his statement captures why the IC is unlikely to invest in cultivating its own superforecasters any time soon. How can you "identify where streams of developments seem to be headed" without making implicit predictions?

Analysts are not the only professionals who balk at acknowledging how riddled their work is with implicit predictions. Consider the journalist Joe Klein: "A professor at the University of Pennsylvania's Wharton School wants to hook me up to a computer and test how well I make predictions," wrote *Time*'s Joe Klein after I invited him and other pundits to participate in a forecasting tournament. "I can save him the trouble. Journalists are terrific when it comes to analyzing the past, pretty good on what's happening right now and embarrassingly dreadful about the day after tomorrow. I stopped making predictions right after I assured CNN's Jake Tapper that George W. Bush would never win the Republican presidential nomination after he lost the New Hampshire primary in 2000"; see http://swampland .time.com/2013/04/11/congress-may-finally-do-a-budget-deal/.

With due respect to Klein—and I do respect those who own up to forecasting flops—he's wrong. He didn't stop making predictions. He just doesn't recognize that the predictions he makes are predictions. "Isn't it interesting that

North Korea's ever more extravagant military threats aren't drawing much media attention in the US?" Klein wrote shortly before he claimed to have sworn off predictions. "No one really expects a war to break out. But what if one does? What if Kim gets so far out on the ledge—with his threats to attack both South Korea and the US—that he can't back down? It's unlikely, but not impossible"; see http://swampland.time.com/2013/03/29/the-kim-who-cried-wolf/.

Well, "unlikely, but not impossible" is a prediction. And there's plenty more like it in Klein's writing, or that of any other pundit. Or in the thoughts of anyone else. We all make predictions, constantly.

Bottom line: it is hard to learn to do something better if you don't even know you are doing it.

12. Ellen Langer, "The Illusion of Control," *Journal of Personality and Social Psychology* 32, no. 2 (August 1975): 311–28.

13. Some examples of this genre are in bad odor in short order—like *Radical E*, a book that urged businesses to follow such models as Nortel and Enron and was published eight months before the latter filed for bankruptcy. But other examples are harder to detect. Their lack of predictive power goes unnoticed for decades, even in the classrooms of leading business schools. In 1994 Jim Collins and Jerry Porras published *Built to Last: Successful Habits of Visionary Companies*, which examined eighteen exemplary companies and from these created "a master blueprint for building organizations that will prosper long into the future." It was a great read that won many accolades. But as the business professor Phil Rosenzweig noted, if Collins and Porras were right, we should, at a minimum, expect that the eighteen exemplary companies would continue to do well. Collins and Porras ended their study in 1990, so Rosenzweig checked how the companies did over the next ten years: "You would have been better off investing in an index fund than putting your money on Collins' and Porras' visionary companies." See Phil Rosenzweig, *The Halo Effect . . . and the Eight Other Business Delusions That Deceive Managers* (New York: Free Press, 2014), p. 98. The dart-throwing chimp strikes again.

14. The size of the father-son correlation determines how much you should move your prediction of the son's height toward the population average of five feet eight inches. If the father-son correlation were perfect, 1.0, base your judgment entirely on the father's height (no reversion-to-mean effect). If the correlation were 0, move all the way toward the average and give no weight to the father's height. In our special-case example, the correlation is 0.5 and the right answer is to move halfway toward the average.

15. Michael J. Mauboussin, *The Success Equation: Untangling Skill and Luck in Business, Sports, and Investing* (Boston: Harvard Business Review Press, 2012), p. 73.

16. http://fivethirtyeight.com/features/the-conventional-wisdom-on-oil-is -always-wrong/.

17. And approximately 90% of all "active" superforecasters, those answering at least fifty questions per year, landed in the top 20% performance category—so, when they did fall, they rarely fell far. This suggests that the skill/luck ratio for superforecasters may well be greater than that for regular forecasters. Exactly esti- mating skill/luck ratios is tricky, however. The values shift across samples of fore- casters, periods of history, and types of questions. If I had to hazard a guess for just the active superforecasters across all four years, it would be at minimum $^{60}/_{40}$ and possibly as high as $^{90}/_{10}$.

5. SUPERSMART?

1. Sanford Sillman, in discussion with the author, February 15, 2013, and May 19, 2014.

2. B. A. Mellers, L. Ungar, K. Fincher, M. Horowitz, P. Atanasov, S. Swift, T. Murray, and P. Tetlock, "The Psychology of Intelligence Analysis: Driv- ers of Prediction Accuracy in World Politics," *Journal of Experimental Psychol- ogy: Applied* 21, no. 1 (March 2015): 1–14; B. A. Mellers, E. Stone, T. Murray, A. Minster, N. Rohrbaugh, M. Bishop, E. Chen, J. Baker, Y. Hou, M. Horowitz, L. Ungar, and P. E. Tetlock, "Identifying and Cultivating 'Superforecasters' as a Method of Improving Probabilistic Predictions," *Perspectives in Psychological Sci- ence* (forthcoming 2015).

3. Item comes from the Forecasting Aptitude Inventory developed by Greg Mitchell and Fred Oswald.

4. The analysis was ordered by the CIA director. It concluded that there would be a cost to losing Vietnam, but nothing like the dire consequences policy mak- ers believed—a forecast that proved prescient. The director handed the report

personally to President Johnson, but with half a million soldiers already neck-deep in the quagmire Johnson did not welcome it. He never shared the report with anyone. McNamara only learned of its existence decades later.

5. Robert McNamara, *In Retrospect* (New York: Vintage, 1996), p. 33.

6. Daniel J. Levitin, *The Organized Mind: Thinking Straight in the Age of Information Overload* (New York: Dutton, 2014).

7. Superforecasters see Fermi-izing—daring to be wrong—as essential to what they do. Consider the superforecaster who goes by the screen name Cobbler. He is a software engineer in Virginia who knew little about Nigeria when he was asked in 2012 whether its government would enter into formal negotiations with the jihadist group Boko Haram. He began with the outside view and estimated the success rates of past efforts to negotiate with terrorist groups in general as well as with Boko Haram in particular. He averaged his two estimates (0% success rate of negotiating with Boko Haram and a 40% guess for negotiations with insurgencies in general). He then shifted to the inside view and assessed each side's options. The government wants to stay on good terms with moderate Islamists who want to be power brokers between the government and the terrorists. Boko Haram might also have an interest at least in appearing to negotiate. He also noted many rumors of pending talks. But he balanced all that against the ferocity of Boko Haram—and guesstimated 30%. He then averaged the outside and inside views, yielding a 25% estimate, and scheduled that number to decline as the deadline approached. Net result of all these dare-to-be-wrong guesstimates: a top 10% Brier score on a question that triggered a lot of false-positive spiking in response to rumors of pending talks.

Or consider superforecaster Regina Joseph, who tackled a question about the risks of another lethal outbreak of bird flu in China, a stretch for a political risk analyst whose free-spirited career includes stints in digital media and training the US Olympic women's fencing team but no background in epidemiology. She also began with the outside view: how often has the casualty toll from bird flu exceeded the threshold value (about 80%)? But the flu season was already one-quarter over—so she cut that to 60%. She then took the inside view, noting improved public health policies and better warning indicators. All that brought her down to 40%, a number she lowered with time. Net result: not a spectacular score but better than 85% of forecasters.

Or consider Welton Chang, a former military officer with combat experience in Iraq, who estimated the likelihood of Aleppo falling to the Free Syrian Army in 2013 by first taking the outside view: how long does it take even a clearly militarily superior attacker to take urban areas as large as Aleppo? Short answer: 10% to 20% base rate chance of success. Welton then took the inside view and found that the Free Syrian Army did not remotely qualify as a superior force, so he ratcheted the chances down. Net result: one of the top 5% of Brier scores on that question.

It is amazing how many arbitrary assumptions underlie pretty darn good forecasts. Our choice is not whether to engage in crude guesswork; it is whether to do it overtly or covertly.

8. Bill Flack, in discussion with the author, August 5, 2014.

9. Peggy Noonan, "The Presidential Wheel Turns," *Wall Street Journal*, April 26, 2013.

10. Amos Tversky and Daniel Kahneman, "Judgment Under Uncertainty: Heuristics and Biases," *Science* 185 (4157): 1124–31.

11. Bruce Bueno de Mesquita in *The Predictioneer's Game* (New York: Random House, 2009) offers an elegant game-theory-grounded approach to assembling inside-view probability estimates. Ask targeted questions like "Who are the key players?," "How powerful is each?," "What does each want?," and "How much do they want it?" Then test possible coalition combinations. Bueno de Mesquita also wisely uses the wisdom of the crowd. He typically gets multiple experts to generate answers to each inside-view question. How his technique matches up against that of superforecasters is unknown but, in principle, quite knowable.

12. The question resolved as yes—so you could argue that David would have gotten a much better Brier score if he had just used the tip-of-your-nose perspective. Ask: how easy is it to imagine another terrorist strike in Europe right after the *Charlie Hebdo* incident? Answer: extremely easy. Conversion into probability: extremely probable. This argument is right but unreasonable, the mirror-image of the reasonable-but-wrong judgment we encountered on Iraqi WMDs in chapter 4. Superforecasters do as well as they do—across many questions—by subjecting their System 1 intuitions to System 2 scrutiny.

13. Stefan Herzog and Ralph Hertwig, "The Wisdom of Many in One Mind," *Psychological Science* 20, no. 2 (February 2009): 231–37.

14. George Soros, *Soros on Soros: Staying Ahead of the Curve* (New York: Wiley, 1995).

15. Researchers often use the integrative complexity coding system to measure this thesis-antithesis-synthesis pattern of reasoning (a system developed by Peter Suedfeld, my first mentor). One common finding is that integratively complex thinkers tend to be more resistant to System 1 biases. See P. E. Tetlock and J. I. Kim, "Accountability and Judgment in a Personality Prediction Task," *Journal of Personality and Social Psychology* 52 (1987): 700–709; P. E. Tetlock, L. Skitka, and R. Boettger, "Social and Cognitive Strategies of Coping with Accountability: Conformity, Complexity, and Bolstering," *Journal of Personality and Social Psychology* 57 (1989): 632–41. But there are situations in which complex thinkers are at a disadvantage. See P. E. Tetlock and R. Boettger, "Accountability: A Social Magnifier of the Dilution Effect," *Journal of Personality and Social Psychology* 57 (1989): 388–98; P. E. Tetlock and R. Boettger, "Accountability Amplifies the Status Quo Effect When Change Creates Victims," *Journal of Behavioral Decision Making* 7 (1994): 1–23; P. E. Tetlock and A. Tyler, "Churchill's Cognitive and Rhetorical Style: The Debates Over Nazi Intentions and Self-Government for India," *Political Psychology* 17 (1996): 149–70.

16. For introductions to the Big Five traits and the openness factor, see Oliver P. John and Sanjay Srivastava, "The Big Five Trait Taxonomy: History, Measurement, and Theoretical Perspectives," in *Handbook of Personality: Theory and Research*, 2nd ed., ed. Lawrence A. Pervin and Oliver P. John (New York: Guilford Press, 1999), 102–38; Robert R. McCrae, "Social Consequences of Experiential Openness," *Psychological Bulletin* 120, no. 3 (1996): 323–37. Need-for-cognition and active open-mindedness scales correlate with generic openness.

6. SUPERQUANTS?

1. Lionel Levine, in discussion with the author, February 14, 2013.

2. Leon Panetta, in discussion with the author, January 6, 2014.

3. The real Maya may also think like a superforecaster. In Panetta's memoir, *Worthy Fights* (New York: Penguin, 2014), he notes that when he called on the

officer who was the model for the character of Maya to say how likely she thought it was that Osama bin Laden was in the compound, she did not answer "one hundred percent," but quickly and firmly said "ninety-five percent."

4. Mark Bowden, *The Finish: The Killing of Osama Bin Laden* (New York: Atlantic Monthly Press, 2012), pp. 158–62.

5. Baruch Fischhoff and Wändi Bruine de Bruin, "Fifty-Fifty = 50%?," *Journal of Behavioural Decision Making* 12 (1999): 149–63.

6. This discussion raises deeper questions about how people use probability estimates in decision making. The classic expected-utility model implies that any shift in probability matters because people multiply the probability of each possible consequence of an action by the utility of each consequence and then sum the cross products to compute the net attractiveness of that option. If we make the simplifying assumption of only a single consequence of the attack option, then a shift from an initial 50% to 75% probability of Osama's presence should raise the net attractiveness of the attack option by 50%. A more qualitative and psychologically realistic model is known as reason-based choice. A shift in probability matters only when it causes a factor either to become a good reason for doing something or to cease being a good reason. If Obama were undecided prior to entering the meeting, his saying "fifty-fifty" after the meeting signaled he had yet to hear anything that would cause him to move his probability dial far enough to choose; see Eldar Shafir, Itamar Simonson, and Amos Tversky, "Reason-based Choice," *Cognition* 49 (1993): 11–36. This is where the application of the earlier described "extremizing" method of aggregating probability judgments could make a big difference. Depending on the diversity of perspectives among the advisers, it might transform a median adviser judgment of 75% into, say, 90%, which might have been enough to cause the president to say, "OK, now I feel I have sufficient reason for action." In this view, probability shifts only matter when they cross reason-based action thresholds.

7. For a persuasive amplification of this point, see Richard Zeckhauser and Jeffrey Friedman, "Handling and Mishandling Estimative Probability: Likelihood, Confidence, and the Search for Bin Laden," *Intelligence and National Security* 30, no. 1 (January 2015): 77–99.

8. For a summary of the research, see Daniel Kahneman, *Thinking, Fast and Slow* (New York: Farrar, Straus and Giroux, 2011).

9. This aversion to uncertainty underlies the Ellsberg paradox, named after Daniel Ellsberg, who discovered it in his undergraduate honor's thesis, long before he became famous for leaking the Pentagon Papers. In the simplest version of the problem, there are two urns. Inside the first urn are 50 white marbles and 50 black marbles. Inside the second urn is a mix of white and black marbles in an unknown proportion. There may be 99 white marbles and 1 black marble, 98 white marbles and 2 black marbles, and so on, all the way to a possible mix of 1 white marble and 99 black marbles. Now, you get to draw a marble from one of the urns. If you draw a black marble, you win cash. So which urn do you choose? It doesn't take a lot of thought to figure out that the odds of drawing a black marble are the same from either urn but, as Ellsberg showed, people strongly prefer the first urn. What makes the difference is uncertainty. With both urns, it is uncertain whether you will draw a black or white marble, but with the first urn, unlike the second, there is no uncertainty about the contents, which is enough to make it by far the preferred choice. Our aversion to uncertainty can even make people prefer the certainty of a bad thing to the mere possibility of one. Researchers have shown, for example, that people given a colostomy they knew was permanent were happier six months later than those who had a colostomy that may or may not be permanent. See Daniel Gilbert, "What You Don't Know Makes You Nervous," *New York Times*, May 20, 2009, http://opinionator.blogs.nytimes.com/2009/05/20/what-you-dont-know-makes-you-nervous/.

10. J. F. Yates, P. C. Price, J. Lee, and J. Ramirez, "Good Probabilistic Forecasters: The 'Consumer's' Perspective," *International Journal of Forecasting* 12 (1996): 41–56.

11. In *Risk Savvy* (New York: Viking, 2014), the psychologist Gerd Gigerenzer has shown how Berliners often misinterpret daily weather forecasts. Misinterpretations of "30% rain tomorrow" include (a) it will rain 30% of the time tomorrow); (b) it will rain on 30% of the landmass of Berlin; (c) 30% of weather forecasters predict rain. The correct interpretation is much harder to wrap our heads around: when meteorologists quantify the weather conditions around Berlin right now and plug in their best models, the equations assign a 30% probability to rain tomorrow. Or another way to look at it, using Lorenzian computer simulations: if we could rerun the weather in Berlin thousands of times, with minor butterfly-effect tweaks for measurement error in antecedent conditions like winds and barometric pressures, it would rain in 30% of the computer-simulated worlds. Small wonder that Berliners resort to more concrete simplifications.

12. David Leonhardt, "How Not to Be Fooled by Odds," *New York Times*, October 15, 2014.

13. Robert Rubin, in discussion with the author, June 28, 2012.

14. William Byers, *The Blind Spot: Science and the Crisis of Uncertainty* (Princeton, NJ: Princeton University Press, 2011), p. vii.

15. Ibid., p. 56.

16. See, for example, Samuel Arbesman, *The Half-Life of Facts: Why Everything We Know Has an Expiration Date* (New York: Current, 2012).

17. Jacob Weisberg, "Keeping the Boom from Busting," *New York Times*, July 19, 1998.

18. Rubin, discussion with the author.

19. Forecasters or algorithms would have a massive advantage if they could predict unpredictability (in financial terms, volatility). For instance, an extremizing aggregation algorithm that "knew" when to throttle back and moderate its forecasts could avoid the big Brier score penalties that await extremizing algorithms that blindly turn every 75% into, say, 90%. I am not implying that superforecasters have mastered this mysterious art/science. Although they outperform regulars in periods of historical turbulence as well as tranquillity, their margin of victory shrinks in turbulence. I return to this issue in chapter 11, which explores Nassim Taleb's critique of tournaments.

20. Novice forecasters often ask why not just say 0.5, coin toss, whenever they "know nothing" about a problem. There are several reasons why not. One is the risk of being ensnared in self-contradictions. Imagine you are asked whether the Nikkei stock index will close above 20,000 by June 30, 2015. Knowing nothing, you say 0.5 chance. Now suppose you are asked whether it will close above 22,000—and you again say 0.5—or between 20,000 and 22,000, and you again say 0.5. The more possibilities the questioner unpacks, the more obvious it becomes that the casual user of 0.5 is assigning incoherent probabilities that far exceed 1.0. See Amos Tversky and Derek Koehler, "Support Theory: A Nonextensional Representation of Subjective Probability," *Psychological Review* 101, no. 4 (1994): 547–67.

Also, even when people feel they know nothing, they typically know a bit and that bit should tip them away from maximum uncertainty, at least a bit. The astrophysicist J. Richard Gott shows us what forecasters should do when all they know is how long something—a civil war or a recession or an epidemic—has thus far lasted. The right thing is to adopt an attitude of "Copernican humility" and assume there is nothing special about the point in time at which you happen to be observing the phenomenon. For instance, if the Syrian civil war has been going on for two years when IARPA poses a question about it, assume it is equally likely you are close to the beginning—say, we are only 5% into the war—or close to the end—say, the war is 95% complete. Now you can construct a crude 95% confidence band of possibilities: the war might last as little as $1/39$ of 2 years (or less than another month), or as long as about 39×2 years, or 78 years. This may not seem to be a great achievement but it beats saying "zero to infinity." And if 78 years strikes you as ridiculously long that is because you cheated by violating the ground rule of you must know "nothing." You just introduced outside-view base-rate knowledge about wars in general (e.g., you know that very few wars have ever lasted that long). You are now on the long road to becoming a better forecaster. See Richard Gott, "Implications of the Copernican Principle for Our Future Prospects," *Nature* 363 (May 27, 1993): 315–20.

21. Brian Labatte, in discussion with the author, September 30, 2014.

22. B. A. Mellers, E. Stone, T. Murray, A. Minster, N. Rohrbaugh, M. Bishop, E. Chen, J. Baker, Y. Hou, M. Horowitz, L. Ungar, and P. E. Tetlock, "Identifying and Cultivating 'Superforecasters' as a Method of Improving Probabilistic Predictions," *Perspectives in Psychological Science* (forthcoming 2015).

23. Charlie Munger, "A Lesson on Elementary Worldly Wisdom," address to the University of Southern California Marshall School of Business, April 14, 1994, http://www.farnamstreetblog.com/a-lesson-on-worldly-wisdom/.

24. The unfortunate expression "good enough for government work" comes to mind. Financial analysts struggle to make fine-grained distinctions about whether options are properly pricing in distinctions among probabilities as fine grained as a $1/1,000$ chance of a market convulsion versus a $1/100,000$ chance. Common sense suggests that if the task is doable and profitable enough, people will eventually figure it out. In this light, though, it is worrisome there is far more interest in probing the limits on granularity in the private than the public sector. Shouldn't

we ask for the same rigor in Homeland Security's estimates of terrorism threats as in Goldman Sachs's estimates of market trends? Of course, there is no guarantee that efforts to boost granularity will boost accuracy. Optimal granularity for many NIC-level problems may turn out to be the five- or seven-point scales they have institutionalized. But the lack of curiosity among anti-quant analysts makes it hard to discover those improvements that are possible.

25. Kurt Vonnegut, *Slaughterhouse-Five* (New York: Dell Publishing, 1969), pp. 116, 76–77.

26. Oprah Winfrey, commencement address, Harvard University, May 30, 2013, http://news.harvard.edu/gazette/story/2013/05/winfreys-commencement-address/.

27. Konika Banerjee and Paul Bloom, "Does Everything Happen for a Reason?," *New York Times*, October 17, 2014.

28. J. A. Updegraff, R. Cohen Silver, and E. A. Holman, "Searching for and Finding Meaning in Collective Trauma: Results from a National Longitudinal Study of the 9/11 Terrorist Attacks," *Journal of Personality and Social Psychology* 95, no. 3 (2008): 709–22.

29. Laura Kray, Linda George, Katie Liljenquist, Adam Galinsky, Neal Roese, and Philip Tetlock, "From What Might Have Been to What Must Have Been: Counterfactual Thinking Creates Meaning," *Journal of Personality and Social Psychology* 98, no. 1 (2010): 106–18.

30. Robert Shiller, interview with the author, August 13, 2013.

7. SUPERNEWSJUNKIES?

1. David Budescu and Eva Chen have invented a contribution-weighted method of scoring forecasters that gives special weight to those who see things before others do; see D. V. Budescu and E. Chen, "Identifying Expertise to Extract the Wisdom of Crowds," *Management Science* 61, no. 2 (2015): 267–80.

2. Doug Lorch, in discussion with the author, September 30, 2014. The Arc-

tic sea ice question, like the Arafat-polonium question (and others), pushed the ideological hot buttons of many forecasters. They saw bigger questions behind the smaller ones. And the bigger ones were incendiary: Is global warming real? Did Israel kill Arafat? They then did the old bait-and-switch routine. They replaced the narrow difficult technical question with an emotionally loaded question that, in their view, called for an emphatic answer. These forecasters paid a steep Brier score price.

3. Bill Flack, in discussion with the author, August 5, 2014.

4. G. Edward White, *Earl Warren: A Public Life* (New York: Oxford University Press, 1987), p. 69.

5. Defenders of Warren could argue that the risks of underestimating the threat outweighed those of overestimating it, so Warren erred on the side of caution. Robert Gates implied something similar in defending his skepticism as a CIA analyst of Gorbachev's intentions. In EPJ, I called this maneuver the "I made the right mistake" defense—and noted that it's sometimes defensible. But Warren's refusal to budge right to the end of the war casts doubt on such a defense. Even years after the war ended, Warren insisted he had been right. Only in his memoirs, written in 1971, did Warren express regret. See G. Edward White, "The Unacknowledged Lesson: Earl Warren and the Japanese Relocation Controversy," *Virginia Quarterly Review* 55 (Autumn 1979): 613–29.

6. John DeWitt, *Final Report: Japanese Evacuation from the West Coast, 1942,* https://archive.org/details/japaneseevacuati00dewi.

7. Jason Zweig, "Keynes: He Didn't Say Half of What He Said. Or Did He?," *Wall Street Journal,* February 11, 2011, http://blogs.wsj.com/marketbeat/2011/02/11/keynes-he-didnt-say-half-of-what-he-said-or-did-he/.

8. Charles A. Kiesler, *The Psychology of Commitment: Experiments Linking Behavior to Belief* (New York: Academic Press, 1971).

9. Jean-Pierre Beugoms, in discussion with the author, March 4, 2013.

10. P. E. Tetlock and Richard Boettger, "Accountability: A Social Magnifier of the Dilution Effect," *Journal of Personality and Social Psychology* 57 (1989): 388–98.

11. For one of the earliest demonstrations of excess volatility in asset market prices, see Robert Shiller, "Do Stock Prices Move Too Much to Be Justified by Subsequent Changes in Dividends?," National Bureau of Economic Research Working Paper no. 456, 1980; Terrance Odean, "Do Investors Trade Too Much?," *American Economic Review* 89, no. 5 (1999): 1279–98.

12. John Maynard Keynes, *The General Theory of Employment, Interest, and Money* (CreateSpace Independent Publishing Platform, 2011), p. 63.

13. Burton Malkiel, *A Random Walk Down Wall Street*, rev. and updated ed. (New York: W. W. Norton, 2012), p. 240.

14. Ibid., p. 241. Note that this comparison of trading frequency involves people making the decisions to trade. So-called high-frequency trading is conducted with computers and algorithms and is an entirely different matter.

15. Tim Minto, in discussion with the author, February 15, 2013.

16. Sharon Bertsch McGrayne, *The Theory that Would Not Die*, Yale University Press, 2011, p. 7.

17. Jay Ulfelder, "Will Chuck Hagel Be the Next SecDef? A Case Study in How (Not) to Forecast," *Dart-Throwing Chimp*, February 9, 2013, http://dartthrowing chimp.wordpress.com/2013/02/09/will-chuck-hagel-win-senate-approval-a-case -study-in-how-not-to-forecast/. Ricks's mistake is a quite common one. In a March 16, 2015, article in the *New York Times*, David Leonhardt warns of pundits' tendency to overreact to gaffes of candidates—like Barack Obama's attributing working-class Americans' interest in guns and religion to economic malaise or George W. Bush's using a curse word to describe a journalist when the tape was still running. Leonhardt rightly reminds forecasters that political fundamentals, like the economy and demographics, largely determine elections ("From the Upshot's Editor: Political Mysteries").

18. In my opinion, Ulfelder got the better of the argument. But that is an *opinion, not a mathematical fact*. One could use Bayes to defend Ricks. How? By finding an alternative defensible base rate to set one's initial probability. Instead of 96% (percentage of secretary of defense nominations that pass the Senate), one could ground one's base rate in the following: When a nomination makes the

news for being troubled, how often does it go through? My guess is 60% to 70% of the time. If we blend the two base rates, we get a prior probability of roughly 80%. Net result: Riggs looks less wrong than before. Never forget: forecasting real-world events is as much art as science. Ulfelder, "Will Chuck Hagel Be the Next SecDef?"

19. Psychologists have run hundreds of lab studies that test how proficient people are as Bayesian updaters. Unlike the messy real-world IARPA problems, there are clear right or wrong Bayesian solutions to these lab problems. Imagine you are randomly drawing balls (with replacement) from an urn—and there is a 50/50 chance that the urn contains either 70 red balls and 30 blue balls or 70 blue and 30 red. You draw 8 red and 5 blue. How much should you change your mind that you are now drawing from the 50/50 urn? The correct Bayesian answer is 0.92 but most people underreact to the evidence and give estimates closer to 70%. Using such tasks, Barbara Mellers has shown that superforecasters are markedly better Bayesians than regular forecasters; see B. A. Mellers, E. Stone, T. Murray, A. Minster, N. Rohrbaugh, M. Bishop, E. Chen, J. Baker, Y. Hou, M. Horowitz, L. Ungar, and P. E. Tetlock, "Identifying and Cultivating 'Superforecasters' as a Method of Improving Probabilistic Predictions," *Perspectives in Psychological Science* (forthcoming 2015).

8. PERPETUAL BETA

1. Mary Simpson, in discussion with the author, April 26, 2013.

2. For a popular summary of Dweck's research, see Carol Dweck, *Mindset: The New Psychology of Success* (New York: Ballantine Books, 2006), pp. 23, 18.

3. One might concede that people with fixed mindsets are at a disadvantage in life because (1) they miss opportunities that those with a growth mindset seize and (2) it is worse never to try than to try and fail. But one might still wonder which view, the fixed or growth, is closer to objective reality. This question leads us into the old "nature-nurture" debate, a sinkhole that I'll skirt, except to warn again against either-or dichotomies. As behavioral genetics is now revealing, nature *or* nurture is a less common reality than nature *and* nurture: the DNA inside each cell of our bodies and the world into which we are born interact in complex ways. On

the nature side of the ledger, not every baby has the potential to become Einstein, Beethoven, a professional basketball player—or a superforecaster. But within these limits, a vast range of outcomes is possible. Who we become and what we achieve depend on the opportunities in our world and our readiness to seize them.

4. John F. Wasik, "John Maynard Keynes's Own Portfolio Not Too Dismal," *New York Times*, February 11, 2014, http://www.nytimes.com/2014/02/11/your-money/john-maynard-keyness-own-portfolio-not-too-dismal.html. See also David Chambers and Elroy Dimson, "Retrospectives: John Maynard Keynes, Investment Innovator," *Journal of Economic Perspectives* 27, no. 3 (Summer 2013): 213–28.

5. Wasik, "John Maynard Keynes's Own Portfolio Not Too Dismal."

6. John Maynard Keynes, *Essays in Biography* (Eastford, CT: Martino Fine Books, 2012), p. 175.

7. Noel F. Busch, "Lord Keynes," *Life*, September 17, 1945, p. 122.

8. Michael Polanyi, *Personal Knowledge* (Chicago: University of Chicago Press, 1958), p. 238.

9. If this analysis is right, all the forecasters who entered the IARPA tournament and stuck with it—not just superforecasters—should improve with practice. Is that true? In an ideal world, it would be easy to find out: put forecasters' Brier scores on a chart and see if they rise over time. But we don't live in that world and nailing this down is tricky. The GJP volunteers are not trying to solve puzzles in a lab in which difficulty can be held constant. That way, if the score rises over time, you know the puzzle solver is getting better. The real-world events being forecast are ill behaved. History is continually changing—and the difficulty of forecasting tasks bounces about. So if we look at a forecaster's accuracy over time, and see improvement, that could mean the forecaster got better—or the questions got easier. One partial solution is to look at the correlation between intelligence and accuracy over time. If it stays about the same, that would suggest the role of tournament-acquired skill is not growing. But if the correlation declines over time, that would imply a shrinking role for raw intelligence, and a growing role for skill. It's far from an ideal measure, but if I held out for Platonic perfection I would have stayed in the lab. The result? The correlation with intelligence did decline. So this gauge is telling us that practice really does make forecasters better.

10. Reading this footnote could save you exponentially more money than the cost of this book. Overconfidence can be expensive. Imagine two people deciding whether to invest $100,000 in retirement savings in either a stock market index fund that yields the base-rate return (the S&P 500 average) or Firm Alpha, an expert-guided actively managed fund that claims to beat market averages. Starting from the stylized facts that there is no consistency in which active funds beat passive funds each year, and that Firm Alpha charges 1% per year to manage funds and the passive fund charges 0.1%, we can compute the cumulative cost, over thirty years, of overestimating one's skill at picking winners. Assuming a 10% before-fee annual return for both funds (implying a 9.9% net return for the passive fund and a 9% return for the active fund), after reinvestment of returns, the more modest investor will have $1,698,973 whereas the overconfident investor will have $1,327,000—a difference of $371,973, a steep price for a cognitive illusion. Of course, the starting assumptions were stylized facts and altering them could yield scenarios that favor hunting for superior active managers. The current weight of evidence does, however, favor the humbler and lazier strategy. See Jeff Sommer, "How Many Mutual Funds Routinely Rout the Market? Zero," *New York Times*, March 15, 2015. This line of research implies that even superforecasters won't be able to beat deep liquid markets in which many very smart and well-capitalized traders are relentlessly second-guessing each other. That proposition has never been tested, but superforecasters can outperform shallower and less liquid markets (see chapter 9).

11. B. R. Forer, "The Fallacy of Personal Validation: A Classroom Demonstration of Gullibility," *Journal of Abnormal and Social Psychology* 44, no. 1 (1949): 118–23.

12. Jean-Pierre Beugoms, in discussion with the author, March 4, 2013.

13. The energy expert Vaclav Smil recalled how, in 1975, he perfectly predicted China's energy consumption in 1985 and 1990, and also how, in 1983, he nailed global energy demand in 2000; see Vaclav Smil, *Energy at the Crossroads* (Cambridge, MA: MIT Press, 2005), p. 138. Impressive? Smil unpacked his forecasts and showed that they were based on judgments that were individually wrong but that, when combined, produced an accurate final figure, by chance. Too many forecasters in Smil's position would have declared "nailed it!" and made more forecasts using the same methods.

14. Devyn Duffy, in discussion with the author, February 18, 2013. My older EPJ

work found that experts with fox-like styles of thinking were more open to the possibility that they just lucked out on their best forecasts. P. E. Tetlock, "Close-Call Counterfactuals and Belief-System Defenses: I Was Not Almost Wrong But I Was Almost Right," *Journal of Personality and Social Psychology* 75 (1998): 639–52.

15. The greater the role of chance in tournaments, the greater the risk that forecasters will give up honing their skills. But chance can also be exciting and there may be an optimal dosage of chance for motivating forecasters to invest problem-solving effort and reach the next performance level. Poker seems to be close to that optimum. Unlike in poker, though, the relative mix of skill and luck can shift suddenly in geopolitical tournaments, from $^{90}/_{10}$ favoring skill to $^{10}/_{90}$ favoring luck. Forecasters need Marcus Aurelius–like levels of grittiness to devote years to cultivating the skills to cope with a world that suddenly morphs into a different world—and this might happen a number of times in a career. Imagine a concert pianist who must occasionally play on pianos with scrambled keyboards. It would be demoralizing.

16. See the PolitiFact.com analysis at http://www.politifact.com/truth-o-meter/article/2008/sep/09/e-mail-heard-round-world/.

17. Anne Kilkenny, in e-mail correspondence with the author, January 5, 2014.

9. SUPERTEAMS

1. Schlesinger is quoted in Irving L. Janis, *Victims of Groupthink: A Psychological Study of Foreign-Policy Decisions and Fiascoes* (Boston: Houghton Mifflin, 1972), p. 20.

2. Ibid.

3. Ibid.

4. Ibid., p.26.

5. Marty Rosenthal, in discussion with the author, November 13, 2014.

6. Elaine Rich, in discussion with the author, November 20, 2014.

7. Paul Theron, in discussion with the author, November 16, 2014.

8. The research of Christopher Chabris and colleagues on collective intelligence underscores this point about the emergent properties of group-level cognitive functioning. See A. W. Wooley, C. Chabris, S. Pentland, N. Hashmi, and T. Malone, "Evidence for a Collective Intelligence Factor in the Performance of Human Groups," *Science* 330 (October 2010): 686–88, http://www.sciencemag.org/content/330/6004/686.full.

9. The giving mindset often extends beyond the superteams. Superforecaster and political scientist Karen Adams joined the project to make a broader contribution to society. She shares lessons learned from the IARPA tournament with her Model United Nations students in Missoula, Montana. Who knows? Maybe she's developing the next generation of superforecasters.

10. Scott Page, *The Difference: How the Power of Diversity Creates Better Groups, Firms, Schools, and Societies* (Princeton, NJ: Princeton University Press, 2008).

11. For details on these tournament-winning strategies, see P. E. Tetlock, B. Mellers, N. Rohrbaugh, and E. Chen, "Forecasting Tournaments: Tools for Increasing Transparency and Improving the Quality of Debate," *Current Directions in Psychological Science* 23, no. 4 (2014): 290–95; B. A. Mellers, L. Ungar, J. Baron, J. Ramos, B. Gurcay, K. Fincher, S. Scott, D. Moore, P. Atanasov, S. Swift, T. Murray, E. Stone, and P. Tetlock, "Psychological Strategies for Winning a Geopolitical Tournament," *Psychological Science* 25, no. 5 (2014): 1106–15; V. A. Satopää, J. Baron, D. P. Foster, B. A. Mellers, P. E. Tetlock, and L. H. Ungar, "Combining Multiple Probability Predictions Using a Simple Logit Model," *International Journal of Forecasting* 30, no. 2 (2014): 344–56; J. Baron, L. Ungar, B. Mellers, and P. E. Tetlock, "Two Reasons to Make Aggregated Probability Forecasts More Extreme," *Decision Analysis* 11, no. 2 (2014): 133–45; V. Satopää, S. Jensen, B. A. Mellers, P. E. Tetlock, and L. Ungar, "Probability Aggregation in the Time-Series: Dynamic Hierarchical Modeling of Sparse Expert Beliefs," *Annals of Applied Statistics* 8, no. 2 (2014): 1256–80.

10. THE LEADER'S DILEMMA

1. Helmuth von Moltke, *Moltke on the Art of War: Selected Writings*, ed. Daniel J. Hughes, trans. Daniel J. Hughes and Harry Bell (New York: Ballantine Books, 1993), p. 175.

2. Ibid., p. 228.

3. Jörg Muth, *Command Culture: Officer Education in the U.S. Army and the German Armed Forces, 1901–1940, and the Consequences for World War II* (Denton, TX: University of North Texas Press, 2011), p. 167.

4. Ibid., p. 169.

5. Bruce Condell and David T. Zabecki, eds., *On the German Art of War: Truppenführung. German Army Manual for Unit Command in World War II* (Mechanicsburg, PA: Stackpole Books, 2009), p. 19.

6. Moltke, *Moltke on the Art of War*, p. 173.

7. Condell and Zabecki, *On the German Art of War*, p. 23.

8. Moltke, *Moltke on the Art of War*, p. 77.

9. Ibid., p. 230.

10. Muth, *Command Culture*, p. 174.

11. Condell and Zabecki, *On the German Art of War*, p. 18.

12. Werner Widder, "Battle Command: Auftragstaktik and Innere Führung: Trademarks of German Leadership," *Military Review* 82, no. 5 (September–October 2002): 3.

13. Condell and Zabecki, *On the German Art of War*, p. 22.

14. Ibid., p. ix.

15. Quoted in *Eisenhower in War and Peace*, Jean Edward Smith, p. 55.

16. Muth, *Command Culture*, p. 174. This was mostly an army problem. The navy and Marines had a different culture and tradition.

17. George S. Patton, *War as I Knew It* (New York: Houghton Mifflin Harcourt, 1995), p. 357.

18. Jean Edward Smith, *Eisenhower in War and Peace* (New York: Random House, 2012), p. 612.

19. Eitan Shamir, *Transforming Command: The Pursuit of Mission Command in the U.S., British, and Israeli Armies* (Stanford, CA: Stanford University Press, 2011), p. 90.

20. Fred Kaplan, *The Insurgents* (New York: Simon and Schuster, 2013), p. 74.

21. Thomas Ricks, *The Generals* (New York: Penguin, 2012), p. 433.

22. Ralph Peters, "Learning to Lose," *American Interest* 2, no. 6 (July/August 2007), http://www.the-american-interest.com/2007/07/01/learning-to-lose/.

23. David Petraeus, in discussion with the author, August 16, 2013.

24. General Petraeus is a controversial figure. And readers may be asking the same questions about him that are often raised about other exemplars of good or bad judgment in this book: Larry Kudlow or Peggy Noonan or Robert Rubin or Helmuth von Moltke or Larry Summers. Remember this book's laser-like focus on accuracy. Don't fall for bait and switch. Don't confuse your judgments of foresight with those of character. It should not matter whether you see the forecaster as an adulterer or an affable television host or a skilled speechwriter or a Wall Street insider or a Prussian imperialist or an Ivy League sexist. It shouldn't even matter whether the forecaster is Adolf Hitler who in the early years of the Third Reich saw more clearly than other German leaders just how far the West would go toward appeasing him. The tenacity with which people raise these irrelevant questions tells us how hard it is to treat forecasting as a pure accuracy game. In another line of my research, I have called this tendency "functionalist blurring." P. E. Tetlock, "Social Functionalist Frameworks for Judgment and Choice: Intuitive Politicians, Theologians, and Prosecutors," *Psychological Review* 109, no. 3 (2002): 451–71.

25. 3M Company, *A Century of Innovation: The 3M Story* (St. Paul, MN: 3M Company, 2002), p. 156.

26. Drake Baer, "5 Brilliant Strategies Jeff Bezos Used to Build the Amazon Empire," *Business Insider*, March 17, 2014.

27. Andrew Hill, "Business Lessons from the Front Line," *Financial Times*, October 8, 2012.

28. Maxine Boersma, "Interview: 'Company Leaders Need Battlefield Values'," *Financial Times*, April 10, 2013.

29. Stephen Ambrose, *Eisenhower: Soldier and President* (New York: Simon and Schuster, 1990), p. 267.

30. Annie Duke, in discussion with the author, April 30, 2013.

31. Joshua Frankel, in discussion with the author, February 13, 2013.

11. ARE THEY REALLY SO SUPER?

1. James Kitfield, "Flynn's Last Interview: Iconoclast Departs DIA with a Warning," *Breaking Defense,* August 7, 2014, http://breakingdefense.com/2014/08/flynns-last-interview-intel-iconoclast-departs-dia-with-a-warning/.

2. See reports by the Stockholm International Peace Research Institute and the Human Security Report Project: *Human Security Report 2013: The Decline in Global Violence* (Vancouver, BC: Human Security Press, Simon Fraser University, 2013).

3. Daniel Kahneman and Shane Frederick, "Representativeness Revisited: Attribute Substitution in Intuitive Judgment," in *Heuristics and Biases: The Psychology of Intuitive Judgment*, ed. Thomas Gilovich, Dale Griffin, and Daniel Kahneman (Cambridge: Cambridge University Press, 2002), pp. 49–81.

4. Nassim Taleb, *The Black Swan: The Impact of the Highly Improbable* (New York: Random House, 2010), p.10.

5. Louise Richardson, *What Terrorists Want* (New York: Random House, 2007), pp. xviii–xix.

6. Taleb, *The Black Swan*, p. 50.

7. J. Bradford DeLong, "Cornucopia: The Pace of Economic Growth in the Twentieth Century," National Bureau of Economic Research Working Paper Series, Working Paper 7602, National Bureau of Economic Research, March 2000.

8. Duncan Watts, *Everything Is Obvious: *Once You Know the Answer* (New York: Crown Business, 2011), p. 153.

9. Donald Rumsfeld, memo to President George Bush, April 12, 2001, http://library.rumsfeld.com/doclib/sp/2382/2001-04-12%20To%20George%20W%20Bush%20et%20al%20re%20Predicting%20the%20Future.pdf.

10. Richard Danzig, *Driving in the Dark: Ten Propositions About Prediction and National Security* (Washington, DC: Center for a New American Security, October 2011), p. 8.

11. *Oxford Essential Quotations* (New York: Oxford University Press, 2014).

12. To take but one example, a big-splash 1993 bestseller, *Head to Head*, by Lester Thurow, the former dean of MIT's Sloan School, drew a portrait of the global economy in the early twenty-first century that was vivid, convincing, and wrong. It featured Japan and Germany as the key challengers to the United States and scarcely mentioned China. *Head to Head* is as forgotten today as it was celebrated in 1993.

13. Fatality estimates for wars sometimes vary widely. There is also room for endless definitional quibbling on what counts as a "war."

14. Given the fast improving technology for mass killing, a prudent policy maker might have pushed his risk assessment of a multimillion-casualty war as high as 20% or 40% or 80%. It is yet another judgment call that requires balancing outside-view, historical base rates against fresher inside-view information about the problem at hand.

15. Nassim Taleb once asked me a tough question: how can you possibly assess the accuracy of forecasters on outcomes that only occur once every few decades?

The short answer is we can't. The longer answer is there are sneaky ways of approaching the problem that at least beat Ouija boards. One approach builds on the scope-sensitivity studies in chapter 11 and assesses how logically consistent forecasters are in estimating the likelihood of rare events, such as being injured in a car accident in one versus ten years. If forecasters give roughly the same answers, they have failed a basic logical consistency test. Teaching them to pass the test will improve the logical coherence of their forecasts, a necessary albeit not sufficient condition for accuracy. Another approach is to develop early warning indicators of rare megaevents, assess forecasters' accuracy on the indicators, and then treat the better forecasters as the better guides to which historical trajectory we are on. Neither approach solves Taleb's problem but each is better than nothing—and better than embracing an extreme form of the precautionary principle that obliges us to reject any change for which anyone can generate a "plausible" worst-case scenario.

16. The Kahneman thought experiment skims the surface of a roiling sea of what-if possibilities. The most incisive alternative histories make strong cases for tiny tweaks yielding big changes, such as Winston Churchill's essay tracing the consequences of a Confederate victory at Gettysburg, a battle often seen as hinging on the actions of a few brave men, through to a German victory in World War I. I enjoy these imaginative excursions into counterfactual history—and have written with the historian Geoffrey Parker on the challenges of judging the plausibility of alternative histories; see P. E. Tetlock, R. N. Lebow, and N. G. Parker, eds., *Unmaking the West: "What-If?" Scenarios That Rewrite World History* (Ann Arbor: University of Michigan Press, 2006). See also P. E. Tetlock and A. Belkin, "Counterfactual Thought Experiments in World Politics: Logical, Methodological, and Psychological Perspectives," in *Counterfactual Thought Experiments in World Politics,* ed. P. E. Tetlock and A. Belkin (Princeton, NJ: Princeton University Press, 1996); P. E. Tetlock and R. N. Lebow, "Poking Counterfactual Holes in Covering Laws: Cognitive Styles and Historical Reasoning," *American Political Science Review* 95 (2001): 829–43.

12. WHAT'S NEXT?

1. How did superforecasters pull this one off? They pieced together a sound cause-effect model that let them zero in quickly on relevant evidence while being only mildly distracted by irrelevant evidence. They knew from patterns

of voting in other nations that the no-change option tends to do better than the polls predicted because some voters are embarrassed to tell pollsters they support the "boring" side. This effect had surfaced in the 1995 referendum on separating Quebec from Canada. Supers also knew the power of aggregation: almost all polls favored no by a narrow margin. Combine these facts and you get a very confident no from the outset. And supers largely stayed the course even when a YouGov poll put the yes vote ahead by 7%. They briefly blipped up to 30% but when later polls did not confirm the YouGov result, they dropped back fast to their 10% starting position. By contrast, on the eve of the election, betting markets in the UK placed the odds at roughly 3:1 against the referendum's success—on the right side of "maybe" but far from the confident 9:1 odds against that the superforecasters were giving at that moment. See Simon Neville, "Scottish Independence: Late Surge at the Bookies as Punters Catch Referendum Fever," *The Independent*, September 18, 2014, http://www.independent.co.uk/news/business/news/scottish-independence-late-surge-at-the-bookies-as-punters-catch-referendum-fever-9739753.html.

2. Daniel W. Drezner, "What Scotland's Referendum Teaches Me About Punditry," *Washington Post*, September 19, 2014, http://www.washingtonpost.com/posteverything/wp/2014/09/19/what-scotlands-referendum-teaches-me-about-punditry.

3. Ibid.

4. "Silver Speaks. Democrats Despair," *Slate*, March 24, 2014.

5. Mac Margolis, "Brazil Threatens Banks for Honesty," *Bloomberg View*, August 1, 2014, http://www.bloombergview.com/articles/2014-08-01/brazil-threatens-banks-for-honesty.

6. This is the most common English transliteration of Lenin's maxim. Its pronunciation is closer to "kto kvo."

7. http://www.nydailynews.com/news/election-2012/dick-morris-offers-explanation-predicting-romney-landslide-article-1.1201635.

8. Ira Rutkow, *Seeking the Cure: A History of Medicine in America* (New York: Scribner, 2010), p. 143.

9. Ibid., p. 145.

10. See the website of the Coalition for Evidence-Based Policy—coalition4evidence
.org—or Ron Haskins and Greg Margolis, *Show Me the Evidence: Obama's Fight
for Rigor and Results in Social Policy* (Washington, DC: Brookings Press, 2014).

11. James Surowiecki, "Better All the Time," *New Yorker*, November 10, 2014,
http://www.newyorker.com/magazine/2014/11/10/better-time.

12. Blame-game ping-pong sheds light on why even the Federal Reserve won't
abandon vague verbiage. I say even because the Federal Reserve, unlike the IC,
already relies extensively on quantitative (macroeconomic) models in its internal
deliberations. If they wanted, they could be far more explicit about their intentions. But they don't—even though former chairman Ben Bernanke had called in
his professorial days, for an end to turgid Fedspeak. Here we run into the limits
of what it is politically possible to do, not what it is scientifically possible to know.
The Federal Reserve has many reasons to hide behind vague verbiage. They don't
want to be blasted for being on the "wrong side of maybe," which is where even
the best-calibrated forecasters often wind up. And they don't want the public to
see how often they change their minds because the public often sees belief updating as a sign one is confused, not rational.
    The Federal Reserve appears thus to have concluded that, although the pub-
lic may clamor for the truth, it is not ready for the truth. Try to imagine the
mild-mannered Ben Bernanke channeling Jack Nicholson's rage from the film
A Few Good Men: "You can't handle the truth." In this view, we just aren't ma-
ture enough to handle the numbers. So we must continue to decode statements
like this from Janet Yellen in February 2015: "It is important to emphasize that
a modification of the forward guidance should not be read as indicating that the
committee will necessarily increase the target range in a couple of meetings." See
James Stewart, "Wondering What the Fed's Statements Mean? Be Patient," *New
York Times*, March 13, 2015, C1.
    The implications for the IC are clear. Even if the IC eventually went as far
as the Fed toward quantifying assessments of uncertainty in its internal deliberations, the IC should stick with sphinxlike external messaging.

13. Often attributed to Einstein, the true author seems to be the sociologist William Bruce Cameron, according to Quote Investigator: http://quoteinvestigator
.com/2010/05/26/everything-counts-einstein/.

14. Leon Wieseltier, "Among the Disrupted," *New York Times*, January 18, 2015.

15. Elisabeth Rosenthal, "The Hype over Hospital Rankings," *New York Times*, July 27, 2013. Efforts to identify "supers"—superhospitals or superteachers or super–intelligence analysts—are easy to dismiss for two reasons: (1) excellence is multidimensional and we can only imperfectly capture some dimensions (patient longevity or test results or Brier scores); (2) as soon as we anoint an official performance metric, we create incentives to game the new system by rejecting very sick patients or ejecting troublesome students. But the solution is not to abandon metrics. It is to resist overinterpreting them.

16. Thomas Friedman, "Iraq Without Saddam," *New York Times*, September 1, 2002.

17. Thomas Friedman, "Is Vacation Over?" *New York Times*, December 23, 2014.

18. Caleb Melby, Laura Marcinek, and Danielle Burger, "Fed Critics Say '10 Letter Warning Inflation Still Right," Bloomberg, October 2, 2014, http://www .bloomberg.com/news/articles/2014-10-02/fed-critics-say-10-letter-warning -inflation-still-right.

19. Some say the Holy Grail project is aptly named because it is so naive. There is too much ill will to bring together clashing camps. Jonathan Haidt has laid out the grounds for pessimism in his insightful 2012 book *The Righteous Mind*. But even a few successes would set wonderful precedents. There are good reasons for supposing that once people start forecasting in tournaments with public postings of winners, they become more open-minded. It is quite remarkable how much better calibrated forecasters are in the public IARPA tournaments than they were in my earlier anonymity-guaranteed EPJ tournaments. And the evidence from lab experiments is even more decisive. Public tournaments create a form of accountability that attunes us to the possibility we might be wrong. Tournaments have the effect that Samuel Johnson ascribed to the gallows: they concentrate the mind (in the case of tournaments, on avoiding reputational death). See P. E. Tetlock and B. A. Mellers, "Structuring Accountability Systems in Organizations," in *Intelligence Analysis: Behavioral and Social Scientific Foundations*, ed. B. Fischhoff and C. Chauvin (Washington, DC: National Academies Press, 2011), pp. 249–70; J. Lerner and P. E. Tetlock, "Accounting for the Effects of Accountability," *Psychological Bulletin* 125 (1999): 255–75.

EPILOGUE

1. Bill Flack, in discussion with the author, August 5, 2014.

APPENDIX:
TEN COMMANDMENTS FOR ASPIRING SUPERFORECASTERS

1. Jo Graven McGinty, "To Find a Romantic Match, Try Some Love Math," *Wall Street Journal*, February 14, 2015.

2. Greg Mankiw, "The Overoptimism of Research Assistants," http://greg mankiw.blogspot.com/2013/11/the-excessive-optimism-of-research.html.

3. There is an alternative hypothesis. One could defend differential treatment of the probability estimates of the basketball advisers and the terrorism advisers on the grounds that sports is repetitive whereas the search for bin Laden was a one-off thing. Obama may have justifiably more confidence that the basketball judgments were driven by hard data on past performance whereas the terrorism judgments appear to have been plucked from thin air. The following sorts of evidence could resolve this issue: (1) Is Obama as precise in talking about clearly repetitive events in national security (e.g., drone strikes) as he is about sports? (2) Would policy makers in general give up their "prejudice" against probability judgments in less repeatable domains if they knew these judgments are just as reliable as those in more repeatable domains? Unfortunately, testing the latter hypothesis will be impossible as long as policy makers see no value in collecting probability judgments of seemingly unique events, less still in assessing their accuracy.

4. Tommy Lasorda and David Fisher, *The Artful Dodger* (New York: Harper-Collins, 1986), p. 213.

5. The oxymoronic Eleventh "Commandment" reminds us of the indispensable role of creativity. For instance, preparing for the "unprecedented"—for Black Swans like the invention of nuclear weapons, super-computers, or genetic engineering—requires lightening up on key Commandments: relying less on historical base rates and running more risks of crying wolf about "far-out" scenarios.

Of course, there are few free lunches. It is usually impossible for imaginative scenario writers to assign higher probabilities to rare high-impact events that do occur (hits) without also assigning higher probabilities to those that never occur (false positives). Whether we deem the price of the improved hit rate too high hinges on how low we can keep our false-positive errors and how well we can hedge against events that others failed to imagine. Again, superforecasting is a nonstop balancing act.

INDEX

Page numbers of illustrations appear in *italics*.

extremizing and, 90, 91 93, 210–11, 307n6
"fate score," 151–52
Holy Grail of, 266, 326n19
joining, 275
launching of, 16
methodology, 90–91
multidisciplinary team for, 16
number of participants, 16, 90, 108–9
participants' reward, 93
performance of, 17–18, 90–91
possible revelations, 90–91
practice and forecasting, 315–16n9
random selection and, 108
recruitment of participants, 89–90
superforecasters in, 94
superteams created, 201–11
synthesizing views, 122–23
training superforecasters, 292–93n7
using teams decision, 197–201
website, 275, 277
Wharton gathering, 106–7, 203
Google, 12, 154
Gorbachev, Mikhail, 50–51, 67, 245
Gott, J. Richard, 309–10n20
Graham, Benjamin, 178
Grant, Asam, 208
Grant, James, 267
granularity, 142, 144, 145, *146*, 146, 153, 168, 281–82, 310–11n24
Great Depression, 177
"Great Rationality Debate, The" (Tetlock and Mellers), 294–95n14
Great Recession of 2007–9, 70–71, 174
policy debate on, 267–69
Greece, finances, 59, 279
grit, 187–90, 192
groupthink, 195–96, 199, 209
Grove, Andy, 199
growth mindset, 174, 176–78, 188, 314–15n3
Guinea elections, 186, 187

Hagel, Chuck, 170–71, 313–14n18, 313n17
Haidt, Jonathan, 326n19
Head to Head (Thurow), 322n12
Hertwig, Ralph, 305n13

Herzog, Stefan, 305n13
Heuer, Richards, 86
heuristics, 35, 294–95n14
"availability heuristic," 35, 40
Hill, Austin Bradford, 28–29
hindsight bias, 184, 245–46, 251, 277, 283
Hitler, Adolf, 220, 248, 320n24
Honduras election question, 204–5
Horowitz, Michael, 300n8
How the Mind Works (Pinker), 294–95n14
humility, 227–29
"Copernican humility," 309–10n20
intellectual humility, 228–29, 271
hunches, 115, 117, 140, 282

Ignatius, David, 95, 301n11
illusion of control, 97–98, 99
illusion of insight, 32
In an Uncertain World (Rubin), 142
information technology, 21–23
evidence-based thinking and, 258
Intelligence Advanced Research Projects Activity (IARPA), 16–17, 85, 87. *See also specific tournament questions*
Cochrane-style experiments and teams, 89
forecasting tournament, 17, 19, 88, 89, 90, 95, 96, 252, 258, 259 (*see also* Good Judgment Project)
forecasting tournament rules, 92
forecasting tournament questions, 262
Goldilocks zone questions, 88, 89, 300n8
mission of, 85
prediction market in tournament, 157
top spot, 166
intelligence community (IC), 82, 85, 310–11n24
accuracy of forecasts, 86–87, 259
analysts vs. superforecasters, 95, 301–2n11
analysts in, 17, 301–2n11
annual budget, 90
blame-game ping-pong, 258–59, 325n12
evidence-based thinking in, 258
granularity in, *146*, 146, 310–11n24
Ignatius story, 95, 301n11

Richardson, Louise, 239

Ricks, Tom, 170–71, 313–14n18, 313n17

Ridgway, Matthew, 221–22

Rieber, Steve, 88

Righteous Mind, The (Haidt), 326n19

Risk Savvy (Gigerenzer), 308n11

Ritholtz, Barry, 48

Rogg, David, 121–22
  methodology, 122, 124

Romney, Mitt, 253, 254–55

Rosenthal, Marty, 202, 203–4, 208

Rosenzweig, Phil, 302n13

Ross, Lee, 298–99n22

Rubin, Robert, 139–40, 142–43, 144, 320n24

Rumsfeld, Donald, 242–43, *243*

Russia (former Soviet Union)
  Cuban missile crisis and, 54, 195–97
  forecasting about, 2, 22, 50–51, 184
  Gorbachev surprise, 50–51, 67, 245
  invasion of Yugoslavia, 54–55

Rutkow, Ira, 28, 255, 256

Saddam Hussein, 58, 81, 82, 83, 84, 85

Saffo, Paul, 261–62

Satopää, V. A., 318n11

Saturday Night Live skit, 183

Saudi Arabia production cuts in oil, 124–25

Schell, Jonathan, 49, 53, 254

scientific testing, 19, 28–29, 66, 89
  randomized controlled trials, 29, 30, 31, 32, 46, 89

scope insensitivity, 234–36

Scotland referendum, 250–51, 323–24n1

Scott, David, 300n9

Seydlitz, Friedrich Wilhelm von, 215

Shiller, Robert, 150–51

Shlaes, Amity, 48

Shula, Don, 257

Sidi Bouzid, Tunisia, 6–7, 9

Sillman, Sanford "Sandy," 105–7, 114

Silver, Nate, 14, 65, 74, 168, 253, 292–93n7

Simon, Herbert, 22, 49

Simpson, Mary, 174, 177

Slaughterhouse-Five (Vonnegut), 147

Sloane, Elizabeth, 188

Smil, Vaclav, 316n13

snap judgments, 42

Snellen charts, 88
  change from 20/100 to 20/40 and, 94, *95*

Sorenson, Theodore, 196

Soros, George, 123, 227

sports
  March Madness predictions, 282
  performance statistics and, 3
  politics vs. baseball, 291–92n3, 327n3

Star Trek (TV series), 75

Stratfor, 292n6

Success Equation, The (Mauboussin), 99

Suedfeld, Peter, 260, 306n15

Summers, Larry, 139–40, 279–80, 320n24

Sun Microsystems, 240

superforecasters, 3. *See also* Flack, Bill; Lorch, Doug; Minto, Tim; *specific individuals; specific questions*
  accuracy of, 144, 303n17
  AOM and, 126, 191
  basic concepts, 18
  black swans and, 242
  Brier scores, 94
  "Cobbler," 304–5n7
  cognitive illusions and, 234, 236
  commitment to forecasts and, 163, 165–66, 191, 311–12n2
  composite portrait of, 191–92
  coping with dissonance, 230
  discovering, 91
  factors that improve foresight, 16, 104, 110–13, 116–27, 129–30, 153–55, 278–79, 304–5n7
  false dichotomies in, 238
  in GJP, 94
  granularity among, 145
  grit and, 187–90, 192
  in groups, 192 (*see also* superteams)
  improved performance of, 103–4, 315n9, 322–23n15
  intelligence and knowledge of, 106–10, 129, 192, 315n9
  intelligence community analysts vs., 95, 301–2n11
  Kahneman's question about, 231

ABOUT THE AUTHORS

PHILIP E. TETLOCK is the Annenberg University Professor at the University of Pennsylvania, with appointments in Wharton, psychology and political science. He is coleader of the Good Judgment Project, a multiyear forecasting study, and the author of *Expert Political Judgment* and, with Aaron Belkin, *Counterfactual Thought Experiments in World Politics*. He has published over two hundred articles in peer-reviewed journals and has won awards from many scientific societies, including the American Association for the Advancement of Science, the National Academy of Sciences, the American Psychological Association, and the American Political Science Association.

DAN GARDNER is a journalist and the author of *Risk: The Science and Politics of Fear* and *Future Babble: Why Pundits Are Hedgehogs and Foxes Know Best*.